VICTORIA MARY SACKVILLE-WEST

(1892–1962) was born at Knole in Sevenoaks, Kent. Her parents were first cousins, her father being the third Baron Sackville and her mother the illegitimate daughter of Lionel Sackville-West and the Spanish dancer Pepita. Knole was to be an abiding passion throughout her life, the inspiration of much of her writing, and the source of great sorrow when, as a woman, she was unable to inherit it on her father's death. Vita was educated at home, except for three years spent at a school in London where she came to know Violet Keppel (later Trefusis) with whom, from 1918–21, she was to have a passionate affair.

In 1910 Vita met Harold Nicolson, the young diplomat whom she married three years later. In 1915 they bought a cottage two miles from Knole where they planned their first garden; three years later Vita Sackville-West's first novel, *Heritage*, was published. A distinguished novelist, poet, short-story writer, biographer, travel writer, critic, historian and gardener, her novels include *The Edwardians* (1930), *All Passion Spent* (1931) and *Seducers in Ecuador* (1924); of her poetry, *The Land* (1926) was awarded the Hawthornden Prize and *The Garden* (1946) won the Heinemann Prize.

During the 1920s her close and influential friendship with Virginia Woolf was at its height, culminating in the publication of Virginia Woolf's novel *Orlando* (1928), a celebration of her friend. In 1930 Harold and Vita bought Sissinghurst Castle in Kent, where they created their famous garden. A Fellow of the Royal Society of Literature and a JP for Kent, Vita Sackville–West was made a Companion of Honour in 1948. She died at Sissinghurst, after an operation for cancer, at the age of seventy.

Virago publishes *The Edwardians*, *All Passion Spent*, *Family History* (1932) and *No Signposts in the Sea* (1961). *Seducers in Ecuador* and *The Heir* (1922) will be published in 1987.

PEPITA

VITA SACKVILLE-WEST

WITH A NEW INTRODUCTION BY
ALISON HENNEGAN

Published by VIRAGO PRESS Limited 1986
41 William IV Street, London WC2N 4DB

First published by The Hogarth Press Ltd, London, 1937
Virago edition offset from The Hogarth Press Ltd edition of 1937

British Library Cataloguing in Publication Data

Sackville-West, V.
  Pepita.
  1. Europe—Social life and customs—
  19th century
  I. Title
  940.2'8'0924   GT146

  ISBN 0-86068-776-7

Printed in Great Britain by Anchor Brendon Ltd
of Tiptree, Essex

INTRODUCTION

Even as Juan Antonio Oliva found you in Madrid and loved you when
you were just nineteen, even as my grandfather found you in Paris and
loved you when you were twenty-two, so did my mother love you and so
do I, for evidently you were a person made to be loved.

So Vita Sackville-West addresses Pepita, the maternal grandmother she never knew: the poverty-stricken Andalusian
daughter of a shadowy father and a gypsy mother who won riches
and international renown as a Spanish dancer (though never in
her own country where her performance was deemed inferior)
and left the stage to live as – or so we are told – the contented
though severely ostracized mistress of Lionel Sackville-West, an
English aristocrat and diplomat. Victoria, the second of the five
illegitimate children she bore him, would eventually become
Lady Sackville, chatelaine of Knole and the mother of Vita.

Pepita stands firmly on a mass of facts, diligently culled by a
harassed and unhappy English solicitor in 1896. Why he was sent
to Madrid, and with what success, Vita herself tells us in an
account where reality continually threatens to outstrip romance:
great inheritances claimed by spurious pretenders; spectacular
court cases; skeletons – of perjury, bastardy and forgery –
clanking in ancestral closets; a lover who deems the world well
lost for love although, somehow, so skilfully does he juggle the
conflicting worlds of diplomatic protocol and the sexual double
standard, he's never quite called upon to make the sacrifice
All this is the raw material of the nineteenth-century novel, a fact
which Vita both acknowledges and uses in her pursuit of the
book's true purpose.

For what appears to be a straightforward joint biography of her
grandmother and mother becomes the means whereby Vita
explores and makes sense for herself of those warring elements in
her own past and temperament which most exercised and
perplexed her. In her mixed ancestry she found, in part created,
twinned pairs of eternal opposites which provided sources and
reassurance for some of her own more bewildering conflicts.
Spanish versus English; gypsy versus aristocrat; Latin passion
versus English reticence; the sprawling volatility of Spain's
peasant working class versus the punctiliously ranked and
ordered line of Sackville ancestors; childlike spontaneity and
happy amorality versus sexual relationships carefully codified and
ratified by legal sanction.

In those apparent oppositions she was to seek the explanation of
her own 'Spanish' self which seemed so often to war with her
'Englishness'. Since early childhood she had been preoccupied
with a Spanish *alter ego*: it 'explained' so many things: her lean,
dark looks which verged upon the androgynous; her sexually
ardent temperament; the capacity for physical cruelty which
shamed her (although many people remember gentleness as her
most characteristic virtue); the rapidly flaring passions which,
once extinguished, could give way to an indifference bordering
on the callous. Characters of Spanish or part-Spanish ancestry
appear as strongly autobiographical protagonists in her novels
Heritage and *Challenge*, and during much of her long love affair
with Violet Trefusis she constructed an alternative persona, called
Julian (after the hero of *Challenge*), through which she explored
and enacted androgynous and 'masculine' elements in her
personality. It was her 'Spanishness' which enabled her to accept
her lesbianism comparatively easily, her 'Englishness' which
forbade anything so 'vulgar' as a public acknowledgement of it.
'Englishness' expressed itself in her passionate love of her
ancestral home, Knole, and in the creation of one of England's
most beautiful gardens: 'Englishness' made her conservative,
traditionalist and patriotic. 'Spanishness' caused her to rail against
the world of male privilege which debarred her, as a woman, from
inheriting Knole; made her reject, in the words of Harold
Nicolson, her husband, 'the institution (not the fact) of marriage';

enabled her to judge the more generous sins of the flesh lightly
and to reserve her horror for the more weighty ones of cruelty,
cupidity, disloyalty and indifference.

And there were conflicts other than her own which she also
sought to resolve. *Pepita* is only half her grandmother's book. Part
II, 'Pepita's Daughter', is devoted to Lady Sackville, Vita's
tormenting and, although Vita can rarely bring herself to say so,
surely tormented mother. Behaviour which might earlier have
passed as charmingly eccentric had become by the end of her life
quite clearly crazy. To plant painted tin flowers has, arguably, its
own logic (no slugs, no falling petals and blossom all the year
round: clearly an improvement on nature). To give total
strangers, met on trains, cheques for £60,000 so that they may
develop their gold mines; to build and then abandon a house
because the central heating system you've demanded consumes
one ton of coal a day; to accuse your daughter's Nannie of having
eaten, at one sitting and in half an hour, three dozen quail which
the poulterer has failed to send (and then still to insist on sacking
Nannie, despite your distraught daughter's tears): these and
innumerable other examples are less comfortingly dismissed as
'eccentricities'.

Throughout her life Vita's relations with her mother were an
uneasy compound of loving exaltation and painful despair. From
the beginning the mother played expertly with the emotions of
her passionate but vulnerable only child. She undermined her
constantly, mocking her appearance. (Vita remained unhelpfully
convinced for much of her life that she was freakishly ugly.) She
lavished and then quixotically withheld affection and, as so often
is the case, the bewildered child only loved the more intensely.
Some of Lady Sackville's grosser brutalities are omitted from this
book. There is no mention of the time when she summoned Ben
Nicolson, Vita's adolescent son, and told him lurid tales of his
homosexual parents' 'perversion', painting a sickening picture of
two obscenely monstrous predators. 'The old woman ought to be
shot' was Virginia Woolf's response. 'It's all very well to say she is
mad. She is not mad, she is just evil', was Harold Nicolson's to an
earlier incident.

Mad or Bad? An intensely loving daughter finds either almost

impossible to countenance. She must either explain it, on the basis
that to understand is to forgive. Or she can recreate it, fashion it
into something different and better. In large part *Pepita* is Vita's
gift to herself of the mother she almost had, is an extended
love-letter to the woman she wanted her mother to be. The central
fact about Pepita, her granddaughter decided, was that 'evidently
you were a person made to be loved.' 'There was,' she continues,
'an old Swede once in Rome, who had known you, and loved my
mother partly for your sake, though partly also for her own.' This
is the language of mythology: the casual anonymity of 'an old
Swede' gives him a curious universality, makes him stand
implicitly for a whole host of old men, dotted all over Europe and
as far from home as this elderly Swedish man cosmopolitanly
displaced in Rome. The Swede who loved a Spaniard in Italy
underlines Pepita's power to inspire a passion which transcends
national boundaries and racial preferences. Pepita is Love. And,
by emphasizing constantly the continuity between Pepita, her
daughter (Vita's mother), and Vita (Pepita's daughter's daughter),
Vita is able to invest her mother with Pepita's own unadulterated
qualities of affection, joyousness, generosity and maternal
tenderness. Lady Sackville, as Pepita's daughter, necessarily
inherits her mother's destiny: she too is 'evidently a person made
to be loved.' Pepita's inheritance is reassuringly free from more
sinister traits, an unblemished gift made possible because we
know so very little about her. As her grandmother says:

It is impossible to fathom the secrets of Pepita's mind. We have the
comments of observers, but no comments of her own. The one person
who never speaks in this whole history is Pepita herself . . . Pepita herself
is never explicit. In order to understand her at all, we have to find a piece
from a different part of the puzzle, to fit it in.

Her silence gives her granddaughter freedom to use techniques
closer to the novel than to biography (although, as Vita herself
reminds us, the distinction is often spurious). Chief amongst her
methods is her creation of a Spain which can encompass
contradictions, beautify that which is elsewhere found morally
ugly, soften and make familiar the frightening and, by the sheer
force of its own vitality, make glamorous a class and a way of life

otherwise found sordid and repellent.

On the very first page Spain is invested with mystery, 'that separate land', whose people have a 'secret heart' whose workings are as difficult and unfathomable as Lady Sackville's own

The description of gypsy dancers whom Vita unexpectedly discovers one evening in Seville demonstrates the personal myth in the making. An elderly matriarch, initially simply 'immensely fat ... the fattest woman I had ever seen', is metamorphosed gradually into a singer of 'primeval sorrow', 'a powerfully obscene goddess immortalised by some sculptor of genius'. All the dancers are preternaturally beautiful, including the 'old and wrinkled' who 'still bore the traces of their youthful beauty in the bony architecture of their features and in the tragic dignity of their sunken eyes'. They are indomitable, untameable, 'like wild things that never ought to have submitted to even the kindliest hand'. They are both superhuman ('goddess') and animal ('both as fine and graceful as a pair of antelopes'). They are creatures of passionate, spontaneous and slightly mysterious emotions ('and as it were impelled by no organised intention, they began to dance'). They are ferocious ('The wild animal in him crouched, waiting to spring') and Children of Nature ('The next thing I knew was that they were all laughing like children at some purely farcical incident'). And in these qualities – the primeval, passionate, animal, childlike, spontaneous, untameable, beautiful and dangerous – they 'all unawares, had brought me nearer to Pepita'. But how much nearer, one suspects, to her mother and to a version of herself.

In that passage those qualities which in her mother were terrifying or grotesque become the stuff of legend and mythic archetype. The gypsies' childlike mirth will find an echo later in the description of Lady Sackville:

As a child can be maddening at one time and irresistible the next, so could my mother be maddening and irresistible by turn.

But the emphasis is allowed to rest upon the irresistible, rather than the maddening. And a child, though domineering, is ultimately impotent against the adult who retains the ultimate

sanctions of life and death. Likening Lady Sackville to a child
neutralizes her true capacity for destructiveness, implies a power
over her which her much tormented daughter never had. Again:

... like a child, she neither analysed nor controlled her moods: they
simply blew across her, and she was first one thing, then the other,
without exactly realising which side was uppermost.

In toddlers that's expected. In an adult woman it's surely
terrifying? Yet here, by implication, childlike is equated with
spontaneity which, in its turn, becomes synonymous with
authenticity and, therefore, truthfulness. Underlying all this is
the suggestion that emotions which are true, however undesirable
they may be, are always to be preferred to those which are
simulated but acceptable. Indeed her daughter ends the book by
saying quite explicitly:

What they never realised was that she was, above all things, herself.
Wrong or right, tiresome, troublesome, turbulent, difficult, generous,
mean, vindictive, revengeful, unjust, kind, lavish, enthusiastic, all in
turn, she was always herself, and to be always oneself to that extent is a
form of genius. 'To thine own self be true', – never have I known
anybody who to their own self was truer, in every detail, creditable or
uncreditable.

That same demand, that people should be true to some essential
self, coupled with an admiration for those who achieve it, surfaces
throughout *Pepita*: in Vita's treatment of Catalina and Lopez
(Pepita's mother and her mother's lover), of Pepita's Andalusian
background and of Madrid's swarming bohemian underworld in
which the young dancer first made her way. In patrician tones
Vita may dismiss characters – as low-bred, vulgarians, loafers,
flashy upstarts – only to recall them with praise because they are
fully and entirely the thing they are. Disreputable bohemian
lovers who reject marriage ceremonies also reject the insulting
assumption that they are incapable of mutual loyalty:

Whether married or not, they kept to one another through years of
trouble, years of poverty and years of prosperity [and for those two there
were more lean years than fat.]

Catalina, it is true, uses her daughter's new found wealth to furnish a house in appalling taste but she and her lover were 'friendly, open-handed, hospitable people'. Lopez did, just as she feared, 'readily break out into flashy garments and cheap gaudy jewellery on the slightest improvement of the family fortunes' but then he and Catalina 'had lived in poverty all their lives and now at last knew the pleasures of having money to spend as they conceived it ought to be spent'. The tone is unequivocally generous and unpatronising and gives fullest acknowledgement to a quality Vita particularly valued: generosity.

And if her strictures upon Lopez's dress-sense sound severe, it's worth reminding ourselves that one of the peasants who gave evidence in 1896 said that Lopez 'looked like a workman dressed up as a gentleman'. Those below you on the social ladder can judge quite as harshly as those above. *Pepita* describes a strictly ordered society and 'being true to yourself' entails knowing your place in it and sticking to it.

Or does it? After all, if we're talking about taste ...: Lady Sackville herself once papered an entire room at Knole with used postage stamps, included cheap reproductions of Dulac in the authentic Turkish room which she always insisted was Persian, and hung an empty whisky bottle, bearing the label "Departed Spirits", in the maze of her villa at Streatham. But then, what *was* the self to which Lady Sackville was to be true? Peasant or aristocrat or some uneasy fusion of the two? And what of Vita's 'true self'? The attempt to establish contrasting sets of 'Spanish versus English', 'Bohemian versus aristocratic' values breaks down time and time again.

From the very beginning Pepita refuses to be her 'proper' ill-bred self. She was 'nineteen, dark, quiet and beautiful', we are told the first time we meet her, and that carefully placed 'quiet' immediately distinguishes her from and elevates her above her vociferously vulgar mother and the uncertainly brash Lopez. Where heredity and lineage are all important, such 'inexplicable' restraint needs explanation. It's ready to hand, in the form of a family rumour which claims one of Spain's grandest grandees, the Duke of Osuna, as Pepita's real father. Using here for the first time a technique which she will employ frequently in the pages that follow, Vita simultaneously dismisses the rumour with light mockery yet manages to retain the glamour it first evoked. Pepita is not, in fact, a Duke's daughter, yet the suggestion, once planted, lingers... It lingered for the 1896 witnesses, too, many of whom asserted that Catalina could quickly be seen to be 'a very different class of woman from Pepita'.

Poor Catalina. Yet she too rejects her proper role. In her relations with the servants whom Pepita's money brought her she shows no sign of those rapid fluctuations between 'too great a tyranny, and then of too great a familiarity' which Vita would have expected from her 'as a woman not born to the habit of command'. Disconcertingly Catalina behaved with a dignity to her servants which her granddaughter, Lady Sackville – who ended her life so furiously enmeshed in litigation with her ex-employees that she renamed her house The Writs Hotel – might well have envied. But Catalina also had her lapses. She once wildly accused a gardener of stealing peacocks (shades of Nannie's quail). Indeed both Catalina and her granddaughter were free with their accusations of theft, although only in Lady Sackville do they seem to have become full-scale paranoia.

Theories based on class, including the ones which Vita herself appears to believe, are constantly exploded or subverted in *Pepita*. So too are those based on national characteristics. It was, for example, Vita's very English father, a 'poetic' man, who encouraged and took utterly seriously Vita's desire to write. There was nothing of 'English' philistinism in his make-up. Lady Sackville, who had Mediterranean 'temperament' in terrifying abundance, had little artistic appreciation. And sexual ardour and a high-handed way of settling amatory disputes is supposedly a 'Spanish' characteristic, but it was Vita's very English grandfather who had to be locked in his room for three days by the British Consul, then despatched in a steamer to prevent him from undergoing a bigamous marriage with Pepita. Altogether unacceptable conduct in an English aristocrat from whom we expect a frigid self-restraint. Yet even that chilly stereotype was itself a comparatively recent creation. Time was when English aristocrats were expected to be passionate, impetuous and violent as any Latin. Lionel's behaviour was, in fact, thoroughly traditional; but the traditions belonged to an earlier age. Yet *in* that age, English Milords had been a byword amongst the nations of Europe for an arrogantly confident eccentricity close to madness. The 'English aristocrat' whom Vita seeks constantly to oppose to 'Spanish raggle-taggle' was itself, in her version, a concept little older than her own lifetime. Some sixty years after the Consul thwarted her grandfather, Vita herself eloped with Violet Trefusis, like her a married woman. Her behaviour was outrageously 'Spanish' or thoroughly 'English', depending on the period from which you take your criteria.

The difficulty – of the defining national and social characteristics which refuse to be definitive – is solved in part by the creation of a new set. Poor Spaniards, by virtue of those qualities identified in the Seville dancers, become 'a natural aristocracy' – of beauty, courage, and a lineage dignified by a tradition of suffering. Pepita herself, as The Star of Andalusia (her stage name), rises above them all as part of the aristocracy of talent. The delirious applause of audiences who pelt her with flowers, take the horses from her carriage to draw it through the street themselves, present her with gifts of gold and gems, echo the rapturous obeisance of loyal subjects to a worthy liege. (Even in 1910 the townspeople of Sevenoaks would take the horses from Lord Sackville's carriage and draw it to the gates of Knole, to celebrate the court verdict which had confirmed him in his inheritance.) Throughout the late nineteenth century Stage and Aristocracy were drawing closer together, culminating in a series of marriages where chorus girls became peeresses and, in their newly acquired hauteur, often out-duchessed dowagers. Strongly hierarchial societies need ritual to sustain them and rituals are essentially theatrical. An hierarchical society in decline – and the old aristocracy's true power was declining rapidly in those years – hovers uneasily between being a real, if weakened, political system and a gorgeously accoutred, but impotent, popular entertainment. And if the entertainment is to work, the actors must be good. So it is, perhaps, not so very surprising after all that a Spanish super-star and her aristocratic English lover should have produced, in Victoria, a daughter in many ways well fitted to play a peeress, despite her much vaunted 'unEnglishness'.

Before her frightening irrationality all but swamped every other quality, Lady Sackville had shown herself to be remarkably competent, astute and gifted. For years she fulfilled, with conspicuous success, her demanding role as her father's official hostess at the British Legation in Washington. Later, as chatelaine of Knole, she administered – and administered well – a great house whose six acres of buildings constituted a village rather than a private home.

These were tasks which most women would find daunting. There are signs that having once conquered them Lady Sackville found them boring. Yet gender debarred her from any more demanding role in public affairs: she could be a valued political hostess but not a valued politician. As it was she had (limited) power without responsibility and, like most people in that position, she abused it. The period's disturbing equation between women and children made it even easier for her to do so. When Vita compares her mother's more distressing mood swings to a child's volatility, she draws, whether consciously or not, upon a contemporary belief that women, like children, are creatures of impulse and naturally amoral. The 'male' concepts of honour, justice and obligation are alien to them. Vita herself, when writing of her mother's Spanishly 'flawed' love for Knole, links herself with her father in their very different, 'pure' and 'English' love for the house. In so doing she brings together Spanishness, delusion, immaturity and femaleness and implicitly opposes them to Englishness, truthfulness, adulthood and masculinity. Nationality takes on gender and here, at least, Vita aligns herself clearly with her English father and against her Spanish mother. She herself saw her mother's difficulties almost entirely in terms of nationality and class:–

Although on one side of her lineage she had the opulent Sackvilles aligned behind her, on the other she had all that rapscallion Spanish background, that chaos of the underworld, tohu-bohu, struggling and scheming and bargaining and even thieving for a living. It was the descendant of all those people – the old-clothes pedlars, the smugglers, the fruit-sellers, the gypsies, the rascals – that her critics expected to behave as an ordinary English lady.

'Struggling and scheming and bargaining and even thieving': well, many a proud aristocratic line can find all those, and murder too, at its roots. I don't believe it was Lady Sackville's murky Spanish ancestry that did for her in the end. I don't believe her daughter entirely believed it, either. Time and again in her biography she approaches the root reason but backs off before she can explore it fully. Lady Sackville, said a wise male friend, was 'a powerful dynamo generating nothing. There was no driving belt attached to her whirling wheels.' Lady Sackville was bored. And her boredom had nothing to do with her ancestors, nothing to do with her nationality, a little, perhaps, to do with her wealth, and a very great deal to do with her gender. Pepita – or so her granddaughter assures us – found her own solution to the same dilemma:

She had given up all the struggle of a professional career, and found herself at last in the happy fulfilment of a woman's life. She was, I think, no feminist.

Vita, wary always of the word 'feminism' but living much of her life according to its principles, found a different and distinctly feminist solution which combined career, motherhood and lesbianism within a deceptively 'ordinary' marriage. Lady Sackville had seen too large a world to renounce it for domesticity, yet had no one particular talent demanding to be perfected. For her, neither her mother's solution nor her daughter's could suffice.

Alison Hennegan, Cambridge, 1986

LIST OF PRINCIPAL CHARACTERS

Spanish

CATALINA ORTEGA, widow of Pedro Duran, a barber of Malaga, by
  whom she has two children:
JOSEFA, known as PEPITA; and
DIEGO, a soldier and adventurer.
MANUEL LOPEZ, a shoemaker of Malaga, living "apparently matri-
  monially" with Catalina.
LOLA, his daughter, who subsequently marries Diego.
JUAN ANTONIO GABRIEL DE LA OLIVA, a dancer of Madrid, who marries
  Pepita.

English

LIONEL SACKVILLE-WEST, subsequently second Lord Sackville, a
  secretary in the British diplomatic service; Pepita's lover. Referred
  to as "my grandfather".
VICTORIA JOSEFA, eldest daughter of Pepita and Lionel Sackville-West.
  Referred to as "my mother". She marries her first cousin (i.e. the
  son of my grandfather's younger brother), another
LIONEL SACKVILLE-WEST, subsequently third Lord Sackville. Referred
  to as "my father".

PART I
PEPITA, 1830–1872

CHAPTER I

COSA DE ESPAÑA

I

SPAIN, in the middle of the nineteenth century, had scarcely been 'discovered' by the foreigner. Indeed, as Richard Ford observed in 1845, "the mere fact of having travelled *at all* in Spain (the italics are his, not mine) has a peculiarity which is denied to the more hackneyed countries of Europe". In saying more hackneyed countries he was doubtless thinking specifically of Italy, which had for so long formed part of the Grand Tour undertaken by young gentlemen of noble birth as to become the commonplace of well-bred and cultured travel; but an acquaintance with Spain, as he and George Borrow were well aware, conferred a distinction upon the English traveller and might reasonably be regarded in the light of an unusual and somewhat hazardous adventure. That proud, aloof, and ruthless nation still dwelt self-contained behind the barrier of the Pyrenees; the expression *cosa de España* (a thing peculiar to Spain) really meant something quite indigenously different from any other part of Europe; the reserve, the austerity, the streak of Oriental secrecy in the Spanish character set them apart even more effectively than the frontier of their mountains. To the rare Englishman penetrating into that separate land, the difficulty of approaching the secret heart of the people soon became as obvious as the external beauty of the country or the picturesque appearance of its

13

inhabitants. It was a time when women still wore the mantilla and the shawl as a matter of course in daily life, not only on festive occasions as they do to-day, and looked as beautiful in them as any woman ought to look with such resources of feminine grace at her command.

II

I should like to explain here that nothing in the following pages is either invented or even embellished. Down to the smallest, the very smallest particular, it is all absolutely and strictly true.

Few English people can have the luck to possess documents which give so intimate and detailed a picture of the daily life of a Spanish family in the nineteenth century—a family obscure and even disreputable, in no way connected with historical events or eminent figures in the world of politics, literature, or art. The interest of this Spanish family is simply human. But for a curious chance, its members would have disappeared entirely as the grave swallowed them one by one, and nothing of their doings and sayings would ever have been recorded. Even as it is, I fear that I may be suspected of introducing some fiction among my facts, just a few touches of circumstantial detail to heighten it all and make it all a little more vivid, a little more picturesque, but I can only repeat that it has not been necessary to fall to this temptation.

The papers which have provided the material for the first part of this book owe their existence to the fact that in 1896 it became legally expedient for my grandfather's solicitors to take the evidence of a number of people in Spain who, some forty years earlier, had been acquainted with the principal characters involved. The point, in short, was the necessity of proving whether my grandmother, Pepita, had ever been married to my grandfather or not. Several issues were at stake: an English peerage, and an historic inheritance. With these important issues, the solicitors had to deal. They dealt with them in their usual dry practical way, little foreseeing that this body of evidence collected in 1896 from voluble Spanish peasants, servants, villagers, dancers and other theatrical folk, would in 1936 be re-read in stacks of dusty typescript by someone closely connected, who saw therein a hotch-potch of discursiveness, frequently irrelevant but always fascinating.

It is upon this evidence which I have principally drawn. I have added nothing, and it is only with great reluctance that the principles of selection have sometimes obliged me to discard. I could not use *all* my material, as it would have become unbearably monotonous and repetitive. Even as it is, I fear that my jostle of Spaniards becomes somewhat confusing; I often got confused amongst them myself while writing this book, although I grew to know them all so well that I could enter with my heart into their separate lives. I can only assert again that I have altered nothing, and that far from inventing anything I have left out a great mass of the evidence at my disposal.

CHAPTER II

GYPSIES IN SPAIN

I

ONE day in the early autumn of 1849, a strange Andalusian trio presented itself at the Teatro del Príncipe, Madrid, and demanded an interview with Don Antonio Ruiz, the Director of the ballet. Antonio Ruiz, by virtue of his calling, was well accustomed to such invasions, and after a suitable delay allowed the suppliants to be admitted to his room. He saw before him "a stoutish well-built woman of middle-age, with a certain style about her whole exuberant personality, yet obviously of inferior origin"; a boastful, excitable, troublesome, warm-hearted woman, not easily or conveniently to be deflected from any purpose she had in hand. The man who accompanied her was far less pleasing. Shorter than she, it was at first sight apparent that he was fussy, insignificant, and self-important. He attracted much attention in Madrid by appearing in Andalusian dress, with tight high-waisted trousers, leathern gaiters, a broad red sash, and the broad-brimmed high-crowned hat with silken tassels. It was clear to any shrewd observer that Manuel Lopez—for that was his name—would readily break out into flashy garments and cheap gaudy jewellery on the slightest improvement of the family fortunes. Even as it was, he wore a heavy watch-chain and a big pin in his scarf. Broad-shouldered, with large goggle eyes of greyish-blue, he attracted the sympathy of his acquaintances far less than did the rather lovable, tiresome, dominating woman who perhaps was and perhaps was not his wife.

This person, who gave her name as Catalina Ortega, lost no time in telling Don Antonio Ruiz exactly what she wanted of him. She wanted dancing lessons to be arranged for her daughter, with a view to that daughter getting an engagement at the Teatro del Príncipe. It was an ambitious request, for the Teatro del Príncipe was at that time the leading theatre in Spain. Josefa was the daughter's name, but her mother referred to her by the colloquial diminutive: "My Pepa", she called her, or, "My Pepita". Antonio Ruiz then transferred his attention to the daughter, the third member of this invasive trio from Malaga. He saw a girl of nineteen, dark, quiet, and beautiful. There can be no question but that Pepita was very lovely indeed. "It was a face divine", said a labourer who had seen her in the vineyards. She had never spoken to him or he to her, yet he had remembered her all his life.

Antonio Ruiz was not easily impressed, but on this occasion he was impressed enough to promise the required lessons, and undertook that a member of his company should attend the girl at her own home for the purpose. The family from Malaga took its departure well pleased, for this journey to the capital had been a great venture and one not to be undertaken without much thought.

II

They were, in fact, living in exceedingly humble circumstances in a mere basement at No. 15 Calle de la Encomienda, peddling old clothes for a living. Some idea of their humble station in life may be gained from their own occupations and those of their relations and friends. Thus, Catalina's father, of gypsy blood, had been

a sandal-maker in Malaga and as a girl she had helped
him in his trade; they were so poor that he had not
even a shop, but worked in his own room. Her first
cousin went about Malaga with a donkey, selling fruit.
Her nephew was a fruit-seller likewise. Another cousin
had married a stevedore. Catalina herself had married
one Pedro Duran, who as a bachelor had existed on any
job he could pick up, as a dock-hand, a journeyman,
and what-not, but who after his marriage opened a
small barber's-shop on the ground floor of their house
in the Calle de la Puente. Catalina had a great friend
during those years in Malaga, and it is to this friend
that we owe much of the information about Catalina's
early life. She was a garrulous person, and her evidence
is abundant. Sometimes a washerwoman, sometimes a
children's nurse, sometimes a general servant at the
Hotel Alameda where she helped the chambermaid,
she lodged with her mother in rooms in Catalina's
house, because it was the cheapest place they could
find. She saw a lot of Catalina at that time, for
Catalina who had tried taking in washing for about a
year abandoned that employment in favour of selling
clothing instead, and prevailed upon her friend to accompany her on her rounds. They used to visit the
wholesale clothing shops together, lay in their stock,
and then go round to private houses selling it.

This friend of course knew Catalina's husband,
Pedro Duran, who is stated rather vaguely to have died
because "he got shot in the finger in a revolution".
More specifically, he is said to have died in the Provincial Charity Hospital of a wound accidentally received during some fêtes held in honour of the memory
of General Torrijos, leaving his widow with two young
children, Diego and Pepita. The washerwoman friend
of course knew these children too. They were said to

resemble one another as much as a boy can resemble a girl. Diego was wild and troublesome from the first, his parents could not induce him to remain at school,—"they wanted him to go to school, but he wouldn't stop. He had set his mind on a soldier's life; he was very harum-scarum and would do nothing. At about sixteen he enlisted and his mother bought him out,"—poor Catalina, with little money to spare!—"but he enlisted again and went away as a soldier to Cuba". This is the first but by no means the last that we hear of Diego.

The daughter Pepita, on the other hand, was far more tractable. Her devotion to her mother was of a nature to be considered excessive by their friends, who on occasion did not hesitate to describe Catalina as Pepita's evil angel. This was perhaps going a little too far, and in any case the expression evil angel, *mal angel*, is too commonly current in the south of Spain for it to carry as sinister a meaning as in English; I would rather say that Catalina lavished on her daughter the fierce and possessive love which Latin women do often display towards their children, injudicious to a degree and mischievous in its consequences, but certainly not malevolent in its intention. In those early days of her widowhood at Malaga she had the girl to sleep in her bed, and never tired of combing and dressing the magnificent hair which even in that southern province was remarkable for its beauty. Catalina's sister, a familiar and constant visitor at the house, was of the opinion that there was no more beautiful girl in Andalusia. "I have seen her when she has got up from bed and put on her dressing-jacket, and with her hair down she was more beautiful than when she was dressed and adorned."

It may seem surprising to read of Pepita as being "dressed and adorned" in that very poor and shoddy establishment of the Calle de la Puente where "the houses were very old and bad", but it appears that the idea of making her daughter into a dancer had already formed in Catalina's mind. She was her jewel, her treasure, and her pride, for whom nothing was too good and no ambition too extravagant. It is rather touching to read that "she was very careful of her and brought her up with great delicacy"; rather touching, too, to find that she not only paid for lessons at a dancing-class, but also provided four silk dresses out of her meagre earnings, different costumes for different dances. Her friend the washerwoman was much impressed by this luxury. She had seen Catalina ten or twenty times taking Pepita to the dancing-class, and had also seen the dresses which were "much adorned and very expensive" hanging up in Catalina's house. Before very long, in fact after Pepita had been having her lessons for about eight months, the washerwoman heard that an opera company had come to Malaga; she heard it said that they were foreigners and sang in a foreign language. She felt proud that her young acquaintance Pepita should be engaged to dance in connection with that company, but regretted that she never saw her dance there, "because I had no money to go with". She did, however, see Pepita's dresses being placed on a tray and carried by a boy sent from the theatre to fetch them.

Catalina's cousin Juan was more fortunate; he went twice to see the child perform; he could not go oftener because, like the washerwoman, he "had not the money to spare"; also he was obliged to go alone, not being able to afford to take anyone with him. He regretted not being able to go oftener, for he came away full of enthusiasm for his young relative. "She danced in company with four or five others. She was the best dancer; I heard everybody saying in the theatre that Pepita was the first dancer. Everybody applauded and said she would be a good dancer. She was just like a bird in the air, she danced so well." He went round to Catalina's house next day and told her what a great success Pepita had made. Catalina replied with commendable modesty that the child had a natural gift for dancing.

III

One might suppose that Catalina was sufficiently occupied with her friends, her relations, her troublesome son, her old-clothes trade, and above all with the daughter whom she adored, but it was not so: she still needed something to fill her life even more. It was then that she found the goggle-eyed Manuel Lopez living three or four doors up the street. He had come, people thought, from Granada. Manuel Lopez, who figures throughout the story as a comic and rather ridiculous character, was a man of precisely the same social standing as Catalina's other associates; in other words, he had always made his living as best he might, sometime as a charcoal-burner, sometime as a bandit, sometime as a smuggler in Valencia and Alicante. At the time of his first acquaintance with Catalina, however, he was practising the respectable trade of a cobbler. As neighbours, they struck up a friendship, and the washerwoman, who envisaged these things simply and without comment, puts the situation into one neat phrase: "After Manuel and Catalina had fallen in love with each other, Manuel took up his abode in her house".

The evidence that they ever troubled to go through a form of marriage is of the slightest, and may I think be disregarded. Whether married or not, they kept to one another through years of trouble, years of poverty and

years of prosperity, years during which they squabbled
and quarrelled and made it up, years during which
Catalina snubbed him mercilessly and he unblushingly
profited by the material advantages which Catalina and
her daughter could offer him. So long as Manuel Lopez
had a cigar to smoke, horses to ride or drive, and servants
over whom he could exercise his swaggering authority,
he cared very little for the snubs he incurred or for the
means by which his pleasures were provided. In the
meantime he adopted Pepita with as much pride as
if she had been his own daughter, showed her off
and boasted about her,—which brings me to another
point: who was the true father of Pepita?

Officially the daughter of Catalina Ortega and Pedro
Duran the barber of Malaga, ex-dockhand and journeyman, Pepita could claim a far more romantic story
current in Spain regarding her birth. Catalina, born a
gypsy, was said to have leapt through paper hoops in
a circus in her youth; and to have been the mistress
of the Duke of Osuna, on whom the existence of
Pepita was unofficially fathered. The obscure barber
of Malaga completely disappears behind this cloud
of wild romance. For the Duke of Osuna is himself
a vivid and well authenticated figure with a terrifying ancestry. I have heard accounts of him from men
who had personally known or seen him. A descendant
of the Borgias on their Spanish side, all Paris had
trembled when he was observed to enter a box at the
first night of Victor Hugo's *Lucrèce Borgia*, for it was
feared that he might rise up in magnificent wrath if any
slight were offered to his illustrious if questionable
forebears. The splendour and extravagance of the old
grandee became proverbial. It was said of him that he
knew no money save gold *ongas*, and never waited for
change in a shop. It was said also that he could travel

from Madrid by coach to Warsaw, sleeping in his own houses every night, where servants in livery awaited him and fires and candles were lighted and dinner prepared daily lest he should happen to arrive without warning and at any time. If Pepita, half gypsy and half aristocrat, were indeed the daughter of such a man, it was not surprising that even the most ignorant observers should comment on the difference between mother and daughter, and remark that although a considerable likeness existed between their features, Catalina, once one had got into conversation with her, was seen to be a "very different class of woman from Pepita".

This, then, was the background story of the family which had presented itself for an interview with Don Antonio Ruiz in Madrid. Of course he knew nothing of it; he did not know that the encampment in the basement of 15 Encomienda included also a small child of five or six, named Lola, the daughter of Manuel Lopez though not of Catalina; and the young man, Diego, the wild tiresome son of Catalina, who was always to go threading his way in and out of their stormy history. Antonio Ruiz could naturally not be interested in such things. As Director of the ballet, he could only be interested in the discovery of a new dancer, and, as such, he had done his duty: he had noted the lovely girl and had detailed his man Perez to give her some dancing lessons at her own home. The Director could scarcely be expected to do more.

IV

The dancing lessons were a complete failure. Pepita might have danced "as a bird in the air" in Malaga, but in Madrid it was found impossible to raise her to the

required level of excellence. The capital evidently had a
higher standard than the provinces, and her career as a
dancer seemed doomed. Antonio Ruiz, who had been
so rash as to sign a contract for her engagement at the
Teatro del Príncipe, cancelled it. This was not the sort of
thing which Catalina would tamely accept. After all, she
had paid for dancing lessons in Malaga when she could
ill afford it; she had provided four silk dresses; she had
succeeded in pushing Pepita on to the Malaguenian
stage in connection with a foreign company; and a
woman of her determination was not likely to abandon
such an enterprise once she had set it in train. There
is no telling what Catalina might have done to Don
Antonio Ruiz for his insult to her daughter, when
luckily a new element entered into the life of the family
occupying the basement of 15 Encomienda, in the
shape of a young man who had fallen violently in love
with Pepita at first sight.

This young man, who was named Juan Antonio
Gabriel de la Oliva, was only a year older than Pepita
herself, in other words, twenty; but he had the advantage of having been on the stage in Madrid and also in
Corunna ever since he was sixteen or seventeen. Destined for the study of medicine when he left school, he
had very soon abandoned that pursuit for his chosen
taste of dancing. He was thus quite a man of the world
compared with the lovely provincial girl from Malaga,
and moreover, being a Spaniard of hot blood and ardent
feelings, he allowed nothing to stand in the way between
himself and the desired acquaintance with Pepita. A reserved young man, not given to confidences even towards
his most familiar friends, he was purposeful and knew how
to get his way when he wanted it. In this case he wanted
it badly. Fortunately for him he had a friend, another
dancer, named Pedrosa, with whom he was so intimate

that "either's purse was always at the disposal of the other". To this friend he now had recourse, and asked him to arrange for him, Oliva, to give lessons to Pepita instead of Perez. He also prevailed upon Pedrosa to persuade Perez to take him, Oliva, to Pepita's home and introduce him. And finally, when the management cancelled Pepita's contract, Oliva cancelled his own contract of his own accord, and left the theatre in a rage.

By these energetic and turbulent methods the young Oliva had succeeded in establishing himself as a recognised friend in the basement. It was an odd household that he had entered, though perhaps it did not seem very odd to him, accustomed as he was to the theatrical circles and irregular lives of that under-world of Madrid. It cannot have troubled him in the slightest to know that Manuel Lopez was living only "apparently matrimonially" with Pepita's mother, or that Pepita herself was at pains to inform her acquaintances that her own father was dead, so that she might not be believed to be Manuel Lopez' daughter.

Oliva had eighteen brothers and sisters, and a correspondingly impressive number of uncles and aunts. His family came from the same class as Pepita's; that is to say, his brother-in-law was a harness-maker, another brother-in-law a tailor, a nephew was also a harness-maker; his uncles were farm-labourers at Ocana in the province of Toledo. There was thus no difference in their social status, and Oliva could be accepted on an equal footing in the Encomienda. The intimacy grew rapidly, so that he fell into the habit of accompanying them on their peddling expeditions when he was not giving a lesson to Pepita. I think Oliva must then have been an attractive, sincere, and likeable young man. A most dutiful son, he lived at home when in Madrid, and whenever he went away on theatrical engagements he frequently wrote to his parents; his father would then read the letters aloud to the rest of the children. As a dancer he was evidently making a successful career, for he never seems to have been without an engagement, and as a character he inspired a remarkably deep affection in his friends. In spite of this, he was said to be unusually reticent, even for a Spaniard, so that they found it difficult to hear anything of his life even when most anxious to help him in his troubles. They recognised and deplored his extravagance, but were always ready to come to his rescue with the price of a fare in the *diligence*, or of a meal, whenever he wanted it. For "he spent every penny he earned as soon as he got it, and as he was fond of good living his money was soon gone". Later in his life we find him doing precisely the things we should expect him to do—living with various women, fathering their children, associating with dancers and bull-fighters, even accepting jobs in connection with the bull-ring when the theatres had closed down after the winter season; but for the moment, that is to say in 1849 at the age of twenty, he appears as a rather serious, determined young man, respectably living with his parents in the Calle Riviera de Cutidores and bent only upon the perfectly honourable idea of marrying Pepita as soon as he possibly could.

These parents were decent people, country-born of peasant stock. The father had left his brothers to carry on their profession of farm-labourers, and had removed himself to Madrid, where he obtained employment in the service of his uncle as a working furrier. He never appears to have risen to be even a master-furrier, but there is no reason to suppose that he was anything but contented with his lot. It was quite a novelty in his family to have a son who insisted on going in for a theatrical career; more usually they adopted some trade such as harness-making, but since Juan Antonio's tastes had lain so very definitely in that direction ever since he was a little boy of ten, no objection had been raised, and indeed by the time the Olivas enter this history they had every reason to be proud of their thoroughly satisfactory son. Juan Antonio himself, like many people of otherwise unconventional and happy-go-lucky life, had a certain respect for orthodox observances, and unquestionably in Spain he would not have stood much chance of success had he proceeded with anything but the most severe propriety in his courtship of the girl he desired to make his wife. Catalina and Lopez themselves, little better than vagrants though they were, would not have permitted any departure from the established rule. Lopez might make his living as a bandit or as a cobbler of old shoes, Catalina might have tumbled in the circus-ring and yielded to the embraces of a grandee so far above herself in station as the Duke of Osuna, but neither Lopez nor Catalina would have tolerated any infringement of the strict Spanish code or any disrespect towards the desirable girl they guarded.

It comes as a surprise to learn how very strict was the standard of conduct observed even by those professional dancers who had passed beyond the supervision of mother or parents. Alexandre Dumas, for simply having attempted with ordinary politeness to kiss the hand of Petra Camara on being introduced to her in her dressing-room, to his great surprise heard the lady scream and instantly afterwards received a sound box on the ear. He is writing from Seville to a friend in Paris during the winter season of the ballet in 1847: "*Pardon, madame*, I had forgotten to tell you something: that these ladies are of ferocious virtue, and when I tell you for whom this virtue is so

carefully preserved, it will make you smile pityingly.
Each one of these ladies has a fiancé *qui plume la dinde
avec elle*,—I crave forgiveness of your amorous sensi-
bility, but in this case *plumer la dinde* means to stand
under the balcony, to sing serenades, and to exchange
glances between the window-bars. This fiancé (who by
the banks of the Guadalquivir is known as the *novio*)
may sometimes be a tailor's boy, or a shoemaker, who,
concerned with waistcoats or gaiters, has managed to
slip his way into the theatre, and who, once in the wings,
watches over his treasure as Argus over Jupiter's. The
only difference being, that Argus was watching over Io
on Juno's behalf, whereas these Arguses of ours are
acting on their own.

"You understand now, madame, what perturbation
I, with my Parisian manners, had introduced into these
bucolic idylls; I kissed a hand at first sight, in other
words, I was filching (*j'escroquais*) a favour which is
usually accorded to the *novio* only after eighteen months
or two years of acquaintance!"

Oliva, once accepted as Pepita's *novio*, of course had
to conform to the prevailing rule, nor would it ever have
entered his head to do otherwise. The two young
creatures were rigorously chaperoned. Whenever visitors went to the basement in the Encomienda, Catalina
was sure to be present, and sometimes Lopez too, and
sometimes the child Lola. Of course in his capacity
as her dancing-master, Oliva had an unusually good
opportunity of improving his acquaintance with his
love, and it is clear that he found the occasion to reveal
his sentiments to her, for Pedrosa, whom curiosity had
driven to the house, was the recipient of Pepita's confidences. "When I arranged with Perez for Juan
Antonio to teach her," he says, "I had not yet made the
acquaintance of Pepita." But he knew Catalina very

well, and after he had effected the introduction of Oliva he continued to frequent the family· "On a few occasions I was present when Juan Antonio was giving her lessons. There was not up to the time of the marriage an open-hearted friendship between Pepita and me so that she would confide to me *everything*, but I used occasionally to go to the house and stop to breakfast and dinner, and she used to confide to me her love affairs with Juan Antonio."

Pedrosa was not at all happy about his friend's infatuation, and cautioned him seriously. "When I found that Juan Antonio was so violently in love, I counselled him to look well what he was doing, as although I had a good opinion of Pepita I certainly did not like either her mother or her stepfather, of whom I had formed my opinion by their general behaviour and their rather gross language." This, naturally, produced a coolness between Oliva and his best friend, which however was not of very long duration. Pedrosa meanwhile kept an anxious eye on the way things were going. He was anything but reassured to witness what he describes as a lovers' quarrel between Oliva and Pepita: Oliva, it appears, was very fond of the bull-fights and never missed attending them if he could help it, and on this occasion when Pepita did not wish him to go, he insisted on going. Neither of them being an easy-going or accommodating person, this particular quarrel lasted for a month or five weeks out of their brief courtship, after which Pedrosa says resignedly that "they made it up and went on as before".

Still according to Pedrosa, no more than three months elapsed between the first lesson and the date of their marriage. Oliva had not wasted his time, but when the moment came for action he conducted himself in the most approved fashion. It is from his sister Isabel

that we learn that he sent his parents formally to ask for
Pepita's hand. They had scarcely known Pepita or her
mother until their son despatched them on this mission,
and when he did speak to them of his intentions they
were anything but pleased. Their sense of propriety did
not at all relish the current rumour that Catalina was not
really married to Lopez; and as for Lopez himself, they
considered that he was far too often seen idling on
horseback with a cigar in his mouth while the women
looked after the family earnings. For the same reasons,
they were most reluctant to allow their daughter Isabel
to frequent the basement in the Encomienda, even after
they had been compelled to accept the engagement
with as good a grace as possible. There is a faint note of
wistfulness in Isabel's evidence; clearly she would have
liked to come closer to the romantic figure who was
about to become her sister-in-law, but even on the rare
occasions when she was allowed to visit there, Pepita,
occupied with her own affairs, remained withdrawn. "I
saw Pepita from two to three times in all before the
wedding . . . my acquaintance with her remained very
slight, either because she was of a very reserved nature
or because she considered me a child. Whenever I went
to Pepita's I saw her mother"—alas, no opportunity for
intimacy there!—"At that time I was about seventeen.
I have an idea that Pepita was then about nineteen or
twenty." What a gulf those two or three years made!
But how intensely the younger girl admired her from
the distance thus imposed! "She was very pretty. Her
eyes were large, black, and almond-shaped,—what the
Spanish call *rasgados*. She had no particular habit or
peculiarity, such for example as twitching of the eyes,
but her way of looking at one was what is called in
Spanish *muy gracioso*, that is to say, very seductive and
agreeable. Her manner of walking was very *airoso*, that

is to say, very airy and graceful; her disposition very
amiable; her mode of speaking was charming, neither
fast nor slow, just like most of the Andalusians, that is
to say, *in tono alegre* (vivacious and animated). She had
small feet like most Andalusians, a dimpled chin, and
small pretty ears. She was the same height as Juan
Antonio; I know this because Juan Antonio was nearly
an inch shorter than my brother Agustin, who has his
exact height stated in his Military Service Ticket as
1666 millimetres. The reason why I say that Pepita was
just as tall as Juan Antonio is that I have often seen
them walking together. Her hair was black and very
shiny. It is common in Spain for women to have long
and abundant hair, but in Pepita's case it was exceptionally so. It was at Pepita's house that I saw her
combing her hair. . . ."

Poor Isabel was not the only one who, with admiration, watched Pepita combing that marvellous hair.
Manuel Guerrero, who, as a ballet-master, was well
accustomed to dealing with decorative women, later saw
her combing it at an hotel window, and thought it
worth while to record his impression: "Long, thick,
luxuriant, it reached down below the knee". But that
was much later; that was after delirious audiences in
Germany had forced her to let it down upon the stage
as they refused to believe it was not false. Guerrero was
not personally acquainted with Pepita at the time of her
engagement to Oliva; he knew her only by sight as the
girl who had had her contract cancelled at the theatre
because her dancing was not up to their standard, but
who nevertheless had been the cause of the promising
young Oliva renouncing his job. He saw her walk
slowly down the street as he stood with a group of his
friends at the door of the Café de Venecia at the corner
of Plaza Santa Ana and the Calle del Príncipe, a café,

as he says, "usually frequented by artists", and through
the bald words of his statement the whole scene comes
to life.   .

She passed down the street accompanied by Catalina,
Lopez, and Juan Antonio Oliva himself. "What a fine
girl", Guerrero said, and one of his friends, he didn't
know which, replied that she was Juan Antonio's
sweetheart. "There", he added, "goes the intended
bride of Oliva." Guerrero, who did not happen to be
employed at the same theatre as Oliva, had no personal
acquaintance then with him either, "but of course I and
all my theatrical friends knew of the marriage. She was
so very handsome that she attracted everybody's attention. We all stood looking at her admiringly. The
distance at which I saw her would have been the width
of the street, which is about the width of two carriages.
She was such a striking person that, once seen, you
could not possibly mistake her. I stood looking at her
as she went down the street. I can even remember the
dress she wore. She had on a dark-coloured gown with
the shawl known as the *manton de capucha* with many
colours, and on her head she wore a black Spanish
mantilla. She wore the *sortijilla*, that is the lock or ring
of hair on the cheek by the ear."

Could more be said? Oh, young and lovely gypsy,
reserved, a promised bride, how glad I am that you
once passed down a street in Madrid, before a café
frequented by artists, so very handsome that you
attracted everybody's attention in your mantilla and
your *manton*, the *sortijilla* on your cheek, and lived to
work out the strange career which after many vicissitudes made you the mother of my mother.

Pepita, can I re-create you? Come to me. Make
yourself alive again. Vitality such as yours cannot
perish. I know so much about you: I have talked to old

men who knew you, and they have all told me the same legend of your beauty. There was an old Swede once in Rome, who had known you, and who loved my mother partly for your sake, though partly also for her own. Why should I be afraid of invoking you or my own mother, who are both dead though you were both once so much alive,—more vividly and troublesomely alive than most people? You both made trouble for everybody connected with you. You were both that sort of person. Yet you were both adored.

Pepita, my grandmother,—it is difficult for me, your grandchild, to think of you as a grandmother, for you seem to me so eternally young,—come back to me. I wish I had known you in the flesh. My mother, who was only nine when you died, told me so many stories about you that she made you into a living person for me from my childhood upwards. She had loved you herself and made me love you in my turn. Even as Juan Antonio Oliva found you in Madrid and loved you when you were just nineteen, even as my grandfather found you in Paris and loved you when you were twenty-two, so did my mother love you and so do I, for evidently you were a person made to be loved.

There was an evening once in Seville, years ago, when your ghost seemed to stand very close behind me, so close as almost to lay a soft hand upon my shoulder. It was a May evening, and the air in the warm narrow streets was overpoweringly heavy with the scent of orange-blossom. It had been heavy all day, but in this velvet dusk it deepened into an actual caress of the senses. I was walking with friends through the silent, shuttered streets to a party. Now there were at that time many places in Seville where foreigners might go to watch gypsy dancing, but this was no such place; this was a private party, given in a private house by an

artist resident in Seville who had for many years been
well acquainted with the gypsies of Triana (the gypsy
quarter), some of whom he had coaxed through long
familiarity into sometimes serving him as models. From
this, they had taken the habit of frequenting his house,
quite at their ease without the suspicion that they were
being in any way exploited.

We knocked, and were admitted. The street door
shut behind us, quickly and secretively.

The *patio*,[1] after the dusk of the streets, seemed
brilliantly lit, but in fact it only glowed with the
coloured lights of many lanterns festooned along the
balconies of the upper storey. So subdued and mellow
were the lights that they gave us only the impression
of a great deal of colour and the indistinct forms of
people grouping in the shadows. Looking up, I could
see other people looking over on the balconies, whisper-
ing together above the gaudy shawls which, after the
fashion of the Andalusian bull-ring in the time of the
fiesta, they had hung over the balconies all round the
patio. There was a fountain splashing in the middle of
the *patio*. The night-sky made a square of black ceiling
with its stars.

Someone struck a few chords on a guitar. An immensely fat woman, the fattest woman I had ever seen,
strode out from under the balcony and, planting herself
down on a perilously small chair beside the fountain,
her knees wide apart and a hand splayed on each knee,
began to sing. She sang what appeared to be an in-
terminable lament, in a voice like a trombone, and as
she sang she began to sway backwards and forwards,
as though she indeed bewailed some personal grief
too intolerable for her mountainous flesh to bear. The
combination of her grotesque appearance and the

[1] Inner courtyard, open to the sky, common to all Spanish houses.

magnificently profound notes of her complaint, suggested some primeval sorrow untranslatable save into the terms of that bellowing song.

She ceased as abruptly as she had begun, and sat there complacently mopping the sweat from her brow. The guitar took up again, in another strain this time, a twanging strain, and one by one the indistinct figures came out from the shadows. I saw then that they were all gypsies, for by their lineaments and their garments they could have been nothing else. They were without exception the most beautiful human beings I ever wish to see. Some of them, of course, were old and wrinkled, but even those still bore the traces of their youthful looks in the bony architecture of their features and in the tragic dignity of their sunken eyes. Others were in their prime, adult and arrogant; but others were divinely young, elusively adolescent, like wild things that never ought to have submitted to the coaxing of even the kindliest hand. There was one pair in particular, a girl of perhaps eighteen, a youth perhaps two years older; they kept close together, suspicious and alert as though the outside world threatened the affinity between them; he watched her with a close and jealous eye, ready to snatch and guard her; and she, for her part, shrank closer to him whenever another man by chance came near; they were both as fine and graceful as a pair of antelopes, and seemed just as ready to bound away.

The guitars by then were twanging in unison; the little *patio* was filled by those strange minor cadences; feet were beginning to tap; the enormous singer, still planted on her tiny chair by the fountain, was beginning to sway again and to clap her hands together in the monotonous, exciting rhythm. Little by little, and as it were impelled by no organised intention, they began to dance. At first it was little more than an instinctive balancing of their bodies, then feet fell into measure, fingers began to snap, and the *patio* was alive with these strangely undulating and sinuous figures, dancing with a curious intensity in which there was no thought of anything but rhythm and dancing. They seemed, indeed, to be part of the rough music and the scented night. There was no thought of sex in it; or perhaps it might be said that the whole thing was an expression of sex, love, passion, so impersonal as to transcend anything trivial or ephemeral in the emotion, and to translate it into eternal terms with which the music, the night, and the colour were inherently mixed. The extraordinary purity and beauty of the performance was only enhanced by the vast black figure seated by the fountain, a powerfully obscene goddess immortalised by some sculptor of genius.

I thought the guitars would never end; they twanged on and on until their effect became almost hypnotic. I noticed then that the centre of the *patio* was emptying, and that most of the dancers had retreated again into the shadows. They crouched there, beating time with the clapping of their hands, and as the music grew faster and wilder they uttered hoarse cries and rose again to their feet with the excitement of the music, pressing round in a narrowing circle until they ringed the solitary pair left dancing in the light of the lanterns. These were the two that I had specially observed. Forgetful of all else, tawny and beautiful, they swayed opposite to one another, as though each dared the other in a mortally dangerous game. Then he sank on to one knee, watching her, clapping softly, half in admiration, half in a menacing derision, as she danced alone. The wild animal in him crouched, waiting to spring. Provocative, she would pass a little closer to him, when he made a half-gesture as though to catch her; elusive, she would glide away, and all the time there was an undercurrent of truth running with a snarl between them.

The next thing I knew was that they were all laughing like children at some purely farcical incident. The two young creatures were gone, and I never saw or wished to see them again. I had seen them once, and that was enough. I had seen unforgettable beauty in human form, and they, all unaware, had brought me nearer to Pepita.

v

On January 10th, 1851, Juan Antonio de la Oliva and Pepita Duran y Ortega were married at the church of San Millan, where Juan Antonio had been baptized nearly twenty-two years previously. Oliva's sister, Isabel, tells us that when once the marriage was seen to be inevitable her parents resigned themselves to it and "everything became pleasant and agreeable". The ceremony provided an occasion for a great gathering of family and friends, and for subsequent festivities which are recorded with appreciation by Isabel. The bride naturally could not produce as many relations in the city where she was, after all, a stranger, as the bridegroom whose native town it was. So far as the records make out, her only contribution to the party consisted of Catalina her mother, Manuel Lopez, her brother Diego, and the child Lola. Oliva, on the other hand, was nobly supported by a host of relations who saw an opportunity for getting not only a breakfast and a dinner at somebody else's expense, but a dance and its attendant jollity thrown in.

At about 8 A.M. on the wedding day Juan Antonio, with all his more immediate relations, went to the house of the bride. There were his father and mother,

his sister Isabel, his brothers Joaquin, Agustin, and
Frederico with his son and daughter, and a friend
named Ramon Acero who was to act as *padrino*. At the
Calle de la Encomienda, Catalina, Lopez, Diego, Lola,
and the bride herself were waiting for them, when they
all proceeded together to the church of San Millan.
Pepita, according to the usual custom, was dressed in
black. She wore a black lace mantilla but no veil, and
drew from one of the Madrilenian guests the comment
that she looked dressed like an Andalusian going to a
bull-fight. A great many more friends and relations
were waiting for them at the church, including "at
least fourteen uncles and aunts" and Pedrosa, who had
come very reluctantly because Oliva had pressed him to
do so, accepting the invitation only on the understanding that he should not be asked to go to Catalina's
house. Oliva seemed surprised to see him, and the first
words he said were, "Oh, I thought you were not
coming". After the ceremony Pedrosa went into the
Sacristy for Oliva's sake and shook hands with Pepita.
He saluted Catalina but avoided shaking hands with
her. Lopez, however, came up to him and shook hands
before he could prevent it. Oliva, who had been paying
the marriage fees while everybody else collected their
hats and coats, came up in his turn and pressed Pedrosa
to come to the wedding dinner; Pedrosa agreed, but did
not go, because of his objection to Catalina and Lopez.

Another very small guest survived to leave a rather
rueful record nearly fifty years later. This was Luisa,
the bridegroom's niece. "I was just six years of age. I
remember having seen my uncle several times before
his marriage and knew him as being my Uncle Juan
Antonio. I recollect being taken to the church of San
Millan and seeing a great number of people. I had some
impression that Mass was being performed. It was the

first wedding ceremony I had ever attended. I think I was too young to be taken notice of."

Agustin Oliva, however, the bridegroom's brother, who had attained the age of seven and a half, preserved quite a definite impression of his new sister-in-law. "She was *muy guapa* (very pretty) and dark." He remembered being taken to some café after the wedding, and having something, but he couldn't remember what. His sister-in-law had evidently made more impression on him than the subsequent cakes.

Luckily we have more to go on than the evidence of these two children. Isabel Oliva leaves a graphic account. "After the ceremony, we all adjourned to the Café Suiza, where some took coffee, others chocolate, and others whatever they pleased. From the Café Suiza, both parties returned to their respective homes and changed their wedding clothes, and afterwards the Oliva family, including Juan Antonio, went to Pepita's house, from whence both families walked about the streets arm-in-arm till three-thirty or four o'clock, when they went to dinner at the Fonda de Europa, where we had the wedding feast in a room specially engaged for the purpose. It is the custom for the *padrino* to provide the wedding feast at his own cost. After dinner we retired to another room and passed the evening dancing till about one o'clock in the morning. Juan Antonio had an engagement at the Teatro Español, and had to leave the wedding party for a short time to go and perform his part. After that we all accompanied the bride and bridegroom to the house in Calle Encomienda and said good-bye to each other at the door.

"As soon as the marriage had been seen to be inevitable, the differences between the families ceased and everything was pleasant and agreeable at the wedding and the dinner."

And pleasantly noisy too, we might credibly add.
The family of a Spaniard associated with the theatre
was not likely to comport itself with much restraint on
such an occasion as the marriage-feast of its brilliant
and successful young scion. We are told that they
danced polkas, waltzes, and quadrilles, and that Pepita
"threw herself with zest into every dance that went
forward". I imagine that they must have been very gay
and uproarious, and that they looked with a good deal of
curiosity at the dark Andalusian swaying in the arms of
her bridegroom.

VI

Between two and three months later, Juan Antonio
Oliva turned up again in Madrid. He went straight
to Pedrosa's house, and found Pedrosa still in bed.
Pedrosa was surprised to see him, although it was no
unusual thing for Oliva to visit him on his return from
fulfilling some dancing engagement, even before he had
called in at the house of his parents, but on this occasion
he had believed him to be far away, touring Spain with
his young wife and her family. Pedrosa knew that after
the marriage they had remained living in the Calle de la
Encomienda with Catalina and Lopez, for although he
had declined to visit them there, he had once or twice
met Oliva and Pepita walking arm-in-arm together in
the street and on each occasion had stopped to converse
with them. He had evidently not noticed what the
Oliva family had noticed, "that almost from the day of
the marriage Juan Antonio appeared to be depressed
and down-hearted". He knew only that they had all left
Madrid together, had heard of them passing through
Ocana and Toledo, and had had news of them again
in Valencia. Now here was Juan Antonio, alone.

They had breakfast together, and over breakfast

Oliva told Pedrosa that he had quarrelled with Catalina and had come away. Pepita had not wanted him to come away, but he had insisted on doing so. "He said", added Pedrosa, "that it was one of those questions which sometimes arise between a man and his wife on account of the mother-in-law." What that question exactly was, we shall never know, nor shall we ever know what exactly had taken place at Valencia to send Oliva flinging away by himself in spite of Pepita's protests; but we do know that Pedrosa always laid the blame at Catalina's door. "I am certain", he says, "that the cause of the separation was Catalina", and it is manifest that in his loyal way he felt deeply indignant on behalf of his injured friend. Oliva, indeed, fully agreed that it was Catalina who had made the trouble, but it was not a question he ever cared to discuss. "He was very reticent in the family circle as to the relations between himself and Pepita"—this is his sister Isabel speaking again;— "He stated that the causes of the separation were not honourable to Pepita, that there were some things which he could not tolerate, and that he blamed mostly her mother." Beyond this, he told his family nothing, though poor Isabel's curiosity was whetted to an unbearable pitch. His state of dejection was obvious to all, and "having once made his reserved revelation, he could never bear to hear even the name of Pepita mentioned by the family". Once, however, when he caught sight of Lopez in a box at the theatre, he started up with the exclamation, "There is that rogue!" (*bribon*). But "so punctilious in matters of honour" was he, that he would never breathe a word of disparagement against Pepita. It is all very mysterious. There is no doubt that he had been very much in love with Pepita; and as for Pepita herself, she had tried to prevent him from leaving her, and it was many months before she could speak of

him without tears coming into her eyes. Whatever it
was that Catalina said or did, or forced Pepita to do in
Valencia in the spring of 1851, it was certainly something which effectively wrecked the married life of her
daughter and son-in-law. They would have been better
off away from the tyranny of that jealous, possessive,
and, I suspect, mercenary, though generous and charitable woman, Catalina Ortega.

CHAPTER III

THE STAR OF ANDALUSIA

I

"THE cholera began to get serious and to kill many people", said Jose Ligeno Castillo. "Most deaths occurred on St. Peter's Day, which is the 29th of June."

It had broken out in Granada, and amongst other refugees who came flying in the heat of summer from the plague to seek safety in neighbouring villages were the ex-peddlers Lopez and Catalina, accompanied by the girl Lola and attended by a down-trodden poor relation named Rafaela, who was said to be a niece of one of them and whom they treated little better than a servant. Catalina's son Diego, who had been with them in Madrid, was no longer with them now, for they had had a quarrel (it will be observed that quarrels were frequent in this family), and he had disappeared from the house. It was to the little village of Chaparral that they first came, but before very long they removed to Albolote, some three and a half miles north of Granada, and there proceeded to dazzle their new neighbours by the luxury and extravagance of their preparations. For the fortunes of the family had undergone a startling change since the days of the basement in Madrid. Lopez had now got a thick gold watch-chain, and rings on his fingers; Catalina had a gold chain too; Lola had a German governess; Catalina had a French maid called Marie; they had horses, carriages, a coachman, and dogs with foreign names. Altogether their arrival

43

aroused great interest and curiosity at Albolote, which was a quiet place, lying a little way off the main road, so that its southern monotony could not be disturbed even by the passing of the public *diligence*, periodically drawing up in a cloud of dust on its way between Jaen and Granada.

Their new neighbours remembered details of the establishment for many years afterwards. The carriage-horses were bright bays called Garbozo and Malagueño; the Galician pony for fetching water was Gallego; the saddle-horses were Esmeralda and Pia, the former a dark chestnut, the latter a white *jaca* (a pony or small horse) with chestnut spots. Andalusian horses were, of course, prized above all others in Spain, with their peculiar loose-limbed gait, flowing tail, and long mane which their owners delighted to plait with coloured ribbons. The principal carriage was a *galera*, which is described as a four-wheeled carriage with a cover over the top, and seats facing sideways,—in fact a sort of roofed-in waggonette,—the ends of which might be closed or opened though the top was permanent. This conveyance was always drawn by at least two horses and sometimes three, but on occasion Lopez substituted mules. He always drove the carriage himself, taking the coachman (who had no livery) to sit beside him on the box.

It is stated that "they used sometimes to drive unicorn". For one wild moment I imagined that the fabulous beast was meant, and that the correct plural of what I had always called unicorns was unicorn, as sheep is the plural of a single sheep, and fish of fish; it seemed to me that so fantastic an equipage would have exactly appealed to Catalina's mind; but then to my chagrin I discovered that it meant only a pair of horses with a third horse in front.

The family had arrived at Albolote in their *galera*, and I am irresistibly reminded of Ford's description of just such a removal as must then have taken place: "The packing and departure of the *galera*, when hired by a family who remove their goods, is a thing of Spain; the heavy luggage is stowed in first, and beds and mattresses spread on the top, on which the family repose in admired disorder". Even if Lopez, Catalina, Lola, their servants and their dogs conducted themselves with a little more dignity as befitted their recent rise to fortune and the fact that the carriage was their own and not a public vehicle which might be hired, one imagines that they still managed to present a sufficiently untidy and raffish appearance. Perhaps even their dogs were carried in the loose open net hanging beneath the carriage, "in which lies a horrid dog, who keeps a Cerberus watch over pots and sieves and suchlike gypsy utensils, and who is never to be conciliated".

II

It appeared at first as though the family intended to take up its residence permanently in Albolote. Money seemed to be no object, and the Casa Blanca in the Plaza Real changed hands. It was a corner house in the principal square, with the parish church on another side of the square, the council-house on another. Thus the Casa Blanca occupied a central position in the village. Its former owner, Don Baltasar Subira y Melero, was fortunate in finding such lavish purchasers for his house, which he watched being "altered and decorated and converted into a perfect palace, changing it almost entirely, having it very well arranged with much and good furniture".

The ideas of the two witnesses I have just quoted,

both of whom had been born in Albolote and lived
there all their lives, may possibly not coincide with ours
as to the "perfect palace" and the "very good furniture". I should imagine that the taste of the ex-circus
gypsy Catalina and the ex-bandit Lopez was profoundly
to be mistrusted. I imagine overcrowded and over-
loaded rooms, very stiff and uncomfortable, and all
arranged with a view to the utmost display of gentility
and ostentation. They had lived in poverty all their
lives, and now at last knew the pleasure of having money
to spend as they conceived it ought to be spent. Catalina
was the one who appeared to be in control of the family
purse, and was not always very delicate in her dealings
with Lopez on the subject. Indeed, the Director of the
Provincial Hospital, who speaks of them with a note
of disapproval throughout, reports that she and Lopez
(who, he has the charity to add, was looked upon as the
only lover of Catalina), used often to quarrel, and that
during these quarrels she would threaten to "kick him
out and send him back to his trade as a shoemaker".
Lopez, it seems clear, was a man who inspired derision
rather than respect. The villagers themselves thought
him funny. He could frequently be observed riding the
saddle-horses for exercise on the Plaza and showing-off
as he rode; was considered "very odd in his mode of
dress"; and before very long got his nickname in the
village: *el tio Caninica*, he was called, meaning one who
wears a belt with a lot of things stuck in it. In Granada
he was known as *el tio zapatero* (Uncle shoemaker),
because "he shod to perfection the members of his
family". The priest summed him up as "the sort of man
who might have risen from the position of an artisan
and had suddenly become better off". Francisco
Ramirez did not think much of him either. "He was just
the kind of man", he exclaimed contemptuously, "who

would get up on the box and take the reins". An agricultural labourer, Pedro Quesada, thought he "looked like a workman dressed as a gentleman". The widow Rafaela Pinel, on the other hand, who had heard Catalina snubbing him, dismissed him as "a short, insignificant, common-looking man who wore a short jacket and a close-fitting cap".

Lola was a spoilt, merry child; people remembered her afterwards as "always skipping and jumping about the house".

This very odd and unexplained lot of arrivals must have seemed like a flock of brilliantly plumaged birds settling down on to the Plaza Real of little Albolote. They puzzled the villagers, the Alcalde (judge), and the parish priest, who were used to rich landowners but not to rich adventurers of such obviously inferior birth. But they were welcome. Catalina was reported as "a very good lady", and both she and Lopez were considered "very charitable, doing much good to the poor". Besides, they gave employment, engaging several local maidservants as well as the labourers employed in the restoration and renovation of the house. They were friendly, open-handed, hospitable people. Don Miguel Reyes Valdivia, who was acting as assistant priest of the parish at that time, noticed that "whenever anyone went to their house, they were immediately regaled with something". Don Miguel lived quite near to them, in the Calle Real, and it was not long before he fell into the habit of calling frequently upon them. Spaniards as a rule are chary of welcoming strangers within their doors, but any such reluctance was noticeably lacking in this odd couple, who in the midst of their prosperity retained their jolly raggle-taggle Bohemianism. They were perhaps a little indiscriminating in their friendships. Señor Corral, the grocer, who supplied Catalina with pork and other articles of food, seems to have been quite as warmly received as the Alcalde. His shop in the Plaza de Aminas was quite near the Casa Blanca, and after becoming acquainted with Catalina, who did her own marketing, he was apparently free to drop in at the Casa Blanca whenever he liked. But of all the friends whom the cheerful adventurers made in Albolote, the most intimate were the members of the Gonzalez family, Manuel Gonzalez, his wife, his daughter Micaela, and his peculiar son, Juan de Dios. The Gonzalez family were next-door neighbours, and so rapidly did the intimacy between the two families advance that they "soon caused a door to be made in the wall between the two gardens".

III

Gossip and speculation in Albolote did not long remain unsatisfied as to the resources of the new arrivals. Catalina made friends, and as fast as she made friends she talked. She talked to the grocer, the priest, the assistant priest, the Alcalde, the Gonzalez family, the labourers, and the servants. The burden of her conversation was ever the same, turn by turn boastful, wistful, vainglorious, touching. Everything was explained: the incongruous wealth, the luxury, the horses, the fine clothes, the fine furniture, the jewellery, the foreign dogs, the French maid, the German governess, the purchase and renovation of the Casa Blanca, the transformation of the gypsy and the cobbler into the prosperous bourgeois. Somewhere in the background was the mysterious romantic figure who paid for it all, "Pepa,—my little Pepa,—my Pepita,—my daughter the famous *bailarina*", Pepita whom she "wished would come, that she might have her at her side"; Pepita of the many, the princely lovers; Pepita, the Star of Andalusia.

For the little Pepa whom they had brought from Malaga to seek her fortune in Madrid, and who had suffered the reverse of having her contract cancelled at the Teatro del Príncipe, was now away from them, out in the great unknown world beyond the Pyrenees, a dancer of European reputation. Some local people already knew her; Don Gabriel de Burgos, for instance, a most respect-worthy lawyer, had lived opposite to her in Granada when she was staying there with her mother in Calle de las Arandas; he had "talked with her several times from their respective balconies, these being opposite to each other, the width of the street being about four metres. Our conversation was always of an indifferent nature. She was beautiful, sympathetic, and of pleasant conversation." She was quite well known already then, and people who saw them passing in the street would take notice and point them out to one another, saying, "That is Catalina", or "That is Pepita Oliva", or, taken together, "That is the family of La Bailarina".

She had left them in Granada and, from the Grand Theatre at Bordeaux, her first engagement, had gone, according to Catalina, all over the world leaving a trail of glory behind her. At Copenhagen she had lived in the most expensive hotel in the utmost luxury with a secretary and a theatrical manager; she had danced a dance called La Farsa Pepita, especially composed in her honour, and the enthusiastic audience had taken the horses out of her carriage and had drawn her through the streets themselves. Germany had acclaimed her, especially at Frankfurt-am-Main, at Stuttgart, and in Berlin; in London she had been billed to appear at Her Majesty's Theatre. There was a newspaper cutting

from *The Times* of May 22nd, 1852. "First appearance
of the Spanish dancer Doña Pepita Oliva. In the course
of the evening a divertissement in which the Spanish
dancer Doña Pepita Oliva (from the Teatro Real del
Príncipe) will appear. It is respectfully announced that
a great extra night will take place on Thursday next,
May 27th, when will be presented Bellini's celebrated
opera *Norma*, after which the admired advertisement
La Tête des Rossières, to be followed by Guecco's celebrated bouffa, *La Prova d'un Opera Seria*, to which
will be added a divertissement in which Doña Pepita
will appear." Here she had danced the Madrilena, the
Aragoneza, and El Haleo de Jerez. She had been a
great success in London as elsewhere. In Germany she
had been such a popular success that the audience had
shouted for her to let down her marvellous hair on the
stage to prove that it was not false.

I have a picture of her dancing the Aragoneza. It is
not a very good picture, being in fact a tinted and somewhat fanciful engraving by a Berlin artist, but it does
contrive to give an impression of the energy and vitality
she flung into her dancing. The short ballet skirt of rose
red silk is flounced with white and blue. She wears a
tight bodice of white satin with panels of dark blue
velvet. Her throat and shoulders are bare, but for the
narrow shoulder-straps provocatively slipping. She is
lightly poised on one toe, her tiny foot pointed in a pink
satin slipper. Two pink roses lie dropped on the ground
beside her; a third one nestles in her dark hair behind
her ear. A heavy gold bangle encircles one wrist; the
castanets are lightly held. Her eyes flash, and her lips
are parted in a smile.

Catalina had always been proud of her daughter and
now had considerable justification for her pride. She
spared no pains in boasting about her to her new

friends at Albolote. In the volubility of her confidences she not only exposed whatever she knew at first hand about Pepita's private life,—"she said that Pepita and her husband had fallen out and were separated; the husband's name was Antonio Oliva, a Madrilenian and a *bolero* or dancer"—but also exposed her own confused ideas of how she might most reputably represent her daughter to the imagination of Albolote. For example, she freely told Micaela Gonzalez (who was only nine years old), that Pepita was "a very famous dancer in Germany", and she said much the same thing to the Coadjutor, to the son of the Alcalde, and to Doña Francisca Navarro. To Señor Corral, the grocer, however,—perhaps with a sense of social difference,—she denied that Pepita was a dancer, but claimed that she gave "mimic representations which were a great success and brought her in large sums of money". It is impossible to fathom the complications of Catalina's mind, which suddenly made her decide that the grocer might not be allowed to think of Pepita as a dancer but only as a mimic, which, so far as I know, she never was. The subtlety of this differentiation escapes me. Why is it more honourable to be a mimic than a dancer? It is a question which I should dearly like to have out with my great-grandmother Catalina, but she unfortunately has been dead for over sixty years.

On the other hand, she was quite prepared to be outspoken on the subject of Pepita's lovers. She never denied that Pepita was "under the protection" of some rich foreigner. Indeed, she seemed proud of this fact which, by her conversation, she spread widely throughout Albolote. Pepita lived, said Catalina, in a palace at Heidelberg. Lopez also would boast about her, saying that she earned quantities of money and was "very intimate" with a foreign prince. The only point where

Catalina varied her story was in the identity of the rich
foreigner. Sometimes he was merely and anonymously
a prince; sometimes the Prince of Metternich; sometimes the Prince of Bavaria; sometimes, on very grand
occasions, the Emperor of Germany himself. That there
was no such person as an Emperor of Germany in 1855
made no difference to Catalina: she had merely invented
him some fifteen years before he came into actual existence. To the simple, snobbish, boastful, circus mind of
the gypsy turned bourgeoise, nothing but an Emperor
could suffice as the protector of her dazzling child. She
created the German Empire prophetically to suit her
story. It seems strange that in spite of the very close
contact she maintained with Pepita during these years,
she should never have known the real truth. Perhaps
the truth, as such, made no appeal to Catalina; perhaps,
temperamentally, she preferred the Imperial fiction. She
would drive into Granada to send telegrams to Pepita in
Germany. Her groom reported that she "used to go into
the Telegraph Office to send the telegrams and when
she came out she would tell Lopez that they had cost so
many dollars. 'Manuel,' she would say, 'the telegram
has cost me eight dollars.' Whenever a letter arrived
from Pepita, Catalina would stop dinner or whatever
we were doing in order to read it. The letter used to be
passed round and Catalina would say, 'Look, here is a
letter from Pepita'." Yet in spite of this extravagantly
sustained relationship she seems to have had no inkling
at all as to what was really shaping Pepita's life.

IV

She knew nothing of the young English attaché at
Stuttgart. Lionel Sackville-West, the fifth son of the
fifth Earl de la Warr, (a title which, according to the

Spanish press later on, had been created by Queen Isabel Tudor), had become an assistant précis-writer to Lord Aberdeen at the age of eighteen, and at the age of twenty had entered the English Foreign Office. It seemed the prescribed career for the younger son of good family, who had then no prospect at all of succeeding to the family inheritance. Appointments followed in due course: Attaché, unpaid, Lisbon, 1847; Attaché, unpaid, Naples, 1848; Attaché, paid, Stuttgart, 1852.

What could Catalina know of such a young man? Even had she remembered the embraces of the Duke of Osuna, she could scarcely have associated them with the upbringing of a young English aristocrat. The Duke of Osuna at any rate, was her own countryman; spoke her own language; understood, however remotely, the shape of her mind. She shared the landscape of Spain with him; knew more than he did about his own peasants, and could follow what he meant when he talked about the year's vintage or olive-crop. But with the young English aristocrat-diplomat she could have had nothing in common. She knew nothing of the English house where he was born, or of the deer flicking their tails beneath the beeches in his English park. She could know nothing of his traditions or his codes.

Pepita, very wisely, kept Lionel Sackville-West as a secret to herself. She was quite willing and ready to pay for everything at Albolote, the house, the furniture, the horses, and the clothes. She was quite willing to let her mother believe in the Prince of Metternich, the Prince of Bavaria, and the Emperor of Germany. Indeed, she personally and lavishly perpetuated these legends. But of the true lover she said not a word.

Yet by the time that Catalina settled in Albolote, she

had known him for three years. It was in the autumn of
1852 that Lionel Sackville-West had travelled from
Stuttgart to meet his parents and his younger brother
William Edward in Paris. Eluding their parents one
evening, the two young men went together to the
theatre, and Lionel pointed out a woman sitting on the
opposite side of the house. He told his brother that this
was the dancer Pepita Oliva; he knew her only by sight,
he said, but hoped to be introduced to her shortly. He
was then twenty-five and she was twenty-two. The
rest of the story can be told practically in his own
words.

She was living at the Hôtel de Bade, situated in one
of the streets leading into the Boulevard des Italiens. He
was under the impression that it was a perfectly respectable hotel. His friend Sir Frederick Arthur took him
there to introduce him, "not as a fast woman, but as
an artiste and a lady and a danseuse. He (that is Sir
Frederick) said, 'This is a famous Spanish danseuse who
is going to dance in Germany'. We treated her with
respect and propriety. For aught I know she was at
that time living a perfectly respectable life."

Then comes the simple statement: "I was in love
with Pepita".

v

They became lovers at once. The passion which swept
over them threw respect and propriety to the winds.
His own shyness and hesitations were overcome by
Pepita herself, for he tells us that "she first suggested
this condition of things to me; I seriously say this",
but adds with engaging naïveté, "I visited her with the
intention of its leading up to that object, though the
actual fact came about at her solicitation". Does it
matter very much? They were both young, she was

intoxicatingly beautiful, he had only a week to spend in Paris, and they spent every night of it together. Pepita was absolutely honest with him from the first. She told him all about her unfortunate marriage and that she was separated from Oliva. This worried him—"I thought it was a wrong thing to have the liaison with her"—but in spite of his scruples he was already too deeply in love to break it off. Before he was obliged to leave Paris and return to duty at the end of the week they had made every arrangement for meeting again in Germany. "I told her I would get an engagement for her at the Theatre at Stuttgart. I used my influence and got her an engagement and she came there and danced. She fulfilled a number of engagements in Germany and during that time she became famous and made considerable sums of money." They were together whenever they could possibly manage it, and with a lack of caution remarkable in a diplomat, he took no trouble to conceal the fact. "I cannot tell you whether it was known in the hotels that I was passing the night with her; there was no secrecy about it whatever. I gave my name at the hotels. Our liaison was a secret from her mother and the rest of the family."

When they were parted, he wrote her letters beginning "Mon ange, bien aimée de mon cœur. . . ."

VI

Meanwhile Catalina, in ignorance of all this in distant Albolote, continued to send telegrams and to wish ardently that her daughter would come for a visit, however brief. Pepita, whose money had paid for everything, had never seen the renovations at the Casa Blanca! They had so much to show her. The spotted *jaca* was waiting for her to ride. The day of her arrival, always

hoped for but ever postponed, was the day for which
Catalina lived. Catalina must have felt, at moments, that
it was a little disheartening to continue boasting about
a daughter who never materialised. Yet Catalina could
have had no justifiable grievance. Pepita was a good
daughter; Pepita had taken her to Paris once; Pepita
had now got Lola in Germany with her and was looking
after Lola; Pepita sent her earnings home and maintained her family in state. There was nothing to complain of, save only that Pepita failed to come to Spain.
And Catalina longed for her to come.

They had been at Albolote for about a year when
Catalina was able triumphantly to announce the imminent arrival of her daughter. Preparations for her
welcome were instantly set afoot. The Gonzalez family,
who by now were so intimate with Catalina and Lopez
that they were to be found almost every day running in
and out of the Casa Blanca, started the idea of "receiving
her with some splendour" and busied themselves with
enlisting the help of the greater part of the village,
including tne Alcalde and the members of the Ayuntamiento (Town Council). It was decided that this tre-
mendous event could best be celebrated with the assist-
ance of a brass band, but as Albolote itself boasted of no
band a message was sent to the neighbouring village of
Atarfe, requesting the loan of theirs. The band of
Atarfe was only too pleased to oblige. Events such as
this were rare in the dusty, sun-baked little southern
villages lying in the rich *vega* of Granada within sight
of the eternal snows of the Sierra Nevada. Not only
were they all inquisitive to see this Star of Andalusia
who by her sobriquet carried the honour of their own
province abroad, but the legend of her wealth was
widespread and Catalina was both popular and generous. The local carpenter remembered "the general

satisfaction and joy expressed in the village the first time she (Pepita) came, because of the good impression her mother had made there; she gave a deal away in charity, and had got a good name". For one reason and another, the village flared into excitement.

They knew exactly the hour at which Pepita would arrive, for she was coming out from Granada by the ordinary *diligence*, which would stop at the point where the road to Albolote branches off from the main road. It would stop there shortly before six o'clock in the evening. Catalina had been busy all day, making ready; amongst other things, Felix Gomez their handy-man, who slept over the stables, and who had heard Catalina telling Lopez that Pepita was soon coming, had been despatched into Granada to buy fish and other provisions. Thus, to his chagrin, he was not present at Pepita's arrival, nor, presumably, at the departure of the whole family in their *galera*, accompanied by the Alcalde, the Ayuntamiento, the band from Atarfe, and most of the people from Albolote, setting out to meet Pepita at the stopping-place of the *diligence*.

It was a double excitement for Catalina. For Lola also was returning after her sojourn in Germany in charge of Pepita; and although Lola was not Catalina's own daughter, but only the daughter of Lopez by another woman, she was fond of the child in her exuberant, affectionate, inclusive way. As she hung her gold chain round her neck, preparing herself for the expedition to meet the *diligence*, she must have felt satisfaction underneath all her excitement: satisfaction at the thought of her family being once more united. That thought probably transcended, at the moment, even the flattering attendance of her neighbours upon the arrival of Pepita.

VII

Pepita alighted from the *diligence* at the expected place and at the expected hour. She was followed out of the *diligence* by Lola, then a child of eleven; by two German servants, who, already slightly bewildered by their journey across Europe, must have emerged completely puzzled by this final stage landing them near a village in the extreme south of Spain; and by two poodles, whom the inhabitants of Albolote described as "dogs of foreign breed, black, with woolly hair, called Prinnie and Charlie". An additional glamour attended these queer animals, for it quickly became known that they had come from Germany, "which was very far away".

Thus followed, Pepita descended from the *diligence* to be enfolded in the arms of her mother.

There are no existing accounts of the actual meeting between mother and daughter, but it is not straining the imagination too far to suppose that many embraces ensued and probably some emotional tears. What we do know for certain is that Pepita, Lola, the two servants, and the poodles then transferred themselves from the *diligence* into the family *galera*, and returned in it to Albolote escorted by the band, the villagers, the Ayuntamiento, and the Alcalde. They then retired into the Casa Blanca for several hours of private reunion before the celebrations of the evening should begin.

Those celebrations were of a nature to be remembered in Albolote forty years afterwards. Witnesses gave evidence lavishly in 1896 relating to the events of that summer evening of 1855. They were most of them old people by then, but the evening still lived vividly in their minds. Perhaps this might be accounted for by the fact that they had been born in Albolote and had lived there all their lives,—as they monotonously and unanimously record at the beginning of their evidence. Anyhow, on the day that Pepita arrived they were all young, gay, excitable Andalusians, ready to enjoy themselves to the utmost on this singular occasion when the star of their province had come amongst them and was willing to give them a party.

The party started after supper and lasted till morning. It was a summer night in Albolote, and the band from Atarfe assembled on the Plaza outside the Casa Blanca to serenade Pepita. It was not long, however, before the band was invited inside, about twenty of them, including the big drum. "A large concourse of people also went in. Catalina kept open house that night." The Casa Blanca threw itself open to all comers. All its windows revealed its lighted rooms, and those who were not fortunate enough to get inside felt themselves rewarded by a glimpse of the dancer, either "as she came out on to the balcony to salute the people" as Maria Ramirez saw her, or as she was seen by Juan Ramirez who was standing out in the Plaza listening to the band. Juan Ramirez saw this *princesse lointaine* in perhaps the most approvedly romantic way of all. "I only saw Pepita once in my life, and that was on the night when she was serenaded. I was in the street, and saw her passing from time to time in the room." One could scarcely touch the fringe of romance more lightly; unless, indeed, Antonio Arantave achieved it, for, on returning from his work in the fields, he was told that Pepita had come, and that the whole Ayuntamiento had gone out to meet her, but although he walked up and down in front of the house hoping to catch a sight of her that evening, he did not succeed in doing so. If the essence of romance is to aspire to the unattainable, then Antonio Arantave and Juan Ramirez certainly deserve to rank with Joffroy Rudel.

Those who got inside, and they were many, for Catalina's hospitality was a byword and this was the occasion for which she had been waiting many months, fell irresistibly under the spell of Pepita's graciousness and charm. How, indeed, could any young man resist her when she came up to him as she did to Jose Galan, and, on hearing that he did not know how to waltz, insisted on his taking several turns round the room with her? "She wore slippers of gold-brocaded velvet", he says. "I thought I should have died of ecstasy." Even Francisca Rivira who was Galan's sweetheart at the time, could bear Pepita no grudge for thus carrying off her *novio*: "Pepita", she says, "showed politeness to all; we were all enchanted with her amiability." Her gaiety and laughter delighted them. "Dressed in rose-coloured silk with flounces, she was doing the honours in and out of the room, saluting and receiving the company all the time." The love-lock lay against her cheek, the dark hair swept back from the forehead in soft glistening waves above the long dark eyes and serenely winged eyebrows. The mouth was curved and voluptuous, with deeply indented corners. She was just slim enough for a dancer, but just plump enough to appeal to Spanish taste with her beautiful shoulders, dimpled arms, and tiny hands. Her foot was surely the smallest ever seen, and she was innocently vain of it. This innocent vanity did not escape the eye of her feminine acquaintances: "She wore her dresses very short in front, to show her foot, though very long behind". Her jewels excited much admiration: "from a gold chain round her neck hung a pendant in the form of a heart of gold, with a large emerald in the centre surrounded by magnificent brilliants. She had in each ear a very good brilliant. She wore on the left hand four or five rings, and one or two on the right hand, and they were magnificent. She also wore a bracelet." Could it be true what rumour said, that the Prince of Bavaria had presented her with jewellery to the amount of twenty-five thousand dollars? Juan de Dios Gonzalez swore that Pepita had told him so herself. But then, as everybody knew, Juan de Dios was a renowned liar.

Pepita, presumably, was not thinking of her lovers, past or present, unless every now and then she wondered what Lionel Sackville-West, whom she had left behind in Berlin, would think of this gay, mixed party going on in Albolote, the Alcalde rubbing shoulders with the grocer's boy. She was the sort of person who throws herself whole-heartedly into whatever she is doing at the moment, and her one preoccupation now was the entertainment of her guests. Refreshments circulated freely; "there were many chocolates, sweets, and liqueurs to be passed round". The guests all noticed and commented in detail on the lavishness of the hospitality. There were no speeches, but there was a good deal of cheering coupled with the name of Pepita. Catalina completely lost her head with over-excitement. Perhaps memories of her circus days came surging over her as the strains of the band from Atarfe filled the rooms of the Casa Blanca and floated out to the Plaza on the warm air through the open windows. Anyway, on hearing Jose Galan, who was known to be studying music with other young men, speak of "the music and the desire the young fellows of Albolote had of playing", she offered to buy up all the Atarfe instruments then and there and present them to Albolote. What with one thing and another, the party was a great success, and the day was beginning to dawn when the last of the guests took their leave. It was, said several of these guests, "a regular fête".

Only one wistful note sounds suddenly in the midst

of all the gaiety. Jose Galan, after being made to waltz
by Pepita, asked her how long she was staying and
whether she would soon come back. She looked at him
sadly, and replied, "God only knows when I shall come
here again".

VIII

It is impossible to fathom the secrets of Pepita's
mind. We have the comments of observers, but no
comments of her own. The one person who never speaks
in this whole history, is Pepita herself. We see her
always objectively, never subjectively, gay, laughing,
rebellious, sometimes sad,—and are always left to guess
the cause. Pepita herself is never explicit. In order to
understand her at all, we have to find a piece from
a different part of the puzzle, and fit it in. Thus I incline to suppose that a few short phrases uttered by
Lionel Sackville-West may explain her sudden lapse into
melancholy after her mood of reckless liveliness. Pepita,
who led no easy ordinary life, was in addition a temperamental person, and, as such, was frequently led
by the varying complications of her existence to betray
herself in an abrupt change of mood. At the back of her
suddenly sad words to Jose Galan I perceive a difficulty
which had arisen between her and Lionel Sackville-
West, and which may perhaps partially account for
her long-awaited visit to Albolote, if, as a wise and
very feminine woman, she had thought it advisable to
absent herself from him awhile. We know how sincerely
they loved one another, and indeed the whole of their
subsequent lives proves it. But Pepita was not an easy
woman to hold, nor Lionel Sackville-West an easy-
going lover. I think the vehemence of their natures had
led to trouble just then: "I was in Berlin," he says, "and
I heard that Pepita was living with Prince Youssoupoff

at Munich. I started from Berlin with the intention of following them to Marienbad where I heard they were. I meant to quarrel with Youssoupoff, but was prevailed upon by my old servant to stay at Frankfort. I wrote to Pepita from there, expostulating with her on her conduct. She answered me by letter, begging me not to come to Marienbad and make trouble, saying that she was going to leave Youssoupoff, which she did."

IX

Accounts differ as to how long she stayed at Albolote; some say one month, some two or three. But all agree that the Casa Blanca was the centre of much merriment while she was there. There were little parties almost every evening, when Lola and the German governess were made to play the piano for the others to dance. The German governess, in accordance with the strict Spanish tradition, had by then been turned into a sort of duenna who accompanied Lola everywhere, never leaving her for a moment. Rafaela, as the poor relation, did a great deal of work about the house, but Lola was never required to do anything. It was noticed with some amusement that, child as she was, the absurd Juan de Dios was paying considerable attention to her. Nobody took this very seriously: they were all far more interested in Pepita.

How often I have longed for a more complete record of Pepita's sojourn at Albolote! How revealing would be one single statement from Catalina's own lips! If only Catalina had not died before all the trouble began and before all the evidence was taken! Her evidence, from what I know of Catalina, I feel sure would have been rambling and expansive, full of rich detail and irrelevant illuminating comments. As it is, I have to content myself with piecing together scraps of outside evidence, just casual remarks to the effect that Pepita had been seen riding the piebald *jaca*; or that someone had seen an oil-painting of her, full length, standing up in a riding-habit; or that she went out driving with Catalina and Lola while Rafaela remained at home; or that Francisca Rivira would call out to them from the window of her house as they went by; or that she could often be seen standing in the doorway or on the balcony of the Casa Blanca; or that Juan de Dios Gonzalez often saw her writing letters; or that,—rather vaguely,—she was very good to the poor. Felix Gomez, the same who had been sent into Granada to buy fish on the day of her arrival, was employed in the house every day so long as she remained, and often saw her about the house and heard her talking to Catalina. She would call out "Mamma!" and Catalina would reply, "Pepa?" One can hear them shouting to one another. On the other hand, she was never heard to call Lopez anything but Don Manuel.

The servants remembered her well. "No," said Felix Carrera indignantly, "my recollection of her is *not* dim." He was only the handy-man who did odd jobs about the house when he wasn't wanted in the stables. "The work I used to do in the house was to sweep the *patio* and draw water from the well. I groomed all the horses myself and cleaned the harness. The horses and carriages were turned out very smart. I remember the Señorita Pepita coming to Albolote. I saw her almost daily, sometimes several times a day. I heard her talk and she used to talk to me; she used to come to the stables to look at her horse. It was a piebald pony, very pretty, named La Preciosa. She used to talk to me about taking care of the horse, keeping the stables clean, etc. She was handsome; you can just imagine, sir, that I took a good deal of notice of her, for I was forty years younger then than I am now. One always likes anything that is good. There were portraits of her hanging up against the walls of the house; I used to notice them. They were good portraits, like her. Everyone in the house thought a great deal of the Señorita and her appearance, as even the Justices came to see her."

Again, she would "show her treasures" to the visitors who came in the evenings, and then would say that "she would like them to have something to remember her by", for, like her mother, she was a generous and giving person. That something would usually be a portrait of herself, which she insisted upon signing. People cherished these portraits, had them framed, and hung them up in their houses. As Catalina also was not averse to distributing similar mementoes of her beautiful daughter, there must at one time have been quite a number of lithographs of Pepita hanging up in the drawing-rooms of Albolote.

Micaela Gonzalez preserved a very vivid recollection of those weeks, during which she had lived in a state of youthful ecstasy. To that simple girl, who had never been further from Albolote than Granada in her life, the advent of Pepita's family had already provided sufficient cause for excitement, but the bewildering presence of Pepita herself was a fairy-tale scarcely to be believed. For one thing, Pepita had brought Lola back with her, and with Lola, a child of almost her own age, Micaela rapidly renewed her friendship. This friendship provided Micaela with an easy passport to Pepita's indulgent affections, for the relations between the two families were already so close that the two children were free to run in and out of each other's houses at any time during the day, and to hang round Pepita's skirts, beseeching her to "show them her things". Pepita loved children, nor was she without an innocent vanity that liked impressing the young or the ignorant when she had nothing better to do. I fancy that, accustomed though she was to the admiration of crowds and princes, she did not altogether scorn the adoration of those two small girls, Lola and Micaela. They would go and find her in her bedroom. "Show us your things, Pepa"; and she would say, "What do you want to see?" Then she would open her boxes and show them things which awed Micaela by their ingenuity and splendour: "a brooch in the shape of a frog with blue stones; another brooch in the shape of a lizard set with streaks of gold and emeralds alternately; a great number of bracelets, one of them shaped like a snake; rings by the handful, the gold of a good colour and heavy, and the stones very bright, and many other things which appeared very good. We used to be all three together looking at the things brought from abroad."

Sometimes Catalina would join them, and would boast that Pepita had a necklet of pearls, with a pendant with an emerald in the centre; but Micaela never saw that jewel. "She had a great many necklets," says Micaela, "but as I never saw her wearing a low dress I cannot describe any necklet with a pendant." This means, of course, that Micaela was too young ever to have attended any of the evening parties. On the other hand, she had her compensation in making Pepita open her cupboards as well as her boxes, to show her the hats, dresses, and finery she had brought from abroad. "We", said Micaela, admiring these things rather enviously, "lived in a country place and dressed very simply." These exhibitions of foreign fashions always ended well for Micaela, for the good-natured and generous Pepita invariably gave her something, a dress, a hat, or even a piece of ribbon: "She was very fond of me, we were very good friends, she used to give me presents out of the things she had brought from abroad".

Undoubtedly, with her youth, her beauty, her warm nature, her simplicity, and the romance of her whole personality, Pepita must have been very charming indeed. The young man Antonio Arantave who had walked up and down outside the Casa Blanca hoping in vain to catch a sight of her on the first evening had his reward later on when she and Catalina came to the house where he lived with his sister, on their way for a walk accompanied by two servant-girls. ("When they went out," he notes, "they always left Rafaela behind, with at least one servant, to take care of the house.") Pepita had called expressly to see his sister Maria's flowers. It was the first time that either Catalina or Pepita had been to their house. As they came up his sister was standing at the door; they stopped, asked if they might look at the flowers, and his sister asked them to step in. He was there all the time they were there, *and in the same room*. The italics are his. His sister cut some of the flowers and gave them to Pepita, who took them away with her. (Luckily, neither Antonio Arantave nor his sister ever saw the evidence of another witness who had known Pepita in Munich: "She received showers of bouquets always". Those showers of bouquets were orchids and lilies, not the humble dusty produce of a Spanish peasant's garden.)

Pepita's interest in Maria Arantave's possessions was not confined to the flowers: she also caught sight of some little fish in a small pond in the garden and immediately wanted to catch them. Antonio, who seems to have been rather an inarticulate though impassioned young man, remained tongue-tied throughout. He could do nothing but observe Pepita and her mother, who "were both very amiable and agreeable, but especially Pepita, who talked much better than her mother. Pepita was very pretty. I did not speak to either of them." Through the curt phrases of his legal evidence, I gather that he went through agonies of shyness and infatuation while Pepita exclaimed adorably over the flowers and the fish.

He was given the chance of seeing that Pepita was neither forgetful of her old acquaintances, however slight, nor unloving as a daughter. She had been absent from Albolote,—perhaps she had gone into Granada for the day, the evidence is not clear on this point,—but anyway she had arrived by the *diligence*, and was on her way on foot to the Casa Blanca, accompanied of course by the inevitable maidservant. It was in the afternoon, some time before dusk. Antonio was there with his sister as Pepita passed. "She stopped and shook hands with my sister and asked how we were. My sister asked her to walk in, but she said she couldn't as she was anxious to see her mother. I did not see her again, nor have I ever seen her since."

One wonders on how many young men during the course of her life Pepita succeeded consciously or unconsciously in making so deep an impression? Wherever she goes, they abound. At Albolote, amongst others, the two brothers Galan fell victims to her charm. Francisco was the more cautious of the two: "I used to go to the friendly evenings at Catalina's house. Pepita was very attractive, dangerously so. I was a young man at the time and she made a great impression on me. If I saw a portrait of her as she then was, I could recognise it without any doubt whatsoever." Jose, his brother, the one who had been taught to waltz by Pepita, expressed himself far more recklessly: "I remember the love-curl that she always wore on each temple, it made her even more attractive. Her teeth were white as ivory; her *tout-ensemble* took away sleep. Her hair was black and wavy, her eyebrows black and beautifully long, her nose fine and sharp. Her face and figure remain engraved upon my memory notwithstanding the lapse of time. After she left Albolote I exclaimed to Catalina, 'God help me, Pepita is gone and I have not even got her portrait!' Catalina said, 'As you like her so much, here, take this portrait as a souvenir of her'. She gave me a portrait of her. I had it for two or three years in a drawer with my papers. I used to look at it sometimes, she was worthy of being remembered."

Then comes a touch of humour, I think unconscious: "Five years after the portrait was given to me, I married. It was after I married that I missed it."

x

Delightful though Catalina and Pepita were, in their different ways, they were not altogether easy people to get on with. They were both high-handed and hot-tempered on occasion. Such an occasion arose over a dispute with the village priest, which ended in the entire family removing itself, lock, stock, and barrel, from Albolote.

Perhaps their heads had been a little turned. Friendly and hospitable as they were, in one respect they showed that they considered themselves as slightly better than their neighbours. Catalina, in short, was in the habit of crossing the Plaza to High Mass, preceded by a procession of servants carrying large, red, luxurious armchairs, one for each member of the family, and a smaller chair for Lola whenever she was at home. These chairs were placed in front of the High Altar, before the general public, and immediately after the service they were carried back again. I do not think that Pepita was wholly to blame; she had arrived to find the objectionable practice already in force, though no doubt she gave it her approval. This naturally caused a great deal of talk and resentment in the village. "They were the only people who have ever made a practice of taking seats like that. Now and then people take a camp-stool or similar seat when they think the seats provided may all be full, but not luxurious seats like the armchairs. I often saw the chairs being carried. I saw them at Mass soon after they came to Albolote, and they were sitting in their own armchairs."

People grumbled, and the extraordinary spectacle of four large armchairs and a smaller one being carried across the Plaza every Sunday and feast-day was watched with black looks, but nothing much was said until the priest himself rebelled. Catalina was heard "having words with the S. Cura as to whether she should be allowed to take chairs into the Church. I heard him telling Catalina that the Church was not a theatre (an unkind cut at Pepita) and that the chairs must not be brought." Catalina could scarcely resist the S. Cura's authority, but she could, and did, refuse to attend Mass again. She kept her word. None of them was ever seen in the Church after that incident, and it soon became known in the village that the family was looking out for another property to buy.

XI

Meanwhile, the Star of Andalusia was preparing to take her departure. Her holiday was over and Germany was awaiting her for the autumn season. Lionel Sackville-West, in Berlin, was awaiting her too. Her family went to see her off by the *diligence*. Contrary to what Juan de Dios Gonzalez said, she travelled alone. Francisca Rivira saw them start: "I saw Pepita, Doña Catalina, Don Manuel, Lola, and the governess all get into the *galera*, and that night all returned except Pepita".

We can follow her as far as Madrid, for several people saw her there, and the accounts are exceptionally amusing and vivid. First we have the two Guerrero brothers, Rafael and Manuel; Manuel is always turning up oddly in Pepita's life, but Rafael we have not met before. He is a dancer, of course, though at the time he first sees Pepita in Madrid he happens to be without an engagement. Still, as though unable to keep away from the theatre even though unemployed, he goes as a spectator to the Teatro Puol with three companions named Vilchis, Carrion, and Mazzoli, and there, during the performance, notices that the public attention is attracted to one of the boxes. "On looking in the same direction, I saw a very beautiful woman. On expressing admiration to my companions, Mazzoli said it was Pepita Oliva, and as he knew her he went to her box to salute her, and remained there till the end of the performance." At the end of the performance, young Guerrero, having lost his friend, returned home and began going to bed. But "as I was getting into bed I heard someone knocking at the street railings below, and Mazzoli's voice calling out, 'Guerrero, Guerrero, get up and give a dancing lesson'. I said, 'What, at this hour of the night?' and he replied, 'What does it matter whether it is one o'clock or two o'clock? Get up and come with me'." Guerrero accordingly got out of bed and dressed himself again, and went with Mazzoli to the Hotel Peninsular in the Calle Alcala; on the way there, Mazzoli told him that the lesson was to be given to the beautiful woman they had seen at the theatre. When they arrived, Carrion and a violinist named

Raenos were waiting in a room with Pepita. It was then two o'clock in the morning, but Pepita declared that she wanted to learn *la Manola* then and there. Guerrero was a little uneasy: he knew, as he puts it, that "in teaching a dance a great deal of time is necessarily occupied in explaining the different steps and movements", but Pepita was determined, the lesson began, and lasted with pauses for the next six hours. During one of these pauses Pepita went out on to the balcony, and Guerrero, following her, found that she was crying. He asked her what she was crying for, and she said, "Nothing, only family troubles". She then came back and resumed her lesson.

They had "plenty of refreshments" while the lesson was going on, and at ten o'clock they all had a meal which Guerrero calls luncheon and which lasted till three o'clock in the afternoon. As none of them had closed their eyes all night, and had been pretty strenuously engaged during all those hours, Pepita dancing, Guerrero directing, the violinist fiddling, and the other two looking on, I imagine that they must all have welcomed their luncheon when it came. Pepita, too, had evidently been overcome by some emotional recollection, but whether it was associated with the mother whom she had left behind in Albolote or with Oliva of whom Madrid perhaps too poignantly reminded her, is impossible to say. All we know is that she stood out on the balcony, as dawn crept slowly over Madrid, surprised in tears by a complete stranger, to whom she murmured something vague about family troubles by way of explanation.

XII

Then there was Manuel Guerrero, who did not have to be dragged out of bed, but who went more or less by appointment as Director of the ballet at the Teatro Real, in response to a suggestion made by his impresario Jose Mayquiz. He was sitting with Mayquiz at the Café Venecia, that "great resort of theatrical people", when Mayquiz told him he had received a message from a dancer staying at the Hotel Peninsular, and invited him to accompany him there and see her and judge of her dancing. She was anxious, Mayquiz said, to take with her to Germany a *cartel* (poster) stating that she had danced in Madrid. Guerrero had no idea of the name of the dancer he was being taken to see. He knew only that the Peninsular was the best hotel in Madrid and that she was staying there in the best apartments. He accepted lazily, and strolled with Mayquiz from the café to the hotel, down the Calle Príncipe and the Calle Sevilla; it took them about half an hour, and they reached the hotel about half-past twelve in the afternoon. On arriving, Mayquiz led the way up to an apartment on the first floor with a window overlooking the Calle Alcala. He knocked, and after calling out "Who is there?" a lady opened the door to them, whom Mayquiz immediately introduced, saying, "Pepita, allow me to introduce *el maestro de baile*". Guerrero recognised her instantly as the girl he had once seen passing down the street outside that very same Café de Venecia, who had been pointed out to him as Oliva's bride.

For obvious reasons he looked at her with more than ordinary attention. She was wearing a light-coloured dressing-gown, a gold necklace with a gold pendant in the shape of a heart with a large emerald in the centre, and several diamond rings on her left hand. She was more polished than when he had first seen her, and he was specially impressed by her jewels, which he considered "extraordinarily fine". And he had good reason to think himself a judge of jewels, for at one time during his career he had worked with "the great tragedienne Mme. Rachel at Marseilles", whose diadem of brilliants and jewelled girdle he remembered, and whom he described rather irreverently as "a walking jeweller's shop". Pepita he evidently did not consider over-dressed, for in speaking of her jewels he adds that there was nothing unusual in artistes wearing jewellery ostentatiously in the daytime. The combination of the dressing-gown and the jewels might well have struck him as a little strange, but he makes no comment.

The three of them sat down together to discuss the somewhat delicate question of how she was to be given a certificate of having danced in Madrid when she had, in fact, never done so. Pepita herself made no bones about the matter: she wanted Guerrero to get her an engagement at the Teatro del Príncipe, so that she might take with her to Germany a poster or a programme showing that she had danced at the first theatre in Spain. Luckily for Guerrero he was able to reply with truth that this would be a difficult thing to accomplish, as neither he nor his friend Mayquiz had any connexion with the theatre in question; nevertheless, he added politely, he would have much pleasure in seeing her dance.

Pepita went into the adjoining room and came back again with her castanets. She was still wearing the dressing-gown, but she had tied it up with a silk handkerchief round the waist so that they might plainly see the movements of her feet. She then, without any music, danced El Ole for four or five minutes (I should have given much to see this performance in the hotel sitting-room!). At the conclusion of the dance she said to Guerrero, "What do you think of it, Maestro?" Poor Guerrero was obviously embarrassed. What he thought privately, and said afterwards to Mayquiz, was that owing to her beauty, her figure, and her personal charm she would probably make a success abroad, but that in his opinion she was no artist at all as regarded dancing, and that although she might be good enough for Germany she would never be good enough for Spain. Aloud, "I replied courteously, 'Oh, very good', although I didn't think so". Pepita, who after all had been told in Malaga that she was like a bird in the air and who had already scored considerable triumphs in Germany and elsewhere, seems to have noticed the lack of enthusiasm in his voice, for "she turned with an interrogative gesture to Mayquiz, who said, 'Well, the maestro likes your dancing very well, but as regards getting you a night at the Príncipe I will do the best I can, but can promise nothing'". This was not very encouraging, and no doubt Pepita saw the Teatro del Príncipe receding again towards the horizon of her ambitions, for this was the second time she had been plainly shown the inadequacy of her standards for it. She was, however, a good-natured creature when not in a temper, and far from bearing Guerrero and his impresario any grudge she rang the bell and invited them both to stay to luncheon. This meal, which was served in the sitting-room, lasted till three-thirty, Pepita meanwhile making no further allusion to her private affairs, but entertaining both men by her conversation on impersonal topics.

The Berlin artist who represented her dancing the Aragoneza has also left a drawing of her dancing El Ole. In the drawing, of course, she is not wearing the dressing-gown, as she danced it for Guerrero, but a tight bodice and short flounced skirt, also a wide sash with long heavily embroidered ends. In her ear is the brilliant ear-ring of which we hear so much; her hair floats loosely far below her waist. Again, as in the other picture, her lips are parted, but this time she is not smiling; there is, on the contrary, something almost threatening in the level glance of the long, dark eyes. She seems to be holding herself in reserve for the rising excitement which is to culminate in the wild dance to follow. Manuel Guerrero recognised the portrait when shown it forty years later; it was exactly the posture in which she used to place herself, he said, although "he did not consider it artistic". However, we already know what Guerrero in his professional way thought of Pepita's performance.

XIII

These were the facts, but Juan de Dios Gonzalez of Albolote had a much more exciting version to tell. There was not a word of truth in it, for Juan de Dios stands high as a fantastic character in this whole story of people none of whom could be described as exactly ordinary. He was a natural liar on the grand scale. As all his neighbours were well aware of this, nobody took any notice of what he said, except to listen with a certain amusement to what Juan de Dios would invent next. The Coadjutor, for instance, had heard him say that he was a Marquis with millions of money in a bank, whereas he was known to be starving at the time. The Coadjutor, in commendably moderate language, added that he had always known Juan de Dios as a "flighty, romancing person", and that he did not consider his statements reliable. Francisco Galan also considered him "a flighty person", and added that he suffered from delusions. He, also, had heard of the Marquisate and of the millions of money in the Bank of Lisbon. "He has always been a little queer," said Galan tolerantly, "and does strange things at times." Pedro

Quesada, less tolerant, roundly calls him "a bad character, in whose statements one can place no confidence".

The story he invented on this occasion was a particularly silly one, since it could be contradicted by dozens of people who had daily seen him going about the village. They knew perfectly well that Juan de Dios had never left Albolote to accompany Pepita to Germany as he claimed. For one thing, he was only in his early teens at the time, but that was not the kind of detail to bother Juan de Dios when he had conceived a picture of himself as the squire of a beautiful and celebrated artiste on her travels. According to his own account, he was already in Pepita's confidence: while still at Albolote, he said, she had told him that she had parted from Juan Antonio Oliva because he had "spent seventy thousand dollars in three weeks in gambling, so that the result was that she said to him, 'You go your way and I will go mine'". This, of course, may or may not be true, but it seems unlikely that Pepita would have told a boy a thing like that. Juan de Dios probably made it up, as he made up all the rest. It was a most romantic story that he evolved, the oddest mixture of circumstantial detail and utter falsehood. It is quite obvious that his strange unreal mind pieced it together from scraps that he had heard, which makes it wear an air of convincingness until we recollect that there was no truth in the story at all. Such as it is, here is the story in his own words: "Pepita left Albolote for Munich. I accompanied her. We went by *diligence* from Albolote to the French frontier. We left Albolote early in the morning and were four or five days travelling to Madrid. We stopped to sleep at Jaen and Bailen and at one other place which I do not recollect. We stayed in Madrid two or three days. It was my first visit to

Madrid, but Pepita told me she had often been there. Pepita did not go to visit anyone in Madrid, nor did anyone go to see her. I went with her wherever she went. She did nothing but take a walk or drive. She was travelling incognita.

"We were from six to eight days travelling by *diligence* from Madrid to the French frontier. We stopped at certain spots to rest, sometimes by day and sometimes by night. From the French frontier we went by railway first to Paris. We stayed there from twelve to fourteen days. The weather was intensely cold. Pepita stopped there to enable me to see all Paris. She accompanied me in all my excursions.

"From Paris we went by a continuous journey with many changes of carriages to Munich. At Munich we stayed at a very fine house, which I think must have been her own. There were four or five servants besides a watchman and footman. She had her carriage and four magnificent horses.

"Pepita performed in the Teatro del Príncipe in Munich every night during the whole time. I used to go with her to the theatre and remain there whilst she was there and return home with her. Almost always the Prince of Bavaria was there. On various occasions when we were passing the play-bills, which were in German, she called my attention to them and said to me, 'Look here, see what that says', and, pointing to one part of it, said the translation of it was, La Estrella de Andalusia.

"She made various calls at times and received many. The calls she made were generally on people of Granada extraction, such as the Count and Countess of Miravilla and the family of General Gavarri. The visitors to her house all appeared distinguished, and were often gentlemen alone. The Prince of Bavaria called several times, often at night time.

"I recollect seeing many letters from time to time from Spain for Pepita.

"From Munich we went direct to Heidelberg. We there stayed at an hotel. I do not recollect the name of it. She danced at a theatre there. I do not remember the name. It was, of course, a German name and strange to me. I accompanied her always to and from the theatre in Munich. She again called my attention to the posters in the same way as in Munich. She was much applauded and received many bouquets there, but not so much as at Munich."

It is a pity to have to destroy the entrancing story of his travels which Juan de Dios invented and perhaps believed himself, but unfortunately some of his contemporaries and fellow-villagers testified contemptuously that to their certain knowledge he had remained at Albolote all the time. Pedro Quesada remarked with justice that a boy of that age could not have left the village without everybody knowing it and asking where he had gone. But it is the Coadjutor who tells us what really became of Juan de Dios, a story quite as dramatic as any which that flighty mind could compose.

"I lived next door to Manuel Gonzalez in Albolote. About the 12th or 13th of June, on the Eve of San Antonio, whilst sitting in my house, I heard a shot, and on going immediately into the house of Gonzalez, I saw his wife lying dead upon the landing and his son Juan de Dios standing on the stairs with his arms folded. He was arrested a few minutes afterwards."

CHAPTER IV

THE HOUSE OF THE ROYAL PEACOCKS

I

CATALINA and Lopez, however, were no longer living in Albolote when Juan de Dios got himself into this trouble. They had already acquired the new house which Pepita had agreed to buy. Pepita had gone away, vaguely authorising them to hold a sale at Albolote and to transfer themselves elsewhere. Pepita, for all her jewellery and the "treasures" she had shown to the visitors at the Casa Blanca, was always singularly casual about her personal property. Very shortly after her departure, Catalina held a sale of all the effects she did not wish to remove. Such dealings were no novelty to Catalina, for her friends well knew that she was "fond of buying furniture and other things, which she speedily tired of and re-sold by auction in order to buy something else"; besides, it is on record that she had sold off most of her effects before leaving Malaga. A volatile nature in some ways, though anything but shallow in others, she loved excitement in any form, whether it came in the shape of quarrels with Lopez and the servants, or in the fascinating occupation of changing and renovating houses. On this occasion she was quite in her element, directing everything and keeping Lopez strictly in his place. "During the sale Don Manuel, as he was called, would attempt to intervene in the bargaining and the lady would stop him and say, 'Not you, Manuel, I will attend to that. You don't know how to manage these things'." It is easy to see the reason for her severity, for the witness adds, "*She* drove a hard bargain, but *he* was more indulgent".

Fortunately for us a certain widow Pinel has left a realistic account of how such sales were conducted. The Señora Pinel, by no means a widow then, was living in Granada at the time, in the Plaza del Matadoro, and although it was not very long before the birth of her first child her curiosity was such that she could not resist going out to Albolote several times with her husband, when she heard that there was a sale in progress at the Casa Blanca. She had not seen any public announcement of the sale, but had heard it spoken of on every side. This was not surprising, for although such sales in private houses were sometimes advertised, it was possible to save money if the people had a sufficiently large circle of friends and could make the thing known merely by talking about it. The arrangements were all somewhat elastic, nor was there any fixed duration for the sale: it just began on a certain day and went on from day to day until everything was sold that could be sold.

Señora Pinel could go out to Albolote only in the evening, after the office hours of her husband, who was then a clerk in the Administration Department in Granada. The first time they went, there were only two or three other intending purchasers in the house. Señora Pinel, who had several times seen Pepita driving in Granada, in "a magnificent open carriage drawn by either two or four horses", was much interested. She and her husband were shown into a large room containing all the articles which were for sale, and there they found a lady who introduced herself as Pepita's mother. In the course of conversation she informed them that she was having the sale because her daughter had gone away; she only referred to her as Pepita, evi-

dently judging that no further explanation was necessary. Whenever the Pinels returned to the sale, which
was on three or four occasions, they always saw the same
lady presiding. Of an auctioneer there is no mention at
all, and it appears that their transactions were all conducted with Catalina in person. We know exactly what
they bought of Pepita's little treasures. There was "a
cut glass toilet bottle, having the name *Pepita de Oliva*
cut in it; a carved wooden egg-shaped case with a rosary
of mother-of-pearl beads; a handsome hair-brush; and
some plated forks and spoons with the initials C.O. engraved on them". When they were buying the forks and
spoons, the lady informed them that C.O. were her
own initials and stood for Catalina Ortega.

Señora Pinel kept the toilet bottle, the rosary and its
case, and the forks and spoons. The hair-brush she gave
away. To whom, she does not say.

Some of Catalina's humbler friends were deeply impressed. One of them went to look, though she dared
not enter the house. "I did not know anyone who
bought the things, because they were all magnificent
things and were bought only by the rich." *El Defensor
de Granada* was impressed too, and later on published
an article headed "El Lord y la Bailarina" (The Lord and
the Dancer), from which the following is an extract:
"The dancer had at various times sales when she lived
at Albolote, at which sales only the wealthy people of
Granada attended, when there were sold pictures of merit,
rich jewellery and gorgeous dresses of the latest fashion
and without having been worn, as well as lovely shoes of
irreproachable make and as to which one does not know
whether they exhibited the skill of Don Manuel Lopez
or of some expensive shoemaker of Berlin or London."

There was also a merchant of Granada, one Enrique
Duran y Manella, whose tone in speaking of some of

Pepita's possessions is almost one of reverent awe: "I bought a tablecloth with a dark ground and raised cloth colours and designs on it which may well be considered a work of art".[1] He bought also a glass dish which he admired equally: "It is glass of foreign manufacture, *not Spanish* [his italics], and is very good. It is a dish of the kind placed in the centre of a table. It is of cut-glass with blue fillets and has engraved on it an inscription which says 'Pepita de Oliva'. The letters are cut into the glass and it is not done by machinery. The glass is of the natural colour except that the base and part of the ornamentation are blue. The servants in the house who handed the dish to me at the sale told me that the words on the dish were the name of the dancer. I also bought a small mother-of-pearl jewel stand with gilt ornament, two candlesticks to match, and a gold ring with a dark flat stone."[2]

Señor Enrique Duran y Manella was still in possession of these things in 1896 when his evidence was taken, but with others he had been less lucky. He had, for instance, bought "a china figure which represented a dancer in ballet costume with her hair hanging down loose and her arms raised; people said that it represented La Oliva". He retained this figure in his possession for some years, until it got broken, he did not know how. (Perhaps, like the young man who missed his photograph of Pepita shortly after he had married, Señor Duran y Manella had also acquired a wife.) He ends his evidence on a rather wistful and very human note: "I bought other things also, but they have been destroyed by time and children".

[1] Opposite p. 83 I reproduce a photograph of the said work of art.
[2] The glass dish, the jewel stand, and one candlestick are shown in the photograph opposite p. 65. Unfortunately I possess no photograph of the ring.

The Director of the Provincial Hospital, in spite of his disapproval of Catalina and Lopez, was another purchaser to make his way into the large and dusty sale-room. Here he bought an album, about eighteen inches by twelve, containing lithograph portraits of musicians and others, views, and comic coloured pictures. Under some of these pictures she had written the words "Souvenir de Frankfurt", or "Brussels, October/55", or "Baden-Baden, August/55"; and sometimes she had written Pepita de Oliva, but sometimes simply Pepita.

I wonder what has happened to all those objects, apart from the ones that were destroyed by time or children? I have some of them in my possession. I have the album which had been acquired by the Director of the Provincial Hospital and which proves all too clearly that Pepita's taste was pathetically atrocious; indeed, it fills me with affectionate embarrassment to look through these glaring coloured pictures of little girls playing with kittens or fitting spectacles on to the noses of puppies, nor do I care at all for the caricatures of bathers at Ostend, with their appropriate jokes underneath. Pepita's taste was naïf; she was a simple, childish soul.

I have the cut-glass toilet bottle with the name engraved on it, a hideous object which I dearly love, and I have also a fork and spoon with the initials C.O. But where is all the rest of the treasures? They may still be somewhere in the world, and I would give anything to handle them. The only other thing I have of Pepita's is a little silver pin-tray, with two almost obliterated initials in the middle, under the coronet to which she had no right. My mother gave it to me, and I value it. I value everything which I have been able to rescue that had any connexion with Pepita.

II

These details of purchases, too few to satisfy my
curiosity, do at least give us some idea of the "treasures"
of the Casa Blanca. It is not possible to deduce very
much from them, save perhaps that Pepita was fond of
recording her own name whenever she could, and that
with a certain sentimental expansiveness she liked pre-
serving things which reminded her of various passages
in her life,—the portraits of friends, the views of places.
As for the comic pictures, I have often enough seen my
own mother laughing till she cried over something she
thought funny, to imagine very vividly Pepita doing the
same. My mother had no sense of humour at all in the
English sense of the word, but the rich Latin sense of
farce was generously transmitted by her Spanish blood.
Over and over again I have seen her standing outside a
village shop, unable to control her laughter (and indeed
not attempting to control it) before a string of funny
postcards dangling in the window. "Mais regarde
donc!" she would say to me, "mais regarde donc, je
t'en prie. Peut-on? Ah non, franchement, peut-on?" and
she would go off again into convulsions of laughter,
heedless of the astonishment of the village children.
Like Pepita, too, she delighted in cutting things out of
newspapers and sticking them into albums; and like
Pepita she liked dating and signing everything. How
clearly I can see Pepita coming out in her!

And Catalina too. Generous soul that Catalina was,
she liked acquiring money as much as she liked spending it on herself and others. My mother was like that
too, and although she might have given away a hundred
pounds to-day (but more often it ran into thousands),
she would still feel that she was to the good if the post
brought her an unexpected postal-order for ten-and-

six next morning. I can thus quite well imagine that a
protracted sale at Albolote furnished Catalina with a
daily store of satisfaction; and can see her after the last
buyers have gone, sitting down to add up the *duros*
and *maravedis* she had managed to collect during the
day. It was not so much greed that inspired her, as a
purely childish pleasure in the game. I am sure that it
gratified her to dispense with the services of an auctioneer, not only on account of the economy thus
effected, but on account of the fun she got out of the
personal bargaining. It is clear enough from the all-too
brief recital of Señora Pinel that the personal element
was very prominently introduced: in strictly business-
like transactions it was not really necessary to inform
the customer that Pepita had gone away, nor that the
initials on the forks and spoons were the vendor's own.
But such things, to Catalina's mind, made everything
much pleasanter and more amicable; they sent a little
warm blood through the dry veins of business; perhaps
also, they sent up the price. . . . My mother would have
felt exactly the same. Of course, in her case, she would
have exerted such charm that anybody would have
given her the last penny out of his pocket, and gone
away, slightly bewildered, to discover only next day
that he had spent more than he meant. I doubt whether
Catalina had it in her to exert an equal charm, but I do
at least believe that she flung herself into the game with
equal zest.

Life in the denuded Casa Blanca must have been very
uncomfortable during that period of transition, for
Catalina had sold the dining-room table on condition
that one leaf was not to be delivered until after they had
left, and in the meantime they ate their meals off that
solitary leaf balanced on packing-cases.

III

Of course Catalina did not put all her goods into the Albolote sale. Far from it. She had the new house to consider, and when the excitement of the sale was over, the excitement of moving into the new house took its place to occupy her mind. This new house was not in a mere village, but was a real country property, with labourers and vineyards of its own. It lay on the road between Granada and Jaen (Camino de Jaen), and was officially known as Buena Vista, but sometimes also as the *Caseria de los Pavos Reales* (the House of the Royal Peacocks), and, after Pepita had bought it, as the *Caseria de la Bailarina* (the House of the Dancer). Both very pretty names, but for the sake of brevity I shall refer to it by its original name of Buena Vista.

It was quite a big property, really a homestead or farm, about nineteen *fanegas* in all. There was a garden, a kitchen garden, some pasture and arable land, and two vineyards, one of them about one hundred yards from the house, the other a little further off, beyond a narrow strip of rough ground. The labourers used a side entrance of their own, but the family had a big important entrance gateway, which they built themselves and over which they presently put the date 1858. There was a fountain in the *patio*, surmounted by a bronze figure of Pepita dancing El Ole. Internal evidence leads me to suppose that there was also a large population of peacocks. Altogether the family might consider itself worthily housed.

Lopez became more and more genteel. He took to using fancy writing-paper, and to enclosing addressed envelopes to his friends for their replies, of so diminutive a size as to be useless. Manuel Gonzalez, annoyed by this new trick, showed two of these envelopes to his

son, saying, "How is it possible to send papers or
letters in such small envelopes?" So whenever he wrote
to Lopez, he used his own envelopes and kept the
others. Why he kept them I don't know; perhaps it was
in order to make fun of Lopez behind his back.

The property was, of course, a Paradise for Lopez.
He could indulge his taste for shooting "such things as
rabbits, or any small birds he could see, dressed anyhow, though when out with the carriage he dressed
luxuriously". The note of contempt and even dislike is
unmistakable in any mention of Lopez; the witness I
have just quoted was Water Guard at Buena Vista. He
could also indulge his taste for lording it over men who
by birth were his equals, but whose superior he had
become owing to circumstances,—the same circumstances as allowed Pepita to take foreign villas and engage the most splendid apartment of the Hotel Peninsular. According to these men he spent nearly all his
time interfering with them at their work among the
vines,—"Don Manuel, who was said to be the husband
of Catalina". Domingo Martirez did not think much
of Don Manuel, though he admitted that his own term
of employment at Buena Vista was irregular, and thus
gave him little opportunity for judging, merely a week's
digging round the roots of the vines in January, then a
second digging in May, and another fortnight in
October for the vintage, about the same thing every
year for three or four years. Fortunately for Manuel
Lopez, he could go shooting his rabbits and little
birds, and give his orders to his subordinates in 1856,
without any anticipation of what those subordinates
would say about him in 1896, when their evidence
was taken.

For Catalina also the new property was a Paradise. It
is easy to see that she was a house-proud woman, with

an insatiable taste for display and also for the fussiness which accompanies the type. Have we not, indeed, expressly been told that she was "much given to alterations and reformation"? a trait which reappears later most faithfully in both her daugnter and her grand-daughter. At Albolote, thanks to Pepita's generosity, she had been able to indulge this taste to a great extent, but now at Buena Vista she was able to indulge it still more. And she did. She had had all the amusement and excitement of the sale, but that was nothing to the excitement and amusement which lay before her now. No sooner had they transferred themselves from the Casa Blanca at Albolote than she started taking the house itself to pieces for the purpose of removing everything removable to Buena Vista. By the time she had finished with it, there was very little left but the shell of the Casa Blanca. She took the doors, the balconies, the marble fireplaces, the grates, the sinks, the iron gates, the windows, and the ornamental iron bars (rejas) from before the windows, in fact she "stripped and gutted the house of everything that was useful. After this they ceased to make any use of the Albolote house." I don't wonder.

Catalina presided in person at the arrival of these effects, and directed where each one was to be placed.

IV

Buena Vista was a far grander house, and I think that Catalina may justifiably have felt that she had scored heavily over the S. Cura of Albolote. Not only had she now a regular estate to herself, but she had a larger number of servants in her new establishment, and that, for a person of Catalina's temperament, was an advantage not to be disregarded. It is rather surprising to learn that Catalina treated her servants with a certain reserved dignity; one would have expected her as a woman not born to the habit of command, to rush first to the extreme of too great a tyranny, and then of too great a familiarity, with all shades of too violent a temper in between, but it was not so. These inconsistencies of behaviour are precisely what make her more credible as a human being and yet more puzzling. The tone is noticeably different when the servants are talking of Catalina or of Lopez. There is no contempt when she is mentioned, but, rather, an affectionate respect. "Doña Catalina was not a proud lady (I think the maid Vicenta Sanchez here means 'not stuck up'). She was very good and kind to her servants, and when I heard her mention Pepita's name it was when she was talking to other members of the family at the table." Perhaps Catalina with the adaptability of the true adventurer had acquired more sense of social behaviour since the days when she admitted Señor Corral the grocer to the intimacy of her friendly evenings at Albolote. And even in the days of Señor Corral she had tried to pretend to him that Pepita was not a dancer, but a mimic, whereas to the Alcalde and her other more elegant friends she had described her frankly as a dancer.

Anyway, she now had plenty of servants over whom to exercise her authority, and as these servants, both indoor and out, play an inevitable part in the life of that pavonian homestead on the outskirts of Granada, I again quote the excellent Richard Ford, this time on the subject of the Spanish domestic, to whom he devotes a great deal of attention. It is indeed irresistible for me to quote Richard Ford, for the period of his acquaintance with Spain corresponds so very nearly with the years covered by this recital, and moreover my own anxiety not to over-romanticise the background of a story already sufficiently romantic in its essence though fortunately realistic in its detail, leads me to welcome the corroboration of an author who can authentically and without prejudice supply such comments as I myself could supply only from the treacherous depths of my own imagination. Let Richard Ford, therefore, speak for the characters represented by Ana Seron Giminez, Antonio Machado Guindo, Jose Ligero Castillo, Antonio Amador, Domingo Martirez Fermandez, Agustin Ballesteros Saes, Arenas Robles, Vicenta Sanchez Ruiz, Felix Gomez Carrera, Juan Hoces Ruiz, Francisco Martin Lopez, Nicanor, Margarita, Josefa, and Juana, surnames unknown, who all at one time or another and in their various capacities faithfully served Catalina and Pepita at Buena Vista:

"The principal defects of Spanish servants and of the lower class of Spaniards are much the same, and faults of race. As a mass, they are apt to indulge in habits of procrastination, waste, improvidence, and untidiness. They are unmechanical and obstinate, easily beaten by difficulties, which their first feeling is to raise, and their next to succumb to; they give the thing up at once. They have no idea indeed of grappling with anything that requires much trouble, or of doing anything as it ought to be done, or even of doing the same thing in the same way—accident and the impulse of the moment set them going. . . . They are very loquacious, and highly credulous, as often is the case with those given to romancing, which they, and especially the Andalucians, are to a large degree. . . . As they have an especial good opinion of themselves, they are touchy, jealous, and thin-skinned, and easily affronted whenever their imperfections are pointed out; their disposition is very sanguine and inflammable; they are always hoping that what they eagerly desire will come to pass without any great exertion on their parts; they love to stand still with their arms folded, while other men put their shoulders to the wheel. Their lively imagination is very apt to carry them away into extremes for good or evil, when they act on the moment like children, and having gratified the humour of the impulse relapse into their ordinary tranquillity, which is that of a slumbering volcano. On the other hand, they are full of excellent and redeeming good qualities; they are free from caprice, are hardy, patient, cheerful, good-humoured, sharp-witted, and intelligent; they are honest, faithful, and trustworthy; sober, and unaddicted to mean, vulgar vices; they have a bold, manly bearing, and will follow well wherever they are well led, being the raw material of as good soldiers as are in the world; they are loyal and religious at heart, and full of natural tact, mother-wit, and innate good manners. In general, a firm, quiet, courteous, and somewhat reserved manner is the most effective. . . . The Spaniards treat their servants very much like the ancient Romans or the modern Moors; they are more their *vernae*, their domestic slaves; it is the absolute authority of the father combined with the kindness."

We may well deduce from all this, that Catalina and her servants could meet and understand one another on several points. Catalina, like them, was free neither from the charge of waste nor of improvidence. Loquacious she certainly was and "highly credulous as is often the case with those given to romancing". Yet, oddly enough, she could also practise the custom observed by Ford, of treating her dependents with an absolute authority combined with kindness. How did she manage it? How did she manage to inspire her servants with the sense of romance in her background, without talking to them with a familiarity which would have diminished their respect? Of course, Pepita unconsciously came to her aid. Everybody in Granada knew about Pepita; had not the House of the Royal Peacocks itself changed its name into the House of the Dancer? They all looked forward to the day when Pepita would come to Buena Vista.

I fancy, however, that some of the servants were of so low a condition that they would never have dared to answer back even if Catalina scolded them. One of them, indeed, Josefa, was in no position to answer back, for she was dumb. Another one, Juana, was little more than a child from the neighbouring village of Castilla la Vieja. Two others, Nicanor and Margarita, were even more to be pitied, for they had been recruited from the miserable ranks of the survivors in the Foundling Hospital. If Ford is to be believed, these hospitals, *casas de espositos* (houses of the exposed), were "scarcely better managed than lunatic asylums; the proportion who died was frightful, it was indeed an organised system of infanticide. The infants were laid in rows on dirty mattresses along the floor and were left unheeded and unattended. Their large heads, shrivelled necks, hollow eyes, and wax wan figures, were shadowed with coming death. About one in twelve survived to idle about the hospital, ill-clad, ill-fed, and worse taught. The boys were destined for the army, the girls for domestic service, nay, for worse." Even their names were not their own, but had been bestowed on them by the matron at the time of their admission, and were usually that of the Saint whose day it was.

Fortunate indeed were those who were adopted by some benevolent or childless person, such as the Nicanor and Margarita whom we find under the rule of Catalina at Buena Vista. Nicanor, who appeared to be about thirteen, helped with the horses and did whatever else he was told; Margarita, who was about a year older, was employed in the house. And of course there was Rafaela, that poor relation, who trailed after Catalina wherever she went and was still treated very much like the other servants.

Naturally, domestic life at Buena Vista was not without its rows and disturbances. The word "dismissed" occurs quite frequently throughout the pages of the evidence. Thus, there is an unfortunate German maid called Maria, who is discovered sheltering with the local greengrocer because she has been sent away by Catalina and is "very lost and troubled owing to her ignorance of Spanish". Then there is Antonio Machado Guindo, who got into trouble with Catalina for taking Pepita's part over a quarrel between mother and daughter. "The next day being Sunday, he asked Catalina for the key of the garden gate to go to Mass, and on her refusing to give it to him, he said he would jump over the railings, did so, and disappeared." And there was Felix Gomez Carrera, who survived only four months of his employment. He tells us the reason for his dismissal himself; it is sufficiently fantastic: "A peacock was lost and I was blamed for it".

A strange young man floats brightly into their lives at this time, and floats out again, never to reappear. "There came a young man to the house, badly dressed and wearing a *capa* such as itinerant shoe-makers wear. He stayed at the house and the following day he appeared well-dressed. People said he was a son of Don Manuel and the servants called him *Señorito*. He was there about a month till the arrival of a woman, when he left with her." Then, apart from one violent quarrel with his family in Granada, he vanishes, so far as we are concerned, for ever.

That disposes of Lopez' son, but Catalina's son Diego is with them again. He had seen military service in both Cuba and Mexico, and appears to have been but little sobered by his experiences. At Malaga his mother's friends had thought him harum-scarum; at Buena Vista her servants thought him light-headed. He was now engaged in courting Lola, seventeen years his junior. Despite the discrepancy in age he insisted on marrying her, and she, having thrown over Juan de Dios Gonzalez in his favour, was not unwilling. The marriage was celebrated by the priest of San Ildefonso at Buena Vista itself; was witnessed by Catalina, Lopez, Rafaela, and several of their servants; and needless to say, turned out most unhappily, for "they were always fighting". This is all that can be recorded of Diego for the moment. We hear no more of him until several years later we find Catalina and Lopez trying to bribe him to assassinate Juan Antonio Oliva.

v

Catalina's relations with her son-in-law had indeed been most peculiar from the first. She had been delighted with the marriage, and then had lost no time in wrecking it, whether by design, folly, cupidity, or jealousy we shall never know. More curious still, we find her apparently making at least one attempt to repair the damage she had done.[1]

She and Lopez were in Paris, sitting together outside a café adjoining the theatre where Oliva was then employed. Suddenly they saw, recognised, and excitedly

[1] I cannot quite make out when this odd incident took place, but it appears to have been two or three years after the marriage. Many of the witnesses were unable to read or write, and some of them could not estimate the years with any accuracy (e.g. "she knows she is 63, but cannot count back to the year in which she was born"), so I have sometimes found it a little difficult to arrive at the correct chronology in the whole story.

summoned Manuel Guerrero, whom they knew to be a
ballet-master in the same company. Guerrero was toler-
ably familiar with Pepita by then, for not only had
he observed her in Madrid just before her marriage,
but had also had that interview with her when she
danced for him so unsuccessfully at the Hotel Peninsular in Madrid. Of course neither Catalina nor Lopez
knew about that. They called him to them, introducing
themselves as the mother-in-law and father-in-law (*sic*)
of Juan Antonio Oliva and invited him to sit down and
drink coffee with them. This, Guerrero refused to do.
He was very fond of Oliva by then, and was not disposed to accept hospitality at Catalina's hands. Lopez
then said, "I wish you would do us a favour". Guerrero
asked what it might be. They then complained that on
several occasions they had seen Oliva passing through
the café on his way to the stage dressing-room, but that
he had passed without taking any notice of them,
although he had evidently seen them. Would Guerrero
please use his influence to induce Oliva to come and
see them, as they wanted to speak to him about important matters? Guerrero went back to the theatre and
spoke to Oliva at once, but met with a flat refusal. He
said that Catalina was the cause of all the trouble; she
had behaved very badly to him at Valencia just after his
marriage and he would have nothing to do with her.
After a great deal of persuasion Guerrero induced Oliva
to come to the café with him, "and there was then a
reconciliation, with much crying and embracing on the
part of Catalina. Catalina said to Juan Antonio that she
had received a letter from Pepita in Berlin in which
the latter requested that Catalina would induce Juan
Antonio to leave the company in which he was then
engaged and go to live with her [Catalina] and Lopez,
and to look after him well, and that she [Pepita] would

soon return to Paris to meet him." By the time the
message had been delivered and the tears and embraces
were over, they were all on the best of terms; they had
been joined by two other members of the company, and
Lopez wound it all up by inviting Guerrero and Oliva
to lunch with him and Catalina at Passy. Guerrero,
for his part, said, "*Me convidad convida a ciento*" (an
invitation to me includes a hundred), meaning that of
course he could take a friend or two with him, which
was the Spanish custom. Lopez said, "Oh certainly,
bring all the company with you", so two days later
Oliva and Guerrero went to luncheon accompanied by
four of their friends. "We all went", says Guerrero
frankly. The part played by the four strangers in this
intimate gathering is hard to imagine exactly. But the
party seems to have been a success. It began at one
o'clock and lasted till late in the evening. Lopez and
Catalina, according to Guerrero, were both "gorgeously
dressed"; they wore the large gold chains and rings which
always seem to have made so deep an impression on all
beholders. During lunch, Lopez rose and gave the toast
of a happy reunion between Oliva and Pepita; they all
drank it with acclamation, Oliva included. Catalina then
referred again to the letter she had received from Pepita,
saying that she was to keep Oliva in Paris and that he was
not to go on dancing any more as she had plenty of money
without that. As all the guests seemed a little doubtful
and disinclined to believe this, Lopez called out, "Bring
out Pepita's letter", when somewhat to their surprise
Catalina went into the adjoining room, produced a letter
with foreign stamps on it, and handed it to one of the
company to read aloud, "when it was found to be to
the effect which the mother had stated. Oliva then
became more cheerful with the prospect of again seeing
Pepita."

There were certain details to be adjusted. Catalina
said Guerrero must use his influence with the management to allow Oliva to cancel his engagement in Paris,
because Pepita's own contract in Berlin would soon
come to an end, and she would then come to Paris to
see him. Meanwhile Oliva should go to live with her
and Lopez at Passy. On this arrangement, the party
happily broke up. They had sat so late over their
celebrations, that the six artistes got back to the theatre
only just in time for the performance.

Guerrero did his best, but could only obtain permission for Oliva to cancel the contract when the company left for Germany, after he had served out his time
in Paris.

Meanwhile Catalina and Lopez kept a close eye on
their recovered rebel. They made him live with them at
Passy during the whole of the remaining fortnight of
his contract, fetching him home every night from the
theatre in a cab lest he should elude them. They kept
him quiet and happy and good by telling him of almost
daily letters from Pepita, saying that she was well, etc.
Oliva was "very pleased and in high spirits", and several
times expressed the hope that she would arrive in Paris
before Guerrero had left.

It seems the most extraordinary arrangement, and
any sensible person would have foreseen that any amicable mode of existence between Oliva and his mother-
in-law in the same house was out of the question. Such
an arrangement might be arrived at through tears,
emotion, reconciliation, and a luncheon-party, but there
was not the faintest hope of its permanence. Guerrero
himself went off to Germany with evident misgivings,
leaving Oliva (for whom he entertained a really deep
affection) in Paris. He went in considerable hope of
finding Pepita in Berlin; to his great disappointment,

however, he arrived in Berlin on the very day she had left. He found nothing but the posters still on the hoardings, ironically announcing Pepita de Oliva as dancing El Ole at the Frederick William Theatre. The posters were left, but Pepita herself was gone.

Perhaps he remembered then the occasion on which Pepita had danced El Ole for him in her dressing-gown, without music, in a sitting-room of the Peninsular.

VI

Guerrero was not altogether sorry to have missed Pepita, for he would have felt obliged to call on her for Oliva's sake and had meanwhile been annoyed by the information that she had been describing his company as "a band of *zincali*" (gypsies) in Berlin. This perhaps came badly from Pepita, who was half a gypsy herself.

Guerrero and his company do not appear to have enjoyed their month in Berlin, for apart from the bitter cold, "we went out very little, being unable to speak German and finding ourselves lost as it were". They had already wandered from Dieppe to Brussels, from Brussels to Aix-la-Chapelle, and from Aix-la-Chapelle to Cologne, finding it "very cold on the Rhine".

In any case, it did not matter very much whether Guerrero saw Pepita or not, for almost immediately after his arrival in Berlin, he received a letter from Oliva, the contents of which he must have divined even before he tore the envelope open. The letter revealed that Oliva had had another quarrel with Catalina,—or, as he put it, "there had been *disgustos*" (unpleasant-nesses). He had been turned out of the house, and now was writing to ask whether Guerrero could get him taken back into the company. Guerrero did his best to oblige, but the company director had had enough of

Oliva's chops and changes. His request was refused on the grounds that the director did not care to incur further expense and had already sufficient members in the company under him.

Guerrero with his company, minus Oliva, then went on to Vienna. It must have been annoying for him to find that Pepita had preceded him there, especially as he was at that time much in love with a rival dancer named Petra Camara, a member of his company, "who like Pepita was an Andalusian".[1] I have in fact been tempted to wonder whether Guerrero's harsh judgment of Pepita's performance was not influenced in some degree by his predilection for La Camara? As Pepita was styled the Star of Andalusia, so was La Camara styled the Pearl of Seville. That there was no love wasted between Guerrero and Pepita is apparent from Guerrero's account, and it is apparent also that there was no love wasted between the two ladies either. Of the two, however, the Camara seems to have been far more civil than Guerrero when it came to the point. Pepita, "dressed magnificently", had arrived "in a carriage and pair of the first order", to call on them.

This is the account of their interview given in Guerrero's own words:

"About four or five days after our company had arrived in Vienna and had made a great success, Pepita came to visit Petra Camara. Our company was staying at the Three Crowns Hotel. Pepita was staying at the most expensive hotel in Vienna.

"This was the first time Petra Camara had ever seen Pepita.

"Petra received her courteously in the presence of her mother and her brother. I was in an adjoining room.

[1] It may be worth noting that the letter from Alexandre Dumas quoted on pp. 27-28 refers to this Petra Camara.

The brother came to me and said, 'Pepita is there and has asked after you; it will look bad if you do not go and say How-do-you-do'. I then entered the room and went up to Pepita and shook hands with her, saying 'How-do-you-do, Pepita?' exchanging the usual courtesies. After that I left the room again almost immediately.

"After Pepita had left our hotel Petra Camara came into the room where I was with other members of the *corps de ballet*, playing cards, and said, 'Pepita Oliva has invited you all to lunch with her, saying she would receive you with much pleasure'. I never went, but two of my companions went.

"Petra afterwards told me that Pepita had asked many questions about Juan Antonio [Oliva], such as, how he was, how he was getting on, whether he was stout or thin, and so on."

Petra Camara in her own evidence adds something significant to all this, which Guerrero omits: "I gathered that the real object of her visit was to get information about Juan Antonio. *She asked me whether he had any lovers.*"

Guerrero picks up the story.

"After Vienna I did not see Pepita again until I saw her in Copenhagen. I only heard from the newspapers and in other ways that she was creating a furore in Germany and Austria.

"Petra Camara and I and our company were performing in Vienna at the theatre situated in the Barrio Trieste, outside the fortifications. We left Vienna for Prague and the train was snowed-up during the night and we arrived in Prague the next day, Christmas Eve." (This poor Spanish troupe! it had encountered bad luck on its European tour, what with the bitter weather on the Rhine and in Berlin, and then the train snowed-up between Vienna and Prague!)

Eventually they arrived at Copenhagen.

"When we arrived at Copenhagen, Pepita was not there. She arrived a few days afterwards. I knew of her arrival from seeing posters in the street announcing as a great event the arrival of the famous dancer Pepita Oliva, who was to perform at the theatre called the Casino. We were staying at the Royal Hotel, but Pepita went to stay at the Hotel de Inglaterra, one of the most expensive hotels. (This always seems to have been a grievance, for it recurs over and over again.)

"The first time I saw her there was on one day when I was passing her hotel. I saw a number of persons looking up at the windows, and on investigating the cause I found that Pepita was combing out her hair in sight of them and that they were all astonished at its magnificence and length."

This is a generous tribute. But then comes the inevitable row with its concomitant backbiting.

"After we had been at the People's Theatre for about a month, Pepita offered her services at less remuneration than Petra Camara wished to accept. Accordingly Pepita was engaged and Petra and our company left. I went with Petra and her brother and other members of our company to see Pepita perform there for the first time. We sat in the back row of the stalls so that Pepita should not see us. She danced El Ole for about ten or twelve minutes. I observed that she did not dance any better than when I saw her dance at the Hotel Peninsular."

Although out of loyalty to my grandmother I am unable to feel any affection for Guerrero as a character, I am still able to esteem myself fortunate in the possession of his album of newspaper cuttings relating to his professional career. It is by now a shabby volume, cheaply bound, with the word A L B U M printed on it in large

and ornate gilt lettering. It seems strange to me to turn
over those tattered pages on to which Guerrero himself
has pasted those cuttings from *El Porvenir de Granada*,
El Dauro, *Die Reform*, *Le Figaro*, *Le Courier du Bas-
Rhin*, *Warszawska Gazeta*, *La Presse*, *Wiener Theater-
zeitung*, *Le Messager de Genève*, *Le Nouvelliste Vaudois*,
l'Indépendance Belge, and many others; old programmes
too, even from the Theatre Royal, New Adelphi, London. As the album does not directly concern Pepita,
except on one or two pages, I must not dwell on it, but
it has its value as showing the kind of life led by these
wandering Spanish troupes all over Europe during the
winter season.

VII

The story of the reconciliation between Catalina and
Oliva, however short-lived, had its sequel in a meeting in Madrid between Pepita and Pedrosa, that old
friend who had originally arranged for Oliva to give her
dancing-lessons; Pedrosa, who might thus in a way consider himself responsible for furthering her disastrous
marriage. Pedrosa was sometimes away, dancing in the
provinces, but he had frequently to return to Madrid, for
he was also a book-binder by trade, and had to look after
his book-binding establishment there. It was on such
an occasion of his return that Pepita's message caught
him: "She sent", he says, "saying that she wished to
see me. I went to see her."

Like Guerrero, he found her in the Hotel Peninsular.
Like Guerrero, he was impressed by the splendour of
her jewels. She was not in a dressing-gown that time,
but was wearing "a very handsome dress". Like Guerrero, he had luncheon with her, for she was always
hospitable. She talked freely about Oliva, speaking of
him "in a most affectionate way but lamenting that his

behaviour prevented them from being together". (I fail to see how she reconciled this regret with the very intimate and passionate existence she was then leading with Lionel Sackville-West whenever they could seize the opportunity, but one cannot expect the Pepitas of life always to be consistent.) Pedrosa was much surprised by these accounts, which did not at all tally with his conception of his friend Oliva, but Pepita insisted that the letters she received from her mother could leave no doubt that Oliva was leading "the same life as ever, a great friend of women and pleasure". Pedrosa protested that from his knowledge of Oliva there was no truth in the saying, and his private opinion was that Catalina kept them apart by these means for her own purposes. "I don't believe anything of the kind," he said; "whatever Juan Antonio may have been before marriage, he has been everything that is right since." Pepita would not have it. "You know very well that I married him for love," she said, "but my mother has not deceived me. How can it be so when in her letter she said she had to forbid him the house at Passy because he was caught with the servants?"

I am afraid this shows Catalina in a very sinister light, besides exemplifying the exaggerated influence she exerted over her daughter.

After luncheon, Pepita gave Pedrosa a portrait of herself,—it was a lithograph, a German production. She signed it for him and wrote what he believed to be "a souvenir" for him at the foot of it, *a mi buen amigo, recuerdo cariñoso*, and added a flourish. When she gave him the portrait he took the opportunity of mentioning Oliva's name again. Tears, he records, came into her eyes. Next day he called at her hotel, but she had already left. He took the portrait to his house, and took the trouble to have it framed and hung up in his sitting-room. Some months later Oliva returned to Madrid and came as usual to see him. "He saw the portrait and immediately exclaimed, 'Ah, that is my Pepita,—give it to me.' I would not give it to him and we had words about it. Four or five days afterwards he induced me to give it up to him, after much pressing and imploring on his part, and we being such old friends I consented. I never saw Pepita again, but I frequently saw the portrait hanging up in the sitting-room of the house of Juan Antonio's parents. It was a very good likeness of her, it is a speaking likeness,—she always wore the *sortijilla*, that is the lock or ring of hair on the cheek by the ear."

From this evidence it is, I think, clear that Oliva and Pepita had been really fond of one another once. Otherwise tears would not have come into Pepita's eyes (even making allowance for her natural emotionality), nor would Oliva have had words with his best friend trying to get her portrait away from him, so long after their marriage and their mysterious quarrel. He always grew indignant with those who attempted to criticise her in his presence, as he did with Guerrero for saying that he considered her dancing inartistic; "I taught her myself," he exclaimed, "so I ought to know". When once he missed her in Granada, he became "very furious and much upset". Pepita, for her part, never forgot him, and never concealed from Lionel Sackville-West that she corresponded with him, sent him money sometimes, and received his replies. I wonder how the English lover relished the constant allusions he says she made to the Spanish husband? It is true that she told him she sent the money to keep Oliva quiet, because she always dreaded his claiming some rights over her or her children.

What a queer pair they were! How strange that Oliva should ever have consented to go back and live with Catalina, or that Pepita should ever have written saying that Catalina must look after him well, until such time as she herself could arrive in Paris to meet him! What on earth was Pepita thinking about, when she made such a suggestion? She must have known quite well that he and Catalina could never come to terms; and besides, she was herself deeply involved with Lionel Sackville-West at the moment. Still, she seems to have preserved that lingering affection for the young man she had married,—a protective affection, which tried hopelessly to establish a home for him with his mother-in-law where he would be well looked after. A case of conscience? Perhaps. She had treated him badly, whether her mother or herself was to blame. She had found another love, of whom her mother knew nothing. I wonder, I continue to wonder, whether it was not some instinct of self-preservation that made her conceal the existence of Lionel Sackville-West from her mother? She was older now, less of a child. She may well have feared lest her mother should wreck her romance as well as her marriage. Tender and passionate by turns, she had swum out into the great world of success and love, leaving all her early youth behind her; she had known both public applause and personal passion; she was a full woman now, as she had not been when the Teatro del Príncipe refused to engage her and she had married her dancing-master as an inexperienced girl. It stands to her credit that she retained even some affection for and some sense of responsibility towards the Juan Antonio Oliva who represented her first essay in the difficult art of love and life. But Oliva and Pepita were now irrevocably parted; neither conscience nor sentiment could heal such a breach; Pepita had passed far beyond the reach of a mere *bolero*; she had passed even beyond the reach of the mother who had originally brought her from Malaga up to Madrid, with un-specified parentage behind her. She was in a position to send for ballet-masters and their impresarios, and to get them to agree to her proposals. She was triumphing in Europe, with contracts in her pocket and villas of her own in Germany and Italy, while Catalina at Buena Vista awaited her return with such loving impatience as she could control.

CHAPTER V

EL LORD Y LA BAILARINA

I

CATALINA had not so very long to wait. Scarcely had she finished building the entrance gateway at Buena Vista with the date above it, than she received word that Pepita was on her way to Granada. There is a noticeable contrast between this occasion and Pepita's gay, light-hearted arrival at Albolote three years earlier. Even the accounts given by the country-people differ; we no longer find young men enchanted and bewildered by her vitality; there are no goldfish to be caught or flowers to be picked; the piebald pony remains idle in the stable; the carriage is never taken out. A grave and silent Pepita wanders alone about the grounds of her new property, watches the men at their work without talking to them, and returns to the house again. The labourers themselves record it; "Every day Pepita used to stroll down to the vineyard. I recollect her very well, for I looked at her with admiration. I had every opportunity of observing her. She came alone and walked about looking at the work going on, but did not speak to any of the men. It was a small vineyard and she kept near to where we were working. She generally stayed about half an hour and then walked back alone."

This was very unlike her, but the reason for this unwonted seriousness and retirement was soon apparent to all. Her first child was born at Buena Vista on May 20th, 1858.

The baby was a boy, and Catalina instantly began to spread extravagant rumours about his parentage. The Emperor of Germany reappears in Catalina's saga, this time as the baby's father and also as Pepita's husband. Catalina came downstairs immediately after the birth, which happened at mid-day, and told her servant Ana to run up and look at the new baby, who was then lying in the bed with his mother. This Ana, who had had ten children herself and several miscarriages, and was therefore a woman of some experience, had recently given birth to her eleventh baby, so was asked to suckle the child as Pepita herself was unable to do so. This duty she obligingly undertook for nineteen days.

During that time she slept in another bed in Pepita's room. She records that Pepita had brought all the baby's clothes with her from Germany. She records also that Pepita confirmed her mother's statement that the baby's father was Emperor of Germany, whereas in fact, Pepita must have known perfectly well that the baby's father was Lionel Sackville-West. There are facets in Pepita's character which still baffle me. . . .

The baptism was celebrated with a display which must thoroughly have gratified the heart of Catalina as a grandmother. For one thing they had the priest of San Ildefonso from Granada to officiate, and that was very grand. For another thing, His Royal Highness Maximilian Duke of Bavaria, father of the Empress of Austria, stood sponsor and was represented by proxy by Don Manuel Lopez and Doña Catalina Ortega, those two adventurers who had never except in saga approached so near to royalty before. The nurse Ana remembered the christening very well, though she evidently did not remember enough to satisfy the examining lawyers. "I can't tell you the name of every priest of that church for the last fifty years," she retorted indignantly when they pressed her; "that is quite impossible. Nor can I say whether or not I held the child in my arms during the whole ceremony—who would think I was going to be asked about such details?" But she remembered well enough that Catalina gave her three dollars and the present of a dress to wear at the ceremony, and that they all drove to the church in the *galera* with Lopez on the box. As the baby was only three days old, Pepita was of course not present, but Catalina's sister remained at home to look after her. The church was decorated as for a grand baptism. When they came out, they found a large crowd, mostly boys, surrounding the carriage, and this crowd followed them, pressing and shouting round them, so that two mounted Civil Guards rode up to escort the carriage, one on each side, all the way back to Buena Vista. For the whole length of the three kilometres, Catalina kept scattering money to the people; this was the usual thing to do, but instead of bringing pence Catalina had brought two straw baskets, one filled with dollars, and the other with pesetas. *El Defensor de Granada* was much impressed: "There was present an immense assemblage who were attracted by the merry pealing of the bells, the cracking of sky-rockets, and the gay tunes of a military band which made pleasant the occasion at the door of the church. Causing much comment amongst the merry gathering that filled the nave of San Ildefonso, was the presence of a foreign gentleman of very distinguished appearance, whom no one knew and who after the ceremony was lost in the crowd and not seen again. (I am afraid this is only a picturesque addition on the part of *El Defensor*, much as I should like to believe that Lionel Sackville-West had slipped away from his diplomatic duties in order to catch a glimpse of his son.) The street boys shouted vigorously the usual *'rona,*

rona', and received a veritable rain of pesetas and napoleons in place of the customary farthings."

The child had been given the names of Maximiliano Leon Jose Manuel Enrique Bernardino, and was known as Max. Catalina was careful to explain that Maximiliano was the name of his father the Emperor; she did not add, probably because she did not know, that Leon was the Spanish equivalent of Lionel.

Pepita adored her baby, but could not nurse it. When Ana's nineteen days came to an end, it became necessary to obtain another nurse, and one was found at the neighbouring village of Santa Fé by Catalina, who drove out with Lopez in the *galera* to bring her back to Buena Vista. This woman, who was a simple peasant, "had much to relate of the grandeur of her sojourn on her return to Santa Fé. It was gathered that she had lived in a palatial house where there was great luxury and many servants." She stayed with Pepita for two years, and reported that she had seen many marvellous things in foreign countries.

It was of course inevitable that Catalina and Pepita should quarrel sooner or later over the baby. It must have been just before Pepita was due to return to Germany; Max was short-coated by then, and she wanted to take him away with her. Catalina opposed the idea, with the result that Pepita lost her temper and left the house, calling to one of the servants to accompany her, which he did, thereby increasing Catalina's fury. They crossed the road to the house of a neighbour, Jose Mendez, and Pepita sent for a carriage to drive her into Granada. The servant returned, to be so soundly rated by Catalina that he immediately went off to join Pepita again. Pepita remained for two days sulking in a hotel in Granada, then suddenly arrived in the *diligence*, sent into the house for her luggage and Max, and took her departure without having alighted. (I wonder how she managed to keep the *diligence* waiting for so long, since it was, after all, a public conveyance?) Catalina, Lopez, Lola and Rafaela all went out to say good-bye to her, so perhaps they did not part on bad terms. Anyhow, she had got her way, for Max and his nurse went with her. They went off to meet Lionel Sackville-West in Germany.

II

After this, the existence of Pepita and Lionel Sackville-West becomes almost domestic. They had a house at Heidelberg and another one at Hackenfeldt; they shared the expenses, Pepita paying the wages and my grandfather paying the household bills; sometimes they were quite alone in the house with their child and the Spanish nurse; at other times they had a proper establishment with a cook and two housemaids. They were both busy, he with his diplomatic engagements, she with her career as a dancer, but whenever they were able to be together their existence appears to have been idyllic. Once they contrived to spend two whole months together; it was the longest time they had ever had.

By this time Catalina must have realised the true state of affairs. I do not see how she can have failed to do so, for her own sister went to stay at Heidelberg,—an incident which reveals Pepita in her most generous and warm-hearted light. This sister, Micaela, had always been devoted to Pepita; as she puts it quite simply in her evidence, "I loved my niece Pepita very much. In my eyes there was no more beautiful woman." She it was who had stayed behind to look after Pepita while Max was being taken to his christening.

This Micaela found herself in great distress, for her husband's eyes began to fail, the doctors in Malaga said he was incurable, and for eight months he was totally blind. "I was in sore trouble and said to myself, 'My God, what shall I do? I will write to my niece Pepita.' A letter was written in my name to tell her that my husband was blind; I cannot write and do not remember who wrote for me, but I told the person who wrote the letter to address it to Doña Pepita Duran, Heidelberg, Alemania. I knew that was her address because she had already sent me money and gifts. I sent her a certificate of the facts signed and sealed by the parish priest, so that there should be no doubt of the truth of what I said. I received a telegram from her, saying that there was a good doctor in Heidelberg, and that she thought he could cure the blindness, and that if we would like to go we were to go. After this I received a letter from her enclosing a sum of money, perhaps about 100 pesetas, for our personal expenses on the way to Marseilles."

With her blind husband and her two daughters aged eleven and four she embarked for Marseilles. In spite of Pepita's promptness and generosity, they must have gone on a small and dilatory boat, for the voyage lasted a fortnight. The boat stopped for two or three days at Alicante, where they disembarked to see the sights, and also stopped at Barcelona, where for an unexplained reason they remained on board. The weather was hot and the Gulf of Lions exceedingly rough. But such a surprise awaited them at Marseilles that their discomforts were soon forgotten.

On arriving in port someone came on board with new clothes for them all to put on, and no sooner were they dressed than who should appear but Pepita herself. She had got Max with her, then a little boy of about a year old. Pepita, evidently determined to give them all a treat, took them out to a hotel on a small islet, at a short distance from the shore, but they only remained there for two or three hours, sufficient time for a meal (these Spanish meals seem to have been habitually protracted), and then "we hastened our removal, for Max yelled very much, and whenever he cried Pepita was ready to die". At dusk they all started in the train for Paris. They went in a first-class compartment, at Pepita's expense of course, and when they got to Paris they stopped there for about four days, staying together at one of the best hotels. Pepita took them everywhere, and they passed the time seeing the sights and walking about the streets, principally the boulevards. The blind husband went everywhere with them.

Even this did not exhaust Pepita's kindness. When they arrived at Heidelberg, which they did in the middle of the night, they found that she had provided a furnished house for them, only a few minutes' walk from her own. Two days later the doctor came, accompanied by one of Pepita's servants; they could not understand a word he said, but presumed trustfully that the servant, who was a German, would understand and would report to Pepita. Each visit was to cost four dollars, and he came every four or five days for two months, but Pepita had told them not to worry as she would pay for everything. She did pay for everything, and gave them a present of 4000 *reals* as well. Moreover, she saw them every day and sent her own servant round with the medicines, and—what was perhaps as thrilling to Micaela as all the fine new sights she was seeing—one day she brought a foreign gentleman with her when she came to call. Micaela did not know his name, and much to her regret could not converse with him as he could not speak Spanish and she of course could speak nothing else; but she did notice that he was "a personage, rather tall, fair, good-looking and handsome, of a distinguished appearance, in the prime of life". She watched Pepita and that gentleman go away together. The gentleman, she observed, took a great deal of notice of Max.

It is pleasant to be able to record that by the time they returned to Malaga, Micaela's husband was completely cured. They had stayed at Heidelberg for nearly a year, and had been much surprised, during their sojourn, to discover that in winter the river Neckar was frozen over. This was a phenomenon to which, as natives of the favoured south, they were not accustomed.

III

Shortly after this little episode, Pepita temporarily abandoned Germany to follow her lover to Turin, where he had recently been appointed secretary at the Legation.

Really these two must either have been very extravagant or very wealthy, for although they still owned the houses at Heidelberg and Hackenfeldt, they proceeded to take Italian villas with a lavishness which is a little startling. The first villa, at Turin, was just outside the city, on the other side of the river, and Lionel Sackville-West used to walk out there in the evening when he had finished his work in the Chancery; another young Englishman, the honorary attaché, Dudley Saurin, often walked with him in that direction to within a short distance of the villa and then my grandfather would go to the right and Mr Saurin to the left. For Mr Saurin knew as well as every other member of the Legation that Pepita was a Spanish dancer and the mistress of their colleague. Even the manager of the Hotel Trombetta knew it. That was the reason why Sackville-West did not go into society like the other members of the Legation, and never called upon anybody in Turin. They knew it, because he had told them so.

It was rather brave of him, I think, thus to flout diplomatic conventions. No one who has not lived in diplomatic society can wholly estimate the pressure of such conventions upon the willing or unwilling victim. Absurd as they may appear to the outside observer, to the inside inhabitant they are the rules and laws of his world. It takes a bold and imprudent man to defy them. It takes a man who is ready to face embarrassing situations and awkward enquiries. Of course it may, with some justice, be said of my grandfather that he was not wholly dependent upon his diplomatic profession for his success in life, but no man light-heartedly endangers his chosen career, and I can only suppose that he preferred Pepita to all worldly considerations, for during his years of service in Turin they were constantly and very openly together. Then, Pepita expressing a preference for the Italian Lakes, they took a villa at Como, moved to another one at Arona, and finally to another one at Genoa. It was easy for my grandfather to get away from Turin, and he "visited her as often as his duties would permit". She was not dancing just then, and had very little to do but to play with Max, stitch at her fancy-work, and wait for her lover's arrival amidst those lovely surroundings. They were very much in love; I think they must have been very happy during those months.

But curious things began then to happen. Catalina had been to stay with them at Heidelberg, and although my grandfather naïvely observes that he does not know whether she is aware of any immoral relationship between himself and Pepita, it seems unlikely that Catalina did not put two and two together as to the connexion between her lovely daughter, the distinguished foreigner and the toddling little boy. At any rate, it seems to have struck Catalina that the distinguished foreigner would make a far more suitable husband for Pepita than that poor penniless scapegrace Juan Antonio Oliva. The next step, in Catalina's simple mind, was to get Oliva out of the way. To this end, she sent for her son Diego, and offered him "some thousands of dollars" if he would go to Madrid and kill his brother-in-law. Diego did go to Madrid, and at once, but for a very different purpose than that designed by Catalina. He appeared unexpectedly in the house of Oliva's parents, while they were all sitting down to their dinner, introduced himself, and told them of his mother's suggestion. He was kind enough to add that he had no intention of carrying it out. He mentioned also that he had recently seen the child Maximilian in Berlin, and that he was "looking very handsome, quite a jewel".

Oliva's brother, who was present, comments that "Diego's visit made a great impression on my family and was often the topic of conversation amongst us". Nevertheless, they were not at all convinced that Diego's motives were as disinterested as he made them appear, and with understandable caution declined to tell him where Juan Antonio was, although they wrote off to him the moment Diego had gone. They had a shrewd idea that Diego's apparent friendliness was due to a grudge against his mother rather than to any protective feeling for Oliva. They had observed that he was "in very bad condition and very poorly clad" and also had expressed himself much incensed against his mother because she had not fulfilled her promise of sending his wife to join him. Alternately, they thought he might have repented at the last moment, or else that he had purposely misled his mother in order to get his expenses

paid to Madrid. One can well imagine that Diego's
visit was "often a topic of conversation" in the Oliva
household.[1]

Catalina certainly exerted a most mischievous influence over the matrimonial affairs of both her daughter
and her son. Perhaps she was not altogether to blame
in Diego's case, for, as we have already learnt, he and
Lola were "fighting always". Indeed, from what we
hear of Lola at odd moments afterwards, and from what
we already know of Diego's harum-scarum career from
his school days onwards, it is quite clear that that
marriage was never destined for success. I don't know
very much about Lola. She has rather a smug, mean,
sly little face on the two photographs I possess of her. I
know she wrote to Pepita for money, because Pepita's
reply exists, saying that she is sending as much as she
can afford at the moment and is sorry she cannot send
more as she is expecting a baby. I know also that at one
time she was living with "a man who was certainly not
Diego" in Madrid in the Calle Jesus Maria, engaged in
a wine-skin business with an inscription on the front
of the shop, *Boteria de Ignacio Rojo*. After that she kept
a stall in a cheap market, where she sold such things as
"umbrellas, articles of clothing, etc., either second-
hand or collected from pawnbrokers". This is all I
know about Lola, until such time as she went to stay
with Pepita. My mother remembered her staying there;

[1] Juan Antonio himself, as a matter of fact, was in Granada at the
time. The witness was quite sure of this, for he remembered that it was
the year of the triumphal entry of the troops into Madrid after the great
battle of Tetuan. What he didn't know, was that Pepita herself had
driven through the streets of Granada during the feasts held in celebration of that victory, in an open carriage decorated with the portrait of
Queen Isabel. "She was the sight of the day in Granada. She went to the
theatre every night in the stage box and attracted universal attention on
account of her beauty and splendid dresses and jewellery."

she remembered being told to call her Aunt Lola. Diego
used to go and stay with Pepita too, he was lame; my
mother remembered him also. Evidently Pepita was
never disloyal even towards the more disreputable of
her relations. I wonder what Lionel Sackville-West,
with his very correct upbringing and his English background, made of them? The situation must have been
further complicated by the fact that Diego could speak
only a few words of French, and Lionel Sackville-West
not a word of Spanish. Diego and Pepita always spoke
Spanish together; my grandfather must sometimes have
felt rather out of it. He and Pepita spoke French
together; she with a strong Spanish accent, and he,
presumably, with an English. Their children spoke
nothing but French.

IV

They all led a queer muddled life during those years
from 1860 to 1866/67. In order to follow their movements at all consecutively, one has to dart about all over
Spain and most of Europe. There is Catalina living at
Buena Vista with occasional visits to Germany; Diego
in Madrid, warning Oliva's parents of Oliva's proposed
assassination; Lola selling wine-skins in a shop and
umbrellas and second-hand clothing in the market,
meanwhile living with another man; my grandfather
taking Italian villas for his mistress, a flat in Paris, a
flat at Bordeaux, and a villa at Arcachon; Pepita herself
bearing successive children, and becoming in a way
of her own more and more domesticated and respectable. And there is Oliva.

Oliva during this time in spite of or perhaps because
of his thwarted love for Pepita, became revengeful. He
had had a great deal to endure, and on the whole he had
endured it all with commendable fortitude, dignity,

and patience. He had resolutely refused to discuss the
early wreckage of his marriage either with his family or
his friends; he had merely stated the fact, leaving them
to understand that although he did not want to enter
into details, he preferred on the whole to put the blame
on Pepita's mother rather than on Pepita. In all this he
behaved very well. He had behaved well, again, in
allowing himself to be persuaded into a reconciliation
with his mother-in-law on the understanding that his
wife would shortly be restored to him. Here again he
had been deceived, and had every reason to suspect that
his mother-in-law had once more made mischief for
reasons best known to herself. Ample confirmation of
this suspicion had then arrived with the news from home
that his mother-in-law was doing her best to arrange for
his assassination.

I for one cannot blame Oliva for the apparently
spiteful steps which he then took. He knew that Catalina was living in luxury at Pepita's expense, while he
himself was leading a precarious existence spending
every penny he got the moment he earned it. He had to
accept any job he could get, whether it was dancing in
provincial towns or bull-fighting at Antequera. On
first hearing of Pepita's liaison with Lionel Sackville-
West he had entered into such a rage that he had made
himself ill for three or four days, and had taken the
extreme step of consulting a lawyer with a view of annulling his marriage. Here again the lack of money
defeated him, for he was warned that it would be a long
and expensive business, and, as he pathetically told his
parents, he needed every dollar he could save to keep
himself supplied with costumes for the theatre. It was
a hard life. Not for him were the comfortable house,
the gardens, the vineyards, the stable full of horses at
Buena Vista. But there was still the shell of the house at

Albolote, and Oliva resolved to take what benefit he could out of the former splendours so contemptuously deserted by Pepita and her family.

As Pepita's husband, he established his right to what remained of the property, and, armed with the necessary papers, presented himself at the house of Manuel Gonzalez, who had been left in charge of the lamentable ruin. In fact, he had written to Pepita for a power of attorney, and she, in her casual easy-going way, let him have it. Oliva was much disgusted to find the condition the house was in; he angrily asked Gonzalez under what authority the family had thus despoiled it, adding that they had left him very little to remove but that he was fully determined to remove that little. He added that he considered he had every right to do as he chose, since Pepita had caused her son to be christened in his name. (This was poor innocent little Max, who had no choice in the matter.)

It was not very easy for Oliva to carry out his schemes, for at that time he was not only *primo mimo* (first dancer) himself but was also Director of the ballet in Granada, and had to go backwards and forwards to Albolote between the rehearsals and the performances. His companions in the troupe remembered him asking for leave to go when the rehearsal had lasted longer than usual, as he had to be back for the performance in the evening. The rehearsal used generally to be over by about eleven in the morning, and the evening performance began at half-past seven. Nevertheless he managed the matter quite well, and soon became a familiar figure at Albolote, where Pepita's old friends would point him out to one another as the husband of their Star of Andalusia. Juan Arantave, for instance, first met him in a shop where he (Arantave) was asking the shopkeeper to change a gold coin for him. Spaniards notori-

ously have a very acute sense of the value and importance of money, and as the shop-keeper had some doubt
as to the genuineness of the coin, he called to Oliva, who
was standing by, to come and give his opinion. After
this, Arantave saw Oliva quite often and they used to
salute each other politely when they met in the street.
He even went on one occasion to load a cart with some
tiles Oliva had sold to his father. His father was present,
and paid cash for the tiles on the spot. His brother
Antonio, the same who had watched Pepita with such
delight trying to catch the goldfish in his garden, was
actually employed by Oliva in the labour of pulling
down the house. Oliva directed all these operations himself, standing in the Plaza while the idle portion of the
population stood round watching with great interest
and amusement. They certainly had had their full meed
of entertainment out of the Casa Blanca, ever since
Catalina had first settled in Albolote.

This time it was no brass band which came from
Atarfe, but bullock-carts from Atarfe instead, to load
quantities of material, tiles, beams, wood and bricks,
and to take them away. Oliva would go back to Granada
in the evening and tell his friends at the theatre about
the progress his sales were making. "One day he would
say, 'I have sold so many cartloads of bricks'; another
day, 'I have sold a doorway', or, 'the frame of a window',
and so forth. Whilst that was going on he had a little
cash in hand, but when he wrote to his wife for the
power of attorney he was dreadfully hard up."

One can imagine what the gay rooms of the Casa
Blanca looked like, windowless, roofless, smothered in
the dust and plaster of their own demolition. The fireplaces were gaping and blackened holes, the doorways
were merely gaps leading from one room into another.
Catalina after her own depredations had not left much,

but after Oliva's operations it looked as though a shell had fallen through the roof and exploded. At this point the Ayuntamiento, not only alarmed but active, intervened and explained to Oliva that he had done enough and must not pull down the external walls as well as everything else, since the house, after all, adjoined the public place and such destruction would be dangerous to the buildings as well as to the passers-by. Oliva cannot have been pleased with this prohibition, but he had filled his pockets and now wound up his business in Albolote by selling the surviving walls and the site to Manuel Gonzalez.

He then took his departure, having got his profit and having also spited Catalina. He was not too much to be pitied, for apart from the cash he carried away from Casa Blanca he had also acquired a woman named Josefa Gallardo, a dancer, who stuck to him in the surprisingly enduring way that these Bohemians did use towards one another. They travelled together, danced together, shared lodgings together, and begat several children. Oliva's friends noticed, however, that he called her Pepa and not Pepita, for short.

v

I do not imagine that either Pepita or Lionel Sackville-West cared very much what Oliva was doing, so long as he left them in peace to pursue their own happiness in their own way. This happiness, as we have seen, they were pursuing in almost idyllic circumstances in Italy with their small Max growing up between them. Max was just over three years old when his parents took a furnished apartment at 4 Avenue de l'Impératrice near the Arc de Triomphe in Paris, for they were awaiting another baby.

This baby was born on September 23rd, 1862, and was named Victoria Josefa Dolores Catalina. Pepita thought it was a nice idea to call her daughter Victoria after the Queen of England; Josefa after herself; Dolores after her aunt and godmother (Lola); and Catalina after her grandmother. I doubt if Queen Victoria had ever found herself in more incongruous company. As she was baptized in France, her names had to be recorded in the French form: Victoire Joséphine Dolores Catherine. She was described on the baptismal register as the daughter of Josefa Duran and of an unknown father (*fille de père inconnu*).

This was my mother.

It was odd for me to read in my grandfather's statement that both Catalina and Lopez were present at the birth and that Lola was invited to be the godmother. These three persons had become so extraordinarily familiar to me, though with a measure of remoteness, that the discovery of their personal association with my mother came to me as a slight shock. It was so odd to think of her being handled by Catalina, prodded by Lopez, crooned over by Lola, those three whose adventures I had followed in such detail ever since they left Malaga to seek fortune in Madrid and who had become such living people to me.

VI

Pepita took her two children to Como with her as soon as she was able to travel, but for about two years her lotus-eating existence with my grandfather was frequently interrupted. I do not know for certain, but I suspect that a temporary coolness then arose between her and my grandfather; at any rate, he alludes rather darkly to "a break" with Pepita, and professes ignorance of what she was doing during most of this time. Even more darkly, he alludes to an urgent telegram which reached him from his banker in Berlin (1864) saying that Pepita was very ill. "I left Turin and went to Baden Baden, where she had gone with Max and Victoria. At Baden she told me she had had a miscarriage and confessed that she had been living with someone else, but who he was I never could find out and never heard."

It was perhaps not to be expected of Pepita that she should remain wholly faithful. Romantically, I would far prefer to draw a picture of her as a single-hearted woman from first to last, but such a picture would show only half the truth. Single-hearted she may have been, but certainly not faithful. There had already been Prince Youssoupoff, even when her love of Lionel Sackville-West had been comparatively young. . . . It is idle trying to gloss over those things. She was a dancer, beautiful, desirable, and temptations were rife. My grandfather seems to have been, to this extent, a realist, for as on a previous occasion, he adds, "I became reconciled with her, and shortly afterwards she joined me at Turin".

This reconciliation was shortly interrupted, and for a double reason. For one thing, she had resumed her dancing, and for another he had been transferred from Turin to (of all places) Madrid. At first sight, one would expect Pepita to welcome this opportunity of returning to live in her own country, but the unexpected happened: she flatly refused to go near Madrid, for fear of meeting Oliva. Meanwhile, my grandfather went off to take up his new duties and also to indulge his personal curiosity in a way with which one is able humanly to sympathise: he went to the theatre to see Oliva perform. "It was a small theatre in a back street. Seeing his name on the

play-bill, I asked a man next to me, who was a Spaniard
and a total stranger to me, to point him out, which he
did. That was all that passed and I never spoke to Oliva
in my life. My curiosity was merely to see Pepita's
husband and it carried me no further."

After the performance was over, Oliva presumably
went home with Josefa Gallardo to their poor lodgings,
ignorant of the young foreigner who had sat among the
audience and who had then made his way back to the
British Embassy wondering, perhaps, where Pepita and
her children lay that night.

VII

The break, if break there was, was presently healed.
It was very completely healed, and several facts confirm
it. Not only do we find my grandfather taking a flat at
Bordeaux for Pepita and her children in expectation of
yet another child, but we also find him involved in one
of the queerest and least orthodox incidents of his
whole very unorthodox diplomatic career. I wish I could
explain my grandfather's character satisfactorily to myself, once and for all. I myself knew him later on as
intimately as a child of eight can ever know a very
reserved old man of nearly eighty. I knew his little
habits and his funny ways. I knew the way in which
he would slam his tweed cap down on to the settee on
the way to the dining-room, stumping along towards
luncheon without speaking a word—for he was without
exception the most taciturn man I have ever known,
which may I think perhaps explain the charm Pepita's
gay volubility held for him,—and I knew also his rare
little phrases which recurred at the appropriate seasons.
"Nice fresh taste", he would say when the first goose-
berries appeared in a "stick tart" on the table; "nice

fresh taste", glaring round at us all lest we had failed to appreciate it. And then again he would suddenly invent the most disconcerting rhymes, aimed suddenly at me in the middle of luncheon: "Rosamund Grosvenor", he would aim at me, "got nearly run overner". This phrase bothered me because I could not see how he could get it to rhyme properly, but at the same time it suggested something alarming, something I had certainly never thought of in connexion with the Rosamund Grosvenor who came daily to share my lessons with me and my governess. I think he addressed these spasmodic remarks to me because he was too shy to speak to anyone else, even though he was sitting at the head of his own table. He had many other little idiosyncratic tricks, and I always, even as a child, recognised him as in some unexplained way an unusual old man. I remember for instance that he used to squirt the juice of orange-peel into my eyes, and when I screamed in agonised protest used to reassure me by saying that Spanish women always did that to their children to ensure their having beautiful eyes,—a hint which he had certainly learnt from Pepita, but which I did not in the least appreciate. I remember, also, that once when I came into his room hanging on to the end of my mother's long plait of hair, he sprang up exclaiming, "Victoria, never, *never* let me see that child doing that again". He was habitually a very mild, meek old man, and this was the nearest I ever got to his feeling for Pepita; I remember my mother looking frightened, dragging me quickly out of the room, and then saying to me at the bottom of the stairs outside, "Remember, darling, we must never let Grandpapa see us like that again". This made a great impression on me. I felt I had entered into some unexplained conspiracy with my mother. I didn't understand, of course; I merely guessed, as children do, at something in the background of which I knew nothing.

All this personal acquaintance with my grandfather leaves me still wondering at that very unorthodox incident which occurred at Malaga during his early diplomatic career. My grandfather, as I knew him, was not a person whom one could readily connect with such romantic and injudicious incidents. Yet the fact remains on record that the English Consul at Malaga was obliged to lock him up for three whole days in a room, in order to prevent him going through a form of marriage with Pepita.

That was a very high-handed thing to do to an English gentleman who was by then quite high up in the Diplomatic Service. Of course the Consul acted rightly, for he must instantly have realised that the Secretary of the Embassy would merely have involved himself in a charge of bigamy, Pepita already being married to Juan Antonio Oliva. The Consul did nothing but save the Secretary from a very awkward ensuing situation. Both Pepita and Lionel Sackville-West owed a great deal to that Consul, although I doubt whether they recognised it at the time. More likely they put it all down to red tape.

I think perhaps I had better let the witness speak. It is the witness whom I have already introduced as the washerwoman friend of Catalina, at the beginning of this book. It may be remembered that she was sometimes employed at the Hotel Alameda in Malaga as a general servant to help the chambermaid. In this capacity she speaks again: "On going one day into one of the rooms of the hotel to arrange the toilet service, I saw there, sitting down, Catalina, Manuel Lopez, Pepita, and a strange gentleman. None of them noticed me except Catalina. She went out with me into the corridor. (That was like Catalina: she never forgot an

old friend.) She asked how I was, and I did the same
to her, and said how glad I was to see them looking
so well. They were all well dressed and wore much
jewellery. They had two female servants, who were
both foreigners.

"All the servants said that the strange gentleman was
a Count. They did not say his name. He was a foreigner.
He wanted to marry Pepita but the English Consul
dissuaded him from it. To prevent the marriage, the
Consul locked the Count into another room overlooking the Alameda. The Consul kept the key and used to
go and unlock the door when the Count had his meals.
After the Count had been locked up for about three
days, the Consul sent him off on a steamer."

No comment is necessary. One can only say, as
Matthew Arnold said of the Shelleys, "What a set!"
Still, it does seem odd to think of Grandpapa trying to
behave in that wildly bigamous way at Malaga in 1865,
and being locked up by his Consul in order to save him
from making a fool of himself. He must indeed have
been very much in love. Heaven only knows what
the Consul thought. It is not usually given to consuls
to lock secretaries of His Majesty's Embassies into a
hotel room for three days, unlocking the door only in
order to introduce food, and then to send them off by
steamer.

VIII

The domestic situation, already sufficiently delicate,
had been complicated during my grandfather's in-
carceration by the arrival of Lopez' wife upon the scene,
making a disturbance in the hotel, so that she had to be
given money to keep her quiet. Apart from this, they
had other occupations; it seems that they held one of
their favourite sales, perhaps of objects dating from the

days when Pepita was a child and they all lived in Malaga; and there were relations with whom acquaintance could be renewed. Catalina's cousin Juan, for instance, received a message to say they were in Malaga and would be pleased if he would come to luncheon. By that time, however, they had tired of living in the hotel and in their impulsive extravagant way had taken a house behind the Church of the Concepcion. The cousin Juan went, and was dazzled by the friendliness and luxury of his entertainment. To his surprise he found them "all dressed like gentlefolk, especially Pepita, who was dressed in silk with jewellery". Last time he had seen them, Catalina was selling old clothes, but now they had silver plates and dishes, and silver forks, spoons, and knives which they had brought with them from Granada and used at luncheon. Catalina explained that they had come to Malaga just for a change of air and to see the family; she told him all about Buena Vista, and was in fact as communicative as usual, but did not forget to ask after the fortunes of her guest. "She asked me how I was getting on, and I told her I went about with my donkey selling fruit, and managed to make a living for my family." Truly Pepita had a mixed existence, between German royalties on the one hand and relations like the fruit-seller of Malaga on the other.

IX

The reader may have observed that my grandfather has by now been raised to the rank of Count in the eyes of his Spanish friends. The explanation of this entirely unjustified title lies with Pepita. Pepita wanted to be a Countess. Pepita, just because she was born a true and not a sham Bohemian, esteemed aristocracy and respectability as her greatest prize. The sham Bohemian rejects respectability with calculated deliberation. The born Bohemian strives after the thing which, to him or her, represents a mixture between security and romance. Romance and respectability, for Pepita, were represented by becoming Countess West. That such a title as Count West did not and could not exist in the English peerage meant nothing to Pepita. It sounded well, and that was all that mattered. It was the childishly snobbish side of her. It fondly amused my grandfather. It was like a toy he had given her to play with, a toy which meant nothing to him but much to her. Countess West,—his English upbringing made him smile when he read those words printed on her visiting-card, and realised how little, how very little, they meant; so little, that he could not even introduce her to his colleagues at the Embassy, because they all knew she was his mistress, not his wife. She put a coronet on her visiting-cards over those words: Countess West. He let her put both the coronet and the words; he said, "it did not matter". The pathetic part is that although she had her visiting-cards, she knew no one to visit; she was not respectable enough to leave cards on any of his friends.

Yet the break was repaired. They had lived apart for nearly two years, and at the end of those two years they came together again. It seems as though they were not able to stay apart. My grandfather was still attached to the Embassy at Madrid, and Pepita still refused to come to Madrid because she was afraid of meeting Oliva there, so between them they arranged to take a flat at Bordeaux, which was not too far across the frontier; and at 105 rue de la Course, Bordeaux, my poor little short-lived aunt Elisa Catalina was born in the hot month of June 1865; was registered as the daughter of Lionel Sackville-West and Josefa Duran, grand-parents Pedro Duran and Catalina Ortega on the mother's side, John and Elizabeth, Earl and Countess de la Warr, on the father's; and died aged seven months in January 1866.

X

After this, they never again parted. Pepita gave up her career as a dancer, and settled down into the life for which I believe she was really best suited: the loving woman and mother of an ever-increasing brood of babies. After the effort and the excitement and the adulation, she was at last finding her natural fulfilment. Those half-English, half-Spanish babies,—what an odd upbringing they had! My mother could remember Pepita covering her and Max with her skirts and screaming at Lola and Diego to go away, for they should never have her children. When they were alone, Pepita alternately raged at them and spoilt them. "Ah, ces pétits maudits!" she would exclaim in French with her Spanish accent when they exasperated her beyond endurance, and she would catch them up and cuff them as one might cuff a litter of unruly puppies. Then when they shrieked in fright she would repent and hug them to her breast: "Mes pétits,—mes amours chéris,—mes pauvrés pétits,"—and then she would make them all sit on a row of hassocks against the wall and would dance El Ole for them till they were comforted. They liked her dancing, and they particularly liked her castanets. My mother remembered this very well. She often told me about it, and I thought she must be romancing, until I met the same story in her legal evidence: "I remember my mother (Pepita) dancing with castanets to amuse us children. I remember her valuable dancing dress covered with black lace. She always spoke French with us; she knew no English. She had very long and abundant black hair; she sometimes wore it in two long plaits, which hung down her back and reached down below her knees." My mother remembered this hair very vividly. (She also remembered her elder brother Max trying to comb her own hair with a fork, which she much resented.) She remembered being made to pick up the plaits to keep them out of the mud when crossing the street, much as a bridesmaid might have picked up the train of a bride. My mother often told me about this, adding that she was Pepita's constant companion on their charitable expeditions, which were called, "going to see *mes pauvres*". "Dieu, qu'elle avait du charme! Dieu, qu'elle était gentille!" my mother would add when telling me these stories; "ils lui racontaient tous leurs malheurs" ("Lord! what charm she had! Lord! how sweet she was! They told her all their troubles").

Pepita must indeed have been very sweet at that last period of her life. She had given up all the struggle of a professional career, and had found herself at last in the happy fulfilment of a woman's life. She was, I think, no feminist. Even her sister-in-law described her as "not dominating, but docile". She might have flown as a bird in the air at Malaga, but her real happiness came among her five or six babies at Bordeaux and Arcachon and Paris, with Countess West printed on her visiting cards and Grandpapa coming as often as he could to see her from Madrid.

He had no business to desert his post. He says so himself: "I ought not to have left Spain without leave, but it was constantly done and whenever I went away without leave I took the opportunity of visiting Arcachon". For Pepita was now installed with the children at Arcachon, in the house he had bought for her at a cost of 100,000 francs. It was known as the Villa Pepa, and true to her family tradition Pepita amused herself by entirely remodelling it. First she added two storeys, then she built two pavilions near the seashore, then a stable and a house for the gardener, then a front wall, then added wrought-iron gates and railings. The gates had a coronet and initials on the top. She evidently got on very well with her builder, M. Desombres, for she told him that she had danced in all the capitals of Europe including London and Paris, showed him her collection of photographs, mentioned that Max's father was the King of Bavaria, told him her Christian name and her age, took him out driving with her and the children in her carriage, sent him in to Bordeaux on messages, made my grandfather give him cigars, and invited him to dinner. It is perhaps natural that M. Desombres should have added: "She was not reserved at all. She used to speak of anything that came into her mind." At the same time, there is a little tribute to her personal dignity, for although "extremely pleasant and friendly, she could still continue to keep one at a distance".

Pepita infallibly rings true to herself. There is another account of her, referring to approximately the same period of her life, an account given by a solicitor (*abogado*) of Malaga. She had apparently been having some trouble connected with an alleged right-of-way over her property at Buena Vista. I can't quite make out what the trouble was, but I suspect it to have been in some way due to an aggression on the part of Catalina, or perhaps Lopez, for an interdict was served to prevent her (Pepita, in whose name the property stood) from obstructing the said right of way. It all sounds to me very like one of the usual rows between Catalina and her neighbours. Anyhow, Pepita had to deal with it. She dealt with it by going to this particular solicitor, telling him that she had consulted him because she was a native of Malaga and had heard that he was a native of Malaga likewise, which flattered him; telling him also that she had been a dancer, and was now living under the protection of an English gentleman to whom she was not married, and whose photograph she showed him; introducing him to Max, who was then five or six years old, and who took a particular fancy to some lozenges which the solicitor was using for an affection of the throat; and finally by giving him, from time to time, presents of boxes of cigars, and, on one occasion, a whip with his initials on it. It is not surprising, after this, to learn that when the proceedings came to a head the solicitor was able to obtain a decision in her favour. Nor is it surprising to find him adding, somewhat gratuitously, that she could overcome the well-known prejudices of the Granadinos and that the best society in Granada went to her house (which was certainly not true).

XI

Arcachon was a small place at that time, of not more than seven or eight hundred inhabitants, and the building activities at Villa Pepa were observed with the greatest interest. Everybody knew Pepita at least by sight, and would watch her strolling about her garden, her hair loosely tied back by a ribbon, her dress often with a train several yards long. Her beauty, her generosity, and her reputation made her the general topic of conversation. It was known of course that she was a Spaniard and had been a dancer, but whether she was married or not to the foreign Count was a subject of endless speculation. On the whole, public opinion decided that they were not married. It was observed that she did not consort at all with those whose equal in social rank she might be considered, and that her children were never to be seen playing with some other

English children who lived in the next villa. "She was better known to the poor than to the rich, for although she was not connected with any charitable society in Arcachon (no doubt on account of her dubious reputation), anybody could go to her house and ask for what they wanted and she would give it." She made use of her butcher's wife to discover what was needed, saying that if clothes or linen were wanted she would give them; they had only to come and ask her. In fact her kindness and gracious manners made her generally beloved, and the smile which so many of the witnesses mention. At the same time, it was known that she changed her servants very frequently, for she would dismiss them for the slightest thing, when they used to go away saying that they could not live with such a lady.

Anyone who had penetrated into the interior of Villa Pepa was closely questioned as to what they had seen there. There were the hairdressers Jean Lagarde and his wife; M. Lagarde used to cut the Count's hair whenever he was at the villa, and described him as a gentleman who did not talk much. Mme. Lagarde had quite lost her heart to Pepita at their first interview, when Pepita received her in her bedroom overlooking the sea and told her she had heard she was a real artist who could dress her hair like the other ladies in that part of the country. Her laundress records that she was fond of changing the style of her hairdressing very often, but that she always remained faithful to the little curl on the cheek. The laundress said she had so much jewellery she couldn't remember a single article, and used to dress like a queen. "She was such a pretty lady that everyone used to stop and look at her."

Whenever a telegram came from the Count, the Countess would start putting everything in order. With the children to help her, she would decorate little trees

by tying red cherries in amongst the dark branches.
She would take a great deal of trouble about ordering
meals, and the butcher noticed that his account was
always higher when "the Count of West" came to stay,
because they lived so much better when he was at home.
Then when all preparations had been made, she would
take the children with her to meet him at the station.

Sometimes there were odd little interludes when
she would take a house at Bordeaux in order to go
to the theatre there. It seems as though, in spite of
all her happy domesticity, she was not able always to
keep away from the absorptions of her youth. The
theatre called to her. She would take the house at Bordeaux for a month, and, being Pepita, "it was a splendid
house with a garden". She never stinted herself. M.
Desombres went there to see her once; he enjoyed his
visit. It did not affect him in the least that some people
said she could not be properly married to the Count,
because she had been married before. "The good-
natured people said they were married, and the bad-
natured people said they were not married." In this
case, alas, the bad-natured people had hit on the right
truth.

XII

This was the situation as the outside observers saw
it, but on looking at it more closely from the inside it is
apparent that Pepita had her sorrows as well as her
joys. She minded terribly about the irregularity of her
position. For instance she greatly wanted to go to a semi-
official party at the Préfecture at Bordeaux, had much
difficulty in securing an invitation, and then when she
got there found that she knew nobody except two or
three young men. On another occasion, in Paris, my
grandfather was going officially to a fête at the Tuileries

and "Pepita cried bitterly because she could not go with me on account of her not being recognised in society". These difficulties affected the children too. My mother in her evidence gives a pathetic account; "I and my sisters never had any children friends at all. Two little girls named Minna and Bella Johnston lived next door, but we saw them very rarely and then always surreptitiously because they were forbidden by their parents to associate with us. The gardens of the two houses adjoined with a low wall between the two. They used to tell us their parents said they were not to speak to us. We went once to a children's ball at the Casino at Arcachon, and I remember no one danced with us and we felt very much out of it. We stood by ourselves and nobody spoke to us. It made such an impression on me that I cried. We were never allowed to go again although these dances constantly took place. At the time of course I did not understand the reason for this." When they were in Paris it was the same story: "It is usual for children to play together in the Champs Elysées. It is the place where children of good families play. We played there but were forbidden to speak to other children. If other children offered to play with us we had to decline." And again: "I can recollect walking with my father to the British Embassy often, but he always made me turn back before getting there."

And there was worse than all this. Pepita of course was a Roman Catholic, but owing to the fact that she was living in adultery she could neither receive absolution nor go to communion. Nor would her conscience permit her to attend Mass, and she was never to be seen at services in the main church at Arcachon. All this was naturally a source of very deep distress to her. It was a source of equal distress when her beloved daughter, on attaining the age of seven (which is the ordinary

PEPITA

CATALINA ORTEGA

JUAN ANTONIO DE LA OLIVA IN 1875

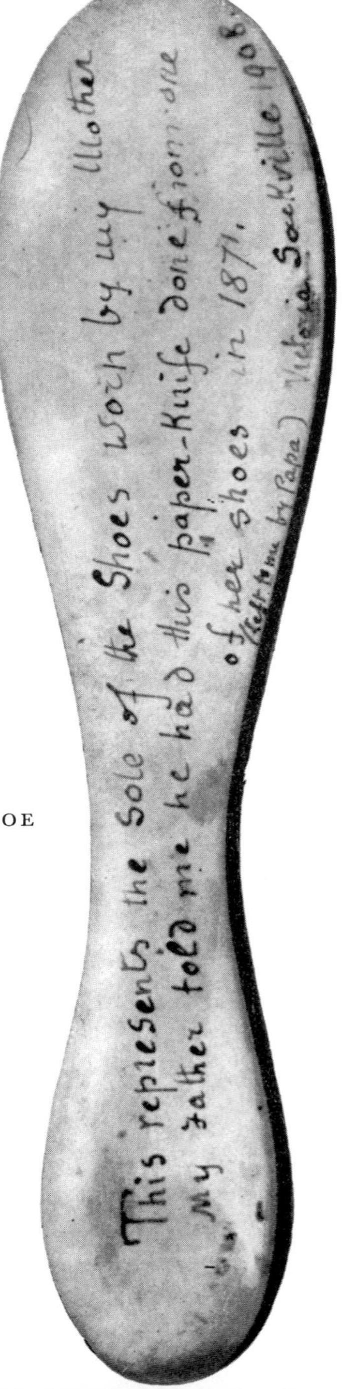
This represents the Sole of the Shoes worn by my Mother
My father told me he had this paper-knife done from one
of her shoes in 1871.
(Left to me by Papa) Victoria Sackville 1908.

THE SOLE OF PEPITA'S SHOE
(*actual size*)

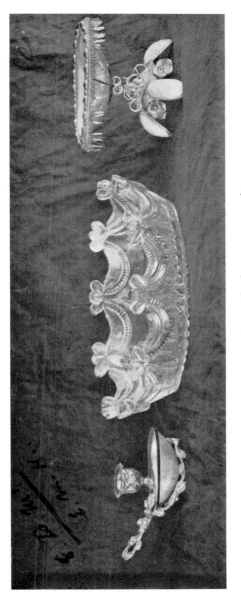

SOME OF PEPITA'S 'TREASURES'

ANOTHER OF PEPITA'S 'TREASURES'—THE TABLECLOTH

LOLA AND HER CHILD

PEPITA AND HER DAUGHTER, IN 1870

MOTHER AND HER SISTERS ON THEIR WAY TO WASHINGTON

MY MOTHER WHEN IN WASHINGTON

KNOLE

MY MOTHER AND I

SIR JOHN MURRAY SCOTT, WITH A POLISH DWARF

MY MOTHER IN 1910

MY MOTHER IN 1917 (SITTING OUT IN THE SNOW)

MY MOTHER AT BRIGHTON, ABOUT 1920

age for a child brought up in the Roman Catholic faith to go to confession), asked to go and had to be told she could not. "I wanted to go, but my mother would not let me. When I asked her to prepare me, she said she could not. I did not know at the time what all this meant." [1]

Unwilling, however, wholly to forego the consolations of her religion, although she might only benefit by them as it were furtively, Pepita used often to drive out to the little church at Mouleau beyond the forest, a tiny chapel frequented by a few pilgrims; it was a very small building, and when she went there in the afternoon she could usually count on having it to herself. She went only to pray, and sometimes to see one of the fathers; she always took my mother with her, and the child used to hear the priest telling her he could not give her communion because she could not be given absolution, although she wanted it.

The priest of course was not to blame: he was only doing his duty according to his precepts, and could not have done otherwise. He could not condone adultery. But when I think of the self-righteous society which rejected Pepita as an improper woman, the words I quoted a few pages back echo in my mind, as I see that lovely, lonely figure kneeling, almost an outcast, in prayer in the deserted chapel: *she was better known to the poor than to the rich, for anybody could go to her house and ask for what they wanted, and she would give it.*

It is only in association with the complete background that these dry words of legal evidence assume their almost Biblical austerity and significance.

---

[1] This, at least, is my mother's version, but I think that somehow she must have got it wrong, for surely the sins of the parents would not thus have been visited upon the children? It seems more likely that Pepita merely thought the child too young and immature. Probably the priest had advised her to this effect.

CHAPTER VI

END OF THE DANCER

I

FROM the material point of view Pepita was prosperous and even happy. And it is not to be denied that the material advantages of this world did count for her. By 1870 she had almost everything she could desire; a villa in Arcachon for the summer, a house in Paris for the winter, a generous lover, and as many children as her very maternal heart could comfortably embrace. Moreover after the births of the two eldest children she had prevailed upon my grandfather to let her register the subsequent children as legitimately his and hers,— a most unfortunate and expensive deception, as it turned out later on, but one which my grandfather weakly accorded, as he could refuse her nothing. There was Max, now a tall boy of twelve; the little girl, my mother, called Mademoiselle Pepita by the servants, aged eight; another little girl aged four, who had been registered as Lydia Eleanor Graciosa, but whose name was subsequently changed to Maria Flor Sophia, called Fleur de Marie; another little girl, Amalia Albertina, aged two, whose godfather was Prince Adalbert of Bavaria and godmother Princess Adalbert, Infanta of Spain; and a little boy, aged one year, Ernest Henri Jean Baptiste, known as Henri. Pepita thus had five children living and two establishments. The house in Paris was in a most fashionable quarter; it was No. 200 avenue d'Eylau, near the Champs Elysées, and it had cost my grandfather 195,000 francs. He, meanwhile, had been transferred from Madrid and appointed First Secretary to the British Embassy in Paris. He does not appear to have lived openly in the house with them, and, as we have seen, reduced Pepita to tears by refusing to let her accompany him to the Tuileries; but beyond these slight concessions to social opinion he was able to see as much as he chose of his happy, illegitimate Spanish family living round the corner. It has always seemed very strange to me that the Foreign Office (and in Victorian days too) should thus have turned so blind an eye towards the private life of their First Secretary, but so it was. He was either very lucky or very skilful at managing his own affairs. And a further piece of good luck was awaiting him, for in 1870 the British Embassy, in fear of the Prussian advance, transferred itself from Paris to Bordeaux, which was quite near Arcachon.

Local gossip said that if the Prussians got as far as Arcachon, the Countess West had everything ready to welcome them. The local gossips slightly confused their facts: the Countess's eldest son, they said, was the son of the King of Bavaria, therefore he was a Prussian, and moreover the Countess had a portrait of the King of Bavaria hanging up in her villa, so whatever happened she would be quite safe. It confused them even more when the Countess started receiving wounded French soldiers into her house, and caring for them personally, until they either died or recovered from their wounds.

II

Pepita's existence, in fact, seemed settled, permanent, and contented, if we except the two sorrows of the social and the religious ostracism, and as we shall presently see she took steps to minimise both these drawbacks as far as she was able. It seemed scarcely likely that Lionel Sackville-West would break now with a woman with whom he had had such intimate and continuous relations for eighteen years, and by whom he had already had six children, five of whom were living. There were bound to be complications, of course, inevitable in so anomalous a situation,—what would happen, for instance, when the children grew up, or when the Secretary rose in the service, becoming a Minister and even an Ambassador?—but on the whole it looked as though they would always be able to find some way of life, not wholly satisfactory perhaps, but tolerable. Money was no anxiety to them, and as for age they were both in the prime of life, he forty-three, she just forty. True, she was getting a little stout, but that was natural to her Spanish race, and in a photograph taken of her at about this time there is a certain mellow serenity about the beautiful brow which speaks of a heart at peace and a life roundly fulfilled. Her hair was as black as it had been in her youth. She often sang as she went about the house, and in the afternoons she would drive out to the sand-dunes with the children and laugh when they filled their drawers with the silvery sand, standing up to let it trickle out at their ankles, for of course according to the fashion of the second Empire they wore the frilly drawers which reached far below their short little skirts.

It is rather alarming to learn that on all these expeditions she carried a fat purse full of gold and notes. The proletarian in Pepita distrusted all banks and all investments, preferring to keep her money in ready cash. This little idiosyncrasy specially amuses me, for my mother inherited it and to the end of her life infinitely preferred to pay her bills by bank-note rather than by cheque. And, like Pepita, she always carried a bulging purse in a pocket let into her petticoat. So long as she could feel it knocking against her leg as she walked, she told me, she knew it was safe.

Pepita spared Max to go to a day school, but the little girls and the baby Henri were always with her, especially my mother, who even slept in her bed.

Nor did she lack for grown-up companionship. Defrauded of the society of those from whom the self-styled Countess West might have expected a welcome, she fell back upon such society as she could provide for herself. We have already seen that she took M. Desombres the builder driving in her carriage, showed him her collection of photographs, and invited him to dinner; but the way in which she acquired the friendship of Henri de Béon was far odder and completely characteristic.

Henri de Béon is a new character, but M. Desombres comes into the story again. The long-suffering M. Desombres is sent into Bordeaux to fetch "a very nice gentleman who was second station-master at Bordeaux". This very nice gentleman had been so kind as to stop the train for Prince and Princess Adalbert of Bavaria on their way to Arcachon, and to see the Prince and Princess and Lionel Sackville-West and Pepita all safely into an empty compartment. Pepita told Desombres that she was very glad to have made de Béon's acquaintance, and sent him to Bordeaux to invite Béon to dinner. Desombres obediently went, found de Béon at the station, and brought him back. The following day de Béon was still to be seen at the villa, so Desombres assumed that he must have stayed there all night.

Scandal inevitably ensued. De Béon, having once got his footing in the Villa Pepa because he had been so obliging as to stop the train for German royalties at Bordeaux, remained at the Villa Pepa as a fixture. The very nice gentleman was taken on as Pepita's secretary and general manager. The laundress, who received her pay from de Béon, used to say to herself, "Yes, you are the superintendent and something more". The good folk of Arcachon, who had already once been scandalised by the spectacle of Pepita living with a foreign Count to whom she was not married, were now doubly scandalised by the spectacle of the under station-master of Bordeaux being taken into the house as *persona grata*. They swung round entirely onto the foreign Count's side, declaring that he ought to throw the station-master into the Bay of Biscay, especially as "he looked to be a lazy fellow". But they all added that Pepita could make the foreign Count do anything she liked. The general opinion was, that the station-master had become Pepita's lover, and that the good-natured Count West was fooled.

I know full well that rumour has made the station-master into the true father of my mother, but chronologically that possibility is dispelled, since Pepita never met the station-master until my mother was four or five years old. As to the rest of the story, I scarcely know what to believe. Pepita is an unfathomable character. But then so are most of us unfathomable characters, even to ourselves. Are we to believe that Pepita, who got herself and the children ready to go and meet Lionel Sackville-West at the station whenever his telegram arrived, and whose house-bills went up because they lived so much better when he was there,—are we to believe that Pepita deceived him, for whom she cared so tenderly, to the extent of importing a new young lover into his house?

All is possible. With people of Pepita's temperament, all is possible. One can neither decide nor judge.

Then, again, they said she took to drink. They said

she drank champagne with de Béon. Well, one knows how easily the tongues of provincial neighbours wag, and one bottle of champagne may innocently have given rise to this particular reproach. I must admit that my mother told me her younger sister, Fleur de Marie, bought, borrowed, or abstracted champagne whenever she could get it, because she had been told it was good for washing the hair, Fleur de Marie being only four years old at the time. For my own part, I think that the picture drawn of Pepita at this time of her life accords ill with what I know of her. It accords ill with her excessive animal love of her babies; her constant companionship with her older children; her pathetic excitement whenever she heard that Lionel Sackville-West was about to arrive; her distress at the ostracism imposed, logically and inevitably, by her Church.

It was in order to mitigate this ostracism that she had recourse to the pathetic expedient of building herself a little chapel in her own garden. The services of M. Desombres were again secured, this time in his true capacity as a builder, and to Pepita's joy when the work was finished the priest from Arcachon consented to hold services on Sundays and feast-days for her and her children. Although she still could not receive the supreme consolation of absolution and communion, she could at least attend Mass without having to endure the inquisitive glances of her neighbours. With her children round her it was very peaceful in the little private chapel, and at any time she could retire there for prayer.

There was yet another purpose for which the chapel had been designed: she proposed to be buried there when the time should come, within sound of the sea.

I think that during the winter of 1870–71 she must have spent some happy months. The staff of the British

Embassy having been transferred to Bordeaux, Lionel Sackville-West could constantly be with her; she had the chapel and her regular services; and she was expecting another baby, her seventh, in March. She cried a little when the ambassador, Lord Lyons, asked my grandfather to go and take charge of the deserted Embassy in Paris, but he explained to her that it was only a temporary absence and, mercurial as ever, she was soon cheerful again. Her baby would be born before he returned, she would be strong again to welcome him, and the spring would be coming.

He left for Paris on February 16th.

On March 6th he received a telegram informing him that Pepita had given birth to a son. Three other telegrams followed in rapid succession. The first stated that she was ill, the second that she was worse, the third that she was dead.

Distraught, he appealed to Lord Lyons for leave of absence, and arrived at Arcachon just two days too late. They had already embalmed the body, so that he might see her once more as he had known her, for it was uncertain when he would arrive. My mother remembered that arrival well. She was in the room, a frightened and heartbroken child of nine, praying beside the bed on which lay the still form of Pepita, a crucifix clasped between her stiffened fingers, the lighted candles burning steadily over the unearthly beauty of the pallor of death. Beside her lay the tiny figure of the dead baby who had cost her her life. As my grandfather reached the room, he stopped for a moment at the threshold, then ran forward and threw himself on his knees beside the bed, sobbing out that it was he who had killed her. It was in vain that they tried to comfort him by telling him that she had died with his name, "Lionel", upon her lips.

III

Fortunately de Béon was there, and so was the excellent M. Desombres, who, in the most practical manner, took charge of everything. He had been present at Pepita's death, and had taken off the diamond necklace she was wearing; he then decided to stay in the villa till after the funeral. There was much for him to do. He put all Pepita's jewellery into a box, including the diamond necklace, the emerald heart which had always been so much admired, and the "brooch shaped like a lizard set with streaks of gold and emeralds alternately", and kept the box in a safe until he could hand it over to my grandfather. He registered the deaths of both little Frederic Charles and his mother. He made the coffin, and, at my grandfather's request, he dug the grave under the chapel where Pepita had wished to be buried.

But this last and surely harmless wish was not to be gratified. De Béon sought permission from the local authorities and, on their refusal, pressed it as far as the Pope himself. It was still refused, and Pepita lies in the general cemetery of Arcachon, with no memorial stone to mark her grave. All the poor of Arcachon, and all the wounded soldiers, attended her funeral.

The keeper of the cemetery records that many years afterwards, to be exact, on September 5th, 1896, two gentlemen came to Arcachon, saying that they were the son and the son-in-law of the Countess and had come with the necessary permission for exhuming the body. They had some difficulty in finding the grave, as there was no headstone, but finally it was identified and opened, and the coffin was taken up. "Mr Henri West appeared to be very much upset and grieved, and wept on the occasion of the opening of the coffin. The body was quite life-like, and as if she would speak."

PART II

PEPITA'S DAUGHTER, 1862–1936

CHAPTER I

PEPITA'S DAUGHTER

I

THE question remained, what was to be done with the children? My grandfather naturally could not look after them himself, and with some relief accepted the suggestion that de Béon's mother should take charge of them and live with them at Villa Pepa, with the exception of Max who was sent to school at Bordeaux. This arrangement lasted for two or three years, during which time my grandfather conveniently disappeared to Buenos Aires in the capacity of British Minister. I mean no disrespect to my grandfather, but I do not think he was the man ever to enjoy dealing with a difficult situation: he far preferred to go away if he decently could and leave it to somebody else. Hitherto, Pepita had ordered his life, and now there was to be an uncomfortable period of transition until Pepita's eldest daughter was of an age to assume the same responsibility.

Meanwhile, all the other characters in this curious story recede from the centre and are discerned henceforth only occasionally wandering round the periphery. Thus Oliva turns up in Arcachon, wearing a dark suit and a black hat-band in mourning for Pepita. He is reported there as a Spaniard who could not speak French, trying to squeeze what benefit he could out of her possessions. A little later we find him in hospital in Madrid with cancer of the tongue, but nevertheless going off to fulfil a dancing engagement in Guatemala,

from whence he returns with a collection of live birds
to show to his friends. As for Catalina, the few last
glimpses of her are tragic compared with the zest she
brought to the renovation of her houses or the praise of
her successful daughter. They tell a story of poverty and
deterioration, for the graph of Catalina's life, after
rising to its peaks of prosperity at Albolote and Buena
Vista, sinks again to the very low level of her beginnings. At one time she and Lopez are found keeping a
provision shop in Malaga, serving in the shop themselves, and then she is seen, still in Malaga, "in an old
furniture shop, greatly changed and simply clad". The
witness did not know if the shop belonged to her or not.
Pressed for further information, he said it was not
exactly a shop but a room used as a shop, for selling old
clothes, old furniture, and other second-hand things.
"There was a great difference in her appearance and
apparel from what I remembered at Albolote. She
seemed crestfallen and in straitened circumstances,—
she seemed decayed. I just bowed to her."

This is painful enough. Then she is seen at Seville,
living "in bad circumstances". And finally, some persons who were in the habit of travelling to and fro between Malaga and Seville, reported to her cousin who
went round with the donkey selling fruit that she had
died at Seville. He could not remember who the
persons were, and he did not know how long she had
been dead.

Thus Catalina takes her exit, and the children are
left with no natural guardians except a father in South
America and, in England, a very different and infinitely more respectable set of relations of whom they
had as yet no knowledge at all.

II

They could not remain for ever in Arcachon, and about two years after their mother's death Mme. de Béon removed them all to Paris, with the exception of Max who continued at his school in Bordeaux. It had become imperative for something to be done about their education which Pepita in her happy-go-lucky way had wholly neglected. The eldest girl (to whom I continue to refer as my mother) was now nearly eleven and had never done any lessons at all. I believe she had never even been taught to read or write. The two other girls, Fleur de Marie and Amalia, were seven and five respectively; Henri was only four. These three therefore remained under Mme. de Béon's charge in Paris, while my mother, older and less fortunate than they, was placed in the Convent of St. Joseph, 17 rue Monceau. She stayed there from the age of eleven to the age of eighteen.

She was miserably unhappy from first to last during those seven years spent in the Convent of St. Joseph. Other characters might adapt themselves to convent life; not so my mother, who was by nature a rebellious and unconventional person. She suffered from the discipline, the restrictions, the cold, the discomfort, the actual harshness imposed. Accustomed to the warm, extravagant, good-tempered, ill-tempered, varying existence at Villa Pepa; to the occasional cuffs administered by Mamma; to the overflowing and spontaneous consolations which followed; to the lax and happy mode of life which included M. Desombres, and the laundress, and the hairdresser, and M. de Béon, and Aunt Lola who quarrelled with Mamma, and Uncle Diego who lodged at the post-office, and Papa who telegraphed his arrival periodically from Paris, creating a stir in the

household so that one tied red cherries on to little trees
and made oneself tidy to go and meet him at the
station,—accustomed to all this, the rigours of a Paris
convent froze the soul. The warmth and storms and
difficulty and humanity had gone out of life. They were
replaced by severe and suspicious supervision. One was
not allowed to talk privately to one's fellow-inmates lest
one might be saying something subversive, or indeed
immoral. If one complained of one's health, as adolescent girls might occasionally and justifiably complain,
one was sent out for a long walk in crocodile, or to an
even earlier church service to teach one not to be self-
regarding. If one fainted in church, from natural causes,
one was reproved and made to do extra lessons. At
night, in bed, one was so cold that one prayed to the
Virgin Mary to warm one. The only happy moments
my mother spent in the convent were the moments
when she could raise her exceptionally pure though un-
tutored voice in the choir. Otherwise it was all chill.
"Oui, ma sœur; non, ma sœur." She had even ceased
to be Mademoiselle Pepita, and had become Mademoiselle quarante-deux.

There were no real holidays. Sometimes in the summer she was taken to Bercq near Boulogne with some
of the nuns, but although there were sand-dunes at
Bercq as at Arcachon she was not allowed to fill her
drawers with the sand as Pepita had allowed her to do.
Her father wrote to her sometimes from South America
and very occasionally he went to see her, for this of
course could only be done when he was on leave. Once
she was allowed to go and see him off at the station; she
thought he was going to Buenos Aires but was not sure.

It was scarcely a life for a much-loved, high-spirited
child, and presently as she grew older she began to
notice certain disquieting facts and whispers which she

felt were vaguely associated in some general mystery, but to which she naturally could not supply the connecting links. First of all some difficulty arose over her confirmation, on account of her baptismal certificate, and there was some talk of her having to be re-baptised. She of course had never seen that baptismal certificate: *fille de père inconnu*. Then, when that trouble was got over, M. de Béon came one day to see her at the convent, and told her never to mention that her mother had been a dancer or that she had been called Pepita after her. He gave no reason. She had already noticed, however, that while she was staying with Mme. de Béon she and the other children had been strictly forbidden to go near the drawing-room when visitors were in the house. A little later de Béon came again, and this time he told her that it would be dangerous for her to go out into the streets as there was a man after her who wanted to kidnap her and her brothers and sisters. He told her the man's name: Oliva. It was the first time she had ever heard it, and as she knew no language but French she understood it as Olivier.

All this was puzzling and even sinister. Children are pathetically helpless at the best of times, with little choice but to acquiesce in the inscrutable arrangements made for them, but these children, with no one to whom they could turn for enlightenment, seem especially lost and at sea. Even Mme. de Béon died, and after her death the two younger girls were also sent to the convent and Henri went to a *lycée*. An unknown hand,—the hand of Providence, as it seemed to them in their ignorance,—swooped down on Max in Bordeaux, lifted him bodily to England, and then set him down on a farm in South Africa. When such things could occur, none of them knew what would happen to any of them next. They realised that they could not stay for the rest of their lives in the convent, unless, indeed, they adopted the religious life, but apart from that the future was completely dark.

It was in 1880 that a Mrs Michel Mulhall appeared at the convent as my grandfather's emissary to remove his children to England. He had met this lady in Buenos Aires, and, as so often happens to helpless men, had attracted her sympathy over the difficult position in which he found himself. Five illegitimate children! and he a Minister in the British Diplomatic Service! True, the eldest son was temporarily provided for, but there remained the three daughters and the little boy with no responsible guardian whatsoever now that Mme. de Béon was dead. Besides, they were Roman Catholics; their father was not, though in his vaguely worried way he expressed a wish that they should continue in their mother's faith; Mrs Mulhall, herself a Catholic, was so much concerned at their possible fate that she travelled to Bercq in order to have a look at the girls who had gone there under the charge of the nuns. When my grandfather called upon her for practical help, she came forward nobly and carried them all off to her own house, Grasslands at Balcombe in Sussex.

My mother, who was then eighteen, left the convent armed with the certificate necessary to enable her to become a governess.

III

When they arrived in England, however, they found a new and most surprising set of facts awaiting them. They discovered that they had an uncle, Lord de la Warr, who owned a large house called Buckhurst, where they were taken to spend the day. It stood in the midst of a park, with a lake and magnificent trees, and was un-

like anything they had ever seen before. They discovered that they had another uncle, Lord Sackville,
who owned an even larger house called Knole. They discovered further that they had two aunts, the Duchess of
Bedford and the Countess of Derby; the Duchess of
Bedford (Aunt Bessie) refused to have anything to do
with them, but Lady Derby (Aunt Mary) treated them
from the first with a kindness my mother never forgot.
She had them constantly to see her at Derby House,
though, with a curious echo of Mme. de Béon, they
were never allowed to meet any visitors and were
always turned away before six o'clock when Aunt
Bessie Bedford came for her daily call. Aunt Mary
Derby, unlike Aunt Bessie Bedford, lent them her
private box at the Albert Hall. She went to see them at
the Convent of the Sacred Heart where they had been
temporarily placed at Highgate, and at the lodgings in
Eastbourne where they had been sent with an English
governess. She told them with the utmost gentleness
that they had better drop the 'Sackville' out of their surname, and be known only by the name of West, also
that my mother had better change her name from Pepita
to Victoria,—it sounded less foreign,—and that Fleur
de Marie likewise had better be called Flora, and Henri
Henry. But by this time there was no need to deal tact-
fully or circumspectly with my mother, for she and she
alone had been told the whole truth. Mrs Mulhall had
told it to her on the boat as they were crossing the
Channel. "She told me she had to say that my father and
mother had never been married. It was a great shock
and surprise to me, though I naturally did not at first
realise the consequences. I was eighteen. I did not tell
my sisters."

But she did tell her brother. He was just going to be
sent to Stoneyhurst, and she thought he might have his

life made unbearable by the other boys. "I said to him, 'Henri, you must not tell any boy that our father and mother were never married. I don't know what it means, but it is a terrible thing', and he said he would not. He seemed to be astonished and probably did not realise what it meant."

The secrecy was over, so far as my mother was concerned, but still her future seemed as undetermined as ever. She once showed me the certificate of her proficiency as a governess, and told me that for a while she had quite made up her mind to adopt that profession; there seemed to be no other path open to her. I must say that I smile to think how she would have turned any employer's household upside-down within a week. Anyone less adapted to the position of a governess I can scarcely imagine. Luckily, Queen Victoria, Lord Granville, and the wife of the American President between them saved her from so incongruous a fate.

IV

My mother appears to have been born with the faculty of attracting the most peculiar and improbable happenings, which trailed after her throughout her career as an ever-lengthening comet's tail of surprise and oddity. One may say, indeed, that they started with her birth, which in itself was picturesque rather than conventional. This, certainly, was due to circumstances over which she could have exercised no influence, conscious or unconscious, but having begun, so to speak, on the right lines she never afterwards fell short of the standard thus prescribed. There are some people to whom unexpected things happen all the time; others to whom nothing ever happens at all. My mother very definitely belonged to the former category. Even she

herself, although one of the least self-conscious and
least analytical of mortals, sometimes became aware of it
and would laugh at herself; "Quelles drôles de choses
m'arrivent, tout de même," she would say. "What
funny things do happen to me, to be sure."

Thus it was quite consistent that such eminent figures
as the Queen of England, the Secretary of State for
Foreign Affairs, and the leaders of American society
should all have been mobilised to rescue the half-
Spanish waif from the life of obscurity and even igno-
miny which threatened. A bastard? A governess? No.
Lady Derby thought otherwise. She had seen the girl's
beauty and the immature charm which was just beginning to expand after the release from the repression
of the French convent. Lady Derby was a kindly woman,
but she was also a woman of the world, and in her young
relative she saw the material for something quite different from a children's governess. Her brother Lionel
Sackville-West had just been appointed British Minister
to Washington, and Lady Derby set herself to use her
position and influence to send his young daughter after
him, to act as his hostess and mistress of his house.

The suggestion caused some consternation, both at
the Foreign Office and among the ladies of Washington, for Washington society was small and excessively
exclusive, and naturally the hostess of the British Legation would play a leading part in social life. To suggest
an illegitimate daughter of eighteen, unable even to
speak English fluently, for such a rôle was asking something which had never been asked before. At first, only
Mrs Garfield had to be consulted, but in the midst
of the negotiations President Garfield was shot,
and the new President Arthur being a widower it became necessary to consult the wives of Secretaries of
State and other influential Washington hostesses. Mrs

Garfield had already given her consent, and although many anxious meetings were called to discuss the matter, not altogether unanimous, it was unlikely that the ladies would in the end refuse to follow Mrs Garfield's lead. One of the gravest difficulties in the way of acceptance was the fact that the Minister's daughter had never been presented in London at Court, and this to the eyes of Washington in the 'eighties was almost as insuperable an obstacle as her illegitimacy. A report however was spread to the effect that Lady Derby had taken her young protegée for a private audience to Buckingham Palace, a report which did much to mollify the conscience of the Washington ladies. I do not know whether there was any foundation for it or not: I know only that it was generally circulated and believed.

Meanwhile, at home, Lady Derby was certainly sending Lord Granville to see the Queen. Nobody was more than slightly surprised when all opposition collapsed and Victoria West, accompanied by a French lady-companion of forbidding appearance and impeccable integrity, sailed for Washington to join her father.

v

Here was a change of affairs indeed. Instead of running at the behest of nuns, or of finding herself bundled out of the drawing-room when visitors were announced, she now found herself at the head of a large house, with a large staff of servants, a number of young secretaries and attachés anxious to do her bidding, distinguished people calling on her in shoals every day—for naturally everybody's curiosity had been aroused—and the prospect of organising balls and official parties ahead of her. She does not seem to have been in the least appalled, but to have taken control of the whole situation as though she had been prepared for it all her life. If Washington society expected a timid little convent girl, it must have received a surprise.

She was lovely, ingenuous, and irresistibly charming. I hope I shall not be accused of prejudice if I say that my mother was a truly beautiful woman. No photograph or portrait ever showed her as she was, for no photograph or portrait could indicate the changes of her expression or the extraordinary sweetness of her smile. If ever the phrase 'turn one's heart to water' meant anything, it meant when my mother looked at you and smiled. I, of course, remember her only in her middle years and her old age, for she was already thirty when I was born, but those who knew her as a girl and a young woman unanimously tell me that seldom have they known such charm allied to such beauty. One of them added, "It really wasn't fair. She did exactly what she liked with everybody." That dark hair, those dark blue eyes, that marvellously curving mouth, those lovely hands and expressive gestures, that broken English, that mixture of innocence and imperiousness —Washington was at her feet, and Mrs Russell Selfridge, who still refused to receive her, found herself in a minority of one.

People fell in love with her right and left. She began dramatically, for the first proposal of marriage she had was from the President himself. Others followed with absurd rapidity. The list of her suitors in America is long and various. Beginning with the President, it included a Red Indian chief whose attentions became so pressing that he had to be pushed out of the Ministerial train, a millionaire who tried to bribe her with a promise of £50,000 a year pocket-money, a financier who puzzled her considerably with his references to Wall Street and to the profits she might make there under his guidance, a Siamese gentleman named Phra Darun, and a rabble of young secretaries in her own and other Legations. Discretion forbids me to mention names, for some of their bearers are still alive, but I may at least say that several of these young men in later life reached the highest ranks in their professions and retained a valued friendship with her to the last. One of them, indeed, whom I knew well and who died nearer the age of eighty than seventy, never failed to write to her on the anniversary of the day when he had first declared his love, invariably ending his letter with the sign (X̄) and the words "votre fidèle R. S." This particular friendship suffered a year's interruption after forty years' duration, when she accused him of eating £100 worth of groceries which she had had sent out to her own flat in Rome (a flat which, incidentally, she rented at great cost and never inhabited for a single day), but after this brief interlude they composed their differences, *anglice*, he apologised to her satisfaction for something he had patently never done—for distinguished diplomats seldom trouble to purloin other people's provisions—and the friendship resumed its course unimpaired.

I think that part of her attraction at that time, apart from her beauty, must have lain in the combination of extreme innocence and determined personality. Fresh from her convent, she was utterly unconversant with the realities of the world in any form. I once asked her why she had never accepted any of the men, young or otherwise, who laid siege to her in Washington. She replied, with the naïve gravity that sometimes overcame her, that she had once indeed consented to become engaged. He was very handsome, and drove her out in his buggy with great dash and speed and *chic* along the flowering avenues of Washington in the late 'eighties.

She fancied herself in love with him, until the lady-companion provided by Lady Derby and Lady de la Warr thought it her duty to explain the facts of married life. After this explanation, my mother instantly broke the engagement, without giving any reason. The poor young man wondered where he had been at fault, he who had done nothing but send her flowers, take her out for drives, and honourably ask her to share his life. She told me herself that he was very much puzzled and upset and that he couldn't understand the sudden change in her at all. When she told me this, perhaps forty or fifty years after it had happened, she suddenly realized how puzzled he must have been. Remorse overcame her. "Ce pauvre Buggy!" she fondly exclaimed——for she had nicknamed him after his carriage, and the nickname had stuck. "Et pourtant," she added, more complacently, "il m'aimait bien——he did really love me." He loved her till he died. This I know, for he told me so himself. He told me that she had been the only woman in his life. He was old when he told me that, and by then he had been married twice. It had turned into a romantic love, of course; he was a romantic person, and she was exactly the sort of woman on to whom a romantic, hopeless love would fasten.

Innocent though she was, she had a will of her own and no hesitation about exercising it. Thus she found certain practices current in Washington of which she disapproved and to which she promptly put a stop. People who came uninvited to large parties at the Legation found themselves politely escorted out. Such a thing had never been done before. It was also made known that people who wished to call on the young hostess of the British Legation could do so only by appointment. This, again, was an innovation; it was high-handed, almost regal; most Legation hostesses

were always accessible at tea-time; they just sat behind
the tea-pot waiting for the *chers collègues* to drop in, and
the more that came, the better they were pleased. Diplomatic receptions were easy and indeed obligatory, but to
be invited to the British Legation became something of
an honour. Another innovation she introduced met with
great approval among the young men, after they had
recovered from their first shocked surprise: she refused
to accept bouquets from them before a dance. The word
went round, "Miss West won't be bunched". It was
surprising, at first, to see the popular Miss West arrive
flowerless in the ballroom, but because Miss West
wouldn't be bunched, all the smart young ladies in
Washington had to follow suit, which proved a welcome
economy to all the smart young men, who hitherto had
gauged a girl's popularity by the number of bouquets
she received, and which they could ill afford repeatedly
to send.

Then a ballot of votes was taken for "the nicest girl
in Washington", and Mrs Bloomfield Moore clasped
the prize of three thousand pounds' worth of pearls
round the white throat of Victoria West. I have not the
faintest idea of what has happened to those pearls. She
wore them for years, and then one day I suddenly
realised that she wore them no longer. She may have
lost them, sold them, or merely given them away. One
never knew, with her, what happened to things, any
more than one ever knew what she was likely to do next.

My mother never cared much for parties or for what
is called Society. For one thing she was curiously fastidious, hated shaking hands, and would do anything
she could to avoid it. Either she would wear a glove, or
else she would enter the room with her arms full of
parcels, which disconcerted everybody and made hand-
shaking impossible. This, of course, she could scarcely

do at Washington, when she had to stand at the top of
the staircase to receive several hundreds of people, and
on these occasions she would dawdle, tearful and rebellious, in her bedroom before going down, while the
French lady-companion fussed round admonishing her,
"Mais voyons, Victoria, voyons!" The French lady-
companion's job was no sinecure; she had been engaged
by Lady Derby, with the recommendation of Lady de
la Warr to back her, to look after that curious sport of
the English aristocracy, Victoria West. It is difficult to
read into the mind of the lady-companion. It is to be
presumed that she took a perfectly orthodox view of the
functions obligatory on her pupil-charge. A daughter
of the English aristocracy,—whether on the right or the
wrong side of the blanket,—had certain obligations to
fulfil. Once pitchforked into Society, she must fulfil
them cheerfully and even with pleasure. It was un-
natural for a young and beautiful girl to dislike those
obligations as vehemently as Victoria disliked them.

Yet by all accounts the young people in Washington
had plenty of fun and a good time. The society, though
exclusive, was by no means rigid or dull. In spring and
summer there were drives and picnics; in winter, on the
all-too-rare occasions of a fall of snow, there were the
sleighs to be brought out of the stable, when the streets
of Washington tinkled to a thousand bells, as clear and
glittering as the sparkling snow over which the horses
trotted noiselessly. Wrapped in huge bearskin rugs, not
only over their knees but round their shoulders also, so
that the frosted fur stood up in great shaggy collars
round their glowing faces, the gilded youth of Washington set off on expeditions, calling gaily to one another as
the silent runners started over the crisp surface. My
mother on these occasions wore a tight-fitting sealskin
jacket and a little sealskin cap; her eyes danced, the

colour came into her cheeks, her laughter rang out, she enjoyed herself with the whole-hearted enjoyment she could throw into anything when she was really amused. The young man who could tuck himself into the narrow seat beside her was esteemed lucky.

Then in the evenings, apart from the big official parties, there was that pleasant institution, the informal after-dinner reunion, when the young could dance and their elders indulge in conversation. The conversation of the elders might be of a serious nature, for diplomatists, Senators, Congressmen would all drift in and out of the well-warmed, well-lighted rooms, but there was no solemnity among the young people enjoying their friendships and their flirtations in the intervals between the polkas and waltzes. They all, of course, knew each other intimately; they had their jokes and their chaff; they "visited" at each other's houses; and they were not above having a laugh at someone else's expense. Thus, when the Chinese Minister determined that the young men of his Legation should learn to dance, there was much speculation on what would be the outcome. A leading beauty flatly declared that nothing would induce her to dance with a Chink. Meanwhile it was known that members of the Chinese Legation staff were obediently taking dancing-lessons in private, and that their curiously shaped shoes had been adjusted in order to meet the new requirements. For in the 'eighties a Chinese gentleman still appeared in his national dress of brightly-coloured silks, with the little round cap and button, and the traditional pig-tail hanging down his back. When the great evening at last arrived an unforeseen difficulty arose. Such was the vigour with which the young Oriental gentlemen displayed their new accomplishment, that their pigtails swung out horizontally, knocking ornaments off mantelpieces and catching their fellow-dancers a smart slap across the face as with a whip-lash.

VI

My grandfather had been Minister at Washington for seven peaceful years, from 1881 to 1888, before events suddenly rushed at him and changed the course of his destiny. My grandfather, as I have indicated, was by nature a peace-loving and indeed a lazy man who liked to have everything arranged for him and did not want to be bothered. Considering the very unconventional private life he had led, running parallel to the most conventional of professions, he had succeeded with remarkable skill in achieving his desire. He had managed to keep Pepita as his mistress and Queen Victoria as his employer concurrently for nearly twenty years. Then, when he had lost Pepita, he had managed to get his illegitimate daughter sent out to look after him, and not only allowed himself and his Legation to be run by her but observed with detached amusement the whole fastidious society of Washington accepting this irregular situation. Up to the autumn of 1888 he must have felt that fate had spared him all the trouble she could; he must have felt that fate deliberately prevented his right hand from noticing what his left hand did. Then, for a few short weeks during the autumn of 1888, fate rapidly played him a series of the most surprising and unsettling tricks.

The first trick took the form of what is known to diplomatic history as the Murchison Letter. It is an absurd story, which in its day created a great commotion, but which now in retrospect appears both uninteresting and unimportant. My poor unwise grandfather, in short, was tricked into a silly indiscretion

which cost him his career. Pepita herself had never done
him so much harm as he then did himself. He had
managed to keep Pepita's existence more or less private,
but the Murchison Letter blazed across the headlines of
England and America:

THE BRITISH LION'S PAW THRUST INTO
AMERICAN POLITICS
* * *
WHAT WILL ENGLAND DO?
* * *
BOTH HOUSES OF PARLIAMENT WILL DISCUSS
THE MATTER
* * *
SACKVILLE SACKED
* * *
THE COUNTRY APPROVES
* * *
HOW EUROPE TAKES IT
* * *
THE FOREIGN OFFICE ASTONISHED
* * *
THE SCREECH OF THE EAGLE
* * *

And so on. Thus the American eagle screeched, but
on the whole recovered its balance and its temper very
quickly, and saw the whole affair for what it was: a
cynical trap into which the victim fell. As somebody
once pertinently though rather brutally remarked to
me, "It was ironical that your grandfather of all people,
the most taciturn of men, should have been sacked for
expressing himself too freely". It was indeed. Nobody
ever committed himself less freely to an opinion,
either by word or on paper, yet nobody ever brought
an otherwise successful career to more sudden or
foolish a conclusion.

It has all been long since forgotten, and concerned a

Presidential Election and the Fishery question. I reproduce the text of the letter and my grandfather's reply,
which was written in his own hand. I cannot imagine
why he should have troubled to reply at all to such an
enquiry, even if he believed it to be *bona fide*,—which
it was not. Nobody ever discovered who Charles F.
Murchison really was, if he ever existed. The *Evening
Express* of Los Angeles said he was a farmer named
Haley living two miles from Pomona, Cal., but it does
not very much matter. What matters is the letter my
grandfather received, and the reply he sent to it.

POMONA, CAL., *Sept.* 4, 1888

To the British Minister, Washington, D.C.

SIR,
      The gravity of the political situation here and the duties of
those voters who are of English birth but still consider England
the mother-land constitute the apology I hereby offer for intrud-
ing for information.

      Mr. Cleveland's message to Congress on the Fishery question
justly excites our alarm and compels us to seek further knowledge before finally casting our votes for him as we had intended
to do. Many English citizens have for years refrained from
being naturalized, as they thought no good would accrue from
the act, but Mr. Cleveland's Administration has been so favour-
able and friendly toward England, so kind in not enforcing the
Retaliatory Act passed by Congress, so sound on the free-trade
question and so hostile to the dynamite school of Ireland, that
by the hundreds,—yes, by the thousands—they have become
naturalized for the express purpose of helping to elect him over
again.   The one above all of American politicians they consider their own and their country's best friend.

      I am one of these unfortunates with a right to vote for Presi-
dent in November. I am unable to understand for whom I shall
cast my ballot, when but one month ago I was sure Mr. Cleveland was the man. IF CLEVELAND WAS PURSUING A NEW POLICY
TOWARD CANADA, TEMPORARILY ONLY AND FOR THE SAKE OF
OBTAINING POPULARITY AND CONTINUATION OF HIS OFFICE FOUR

YEARS MORE, BUT INTENDS TO CEASE HIS POLICY WHEN HIS RE-
ELECTION IS SECURED IN NOVEMBER AND AGAIN FAVOR ENG-
LAND'S INTEREST, THEN I SHOULD HAVE NO FURTHER DOUBTS,
BUT GO FORWARD AND VOTE FOR HIM.

I know of no one better able to direct me, sir, and I most
respectfully ask your advice in the matter. I will further add that
the two men, Mr. Cleveland and Mr. Harrison, are very evenly
matched and a few votes may elect either one. Mr. Harrison is
a high-tariff man, a believer on the American side of all questions and undoubtedly an enemy to British interests generally.
This State is equally divided between the parties, and a mere
handful of our naturalized countrymen can turn it either way.
When it is remembered that a small state (Colorado) defeated
Mr. Tilden in 1876 and elected Hayes, the Republican, the
importance of California is at once apparent to all.

As you are at the fountain head of knowledge on the question,
and KNOW WHETHER MR. CLEVELAND'S PRESENT POLICY IS
TEMPORARY ONLY, and WHETHER HE WILL, AS SOON AS HE
SECURES ANOTHER TERM OF FOUR YEARS IN THE PRESIDENCY,
SUSPEND IT FOR ONE OF FRIENDSHIP AND FREE TRADE, I apply
to you privately and confidentially for information, which shall
in turn be treated as entirely secret. Such information would put
me at rest myself, and if favorable to Mr. Cleveland enable me,
on my own responsibility, to assure any of our countrymen that
THEY WOULD DO ENGLAND A SERVICE BY VOTING FOR CLEVE-
LAND AND AGAINST THE REPUBLICAN SYSTEM OF TARIFF. As I
before observed, we know not what we do, but look for more
light on a mysterious subject, which the sooner it comes will
better serve true Englishmen in casting their votes.

Yours very respectfully,

CHARLES F. MURCHISON

(PRIVATE)

BEVERLY, MASS.
Sept. 13, 1888

SIR,
I am in receipt of your letter of the 4th inst. and beg to say
that I fully appreciate the difficulty in which you find yourself
in casting your vote. You are probably aware that any political

party which openly favoured the mother country at the present moment would lose popularity, and that the party in power is fully aware of this fact. The party, however, is I believe, still desirous of maintaining friendly relations with Great Britain, and is still as desirous of settling all questions with Canada, which have been unfortunately reopened since the retraction of the treaty by the Republican majority in the Senate, and by the President's message, to which you allude. All allowances must, therefore, be made for the political situation as regards the Presidential election thus created. It is, however, impossible to predict the course which President Cleveland may pursue in the matter of retaliation, should he be elected; but there is every reason to believe that, while upholding the position he has taken, he will manifest a spirit of conciliation in dealing with the question involved in his message.

I enclose an article from *The New York Times* of August 22, and remain,   Yours faithfully,

L. S. SACKVILLE-WEST

My mother always maintained that she three times prevented him from sending his reply, but that he eventually despatched it without her knowledge. Whether this was true or not, I am not in a position to say. She had told a different story to her friends at the time, to the effect that she was away on a visit, and that her father, left to his own devices in the small house where they were spending their summer holiday, had written because he was bored and could find nothing better to do.

VII

It became quite clear that he could no longer retain his position as Minister and it seemed doubtful whether any other country would welcome an envoy recalled owing to an indiscretion; Lord Salisbury in London, in fact, was wondering what on earth he should do with Sackville-West. Fate, however, had another trick up her sleeve, and intervened by suddenly transforming Sackville-West into Lord Sackville, in succession to his brother, only a month after the unfortunate correspond- ence had passed.[1] He now had an admirable pretext for offering his resignation and quitting his post with the minimum loss of dignity, even after the reception of a note issued by Mr Secretary Bayard by direction of the President, to the effect that "for causes heretoiore made known to Her Majesty's Government, Lord Sackville's continuance in his present official position in the United States is no longer acceptable to this Government and would consequently be detrimental to the relations be- tween the two countries". This was plain speaking, but everything was carried out in as gentleman-like a spirit as possible; the American statesmen were courteously anxious to spare the feelings of their hapless friend; no pressure was put on the Minister to hurry his departure, and the sale of his effects at the Legation was arranged at leisure. The silent, reserved man had been well liked, even though the more voluble Americans did declare that he was as tightly shut-up as an oyster; the popularity of his three daughters had never been in question. The success of the sale was due in part to the determination of the souvenir-hunters. Any objects bearing the family crest fetched absurdly high prices, even if they were horse-cloths so moth-eaten as to be of no practical use at all. The big ballroom, it was said, "looked for all the world like a bazaar, with a junk shop extension". Two thousand five hundred cards of ad-

[1] This change of name and style puzzled the Americans, and some of the superscriptions to his envelopes at this time are remarkable. One of them runs: "To His Excellency and Imperial Highness, the Baron and Earl of West, Ambassador Plenipotentiary of Her Majesty the Empress of Great Britain and Ireland, the Cape of Good Hope, Canada, Australia, and also the Indies, at his residence 1300 Connecticut Avenue, Washington, D.C."

mission had to be supplemented by a further five hundred before the sale had even begun. The reserve prices which had been fixed by my mother,—who was not Catalina's grand-daughter for nothing,—were in most cases far exceeded.

The break-up of this Victorian Legation offers as suggestive a 'period' document as the sales of the treasures at Albolote and Buena Vista. There were small work-tables inlaid with marqueterie, little tea-services ornamented with Victoria West's monogram, bamboo flower-holders, old parasols, a Japanese dinner-gong, an immense French picnic umbrella, material for fancy dresses, and endless bric-à-brac, all of which speak eloquently of the gay life, half intimate and half social, which had flowed through those no doubt atrociously furnished rooms. In the stables, too, there were the horses and carriages which had served on many a pleasant drive over the then uncultivated heights of Rocky Crags or on expeditions into the wooded hills of Virginia. The family landau, the victoria, the phaeton, the buggy with its red wheels, the sleigh with its reversible robes and harness bespangled with little silver plates and bells, the English saddle which had lost half its padding, all came under the hammer and were bought for reasons more sentimental than practical. I wish I had the complete catalogue, but my only source of information lies in some old newspaper cuttings of the day.

VIII

Thus ended the affair of the Murchison Letter, and, accompanied by his two unmarried daughters,[1] "Minister West" left for Europe and the splendid inheritance which had fallen to him. From my mother's point of

1 Flora had married a M. Gabriel Salanson, a French banker.

view, she knew that she was now about to become the
mistress of one of England's most magnificent country-
houses. For an absurd reason, however, highly characteristic of a family which was always cursed by litigation,
they preferred not to go straight to England but to
spend several months in Paris and on the Riviera. My
grandfather's predecessor, in fact, after a lifetime spent
in quarrelling violently with his relations and his neighbours, endeavoured to complicate matters as much as
possible for his heir by leaving an extraordinary will
behind him, to the effect that all his personal estate
should be equally divided between the Queen's four
maids-of-honour. It was supposed that he had private
reasons for wishing to benefit one of them, and hit on
this method of doing it without singling her out into a
scandalous publicity. It was ingenious, but it produced
consternation among his relations. They could not
submit to this wanton ruin of Knole. Eventually the
matter was settled out of court, but in the meantime the
new owner and his family were forced into something
like a voluntary exile. Exile it might be, but it was
only temporary and by no means unpleasant. From
my mother's diaries, all of which I possess from this
time (1889) onwards, and kept, of course, in French,
I learn how gaily she enjoyed herself in the country
of her birth. True, the diary opens on a wistful note:
"My first thought was to offer this year to God (*le
bon Dieu*). I have passed through so many sorrows; let
us hope that they will not be renewed. I am so anxious
about the future . . ."; but the wistfulness quickly disappears under the influence of the southern sun and
the amusing company she found in the villas of her
friends. There were so many diverting things to do,
and such an odd assortment of people to observe! There
were battles of flowers at Nice; there were luncheon-

parties and cotillons (she seems to have forgotten her
dislike of society for the time being); there was the *tir
aux pigeons*; picnics, and parties on luxurious yachts
lying in the harbours; drives in landaus along the
Corniche road, with such ravishing views opening at
every corner, and such a blue, blue sea, and flowers
pouring in such profusion over the white walls; Monte
Carlo especially was *"féerique le soir avec toutes ses
lumières se reflétant dans l'eau"*. Then there were the
people, from the Prince of Wales downwards. Jovial,
genial, pleasure-loving, he escaped from his own country and from the supervision of his mother to enjoy himself freely in foreign parts. He was the leading figure,
socially, on the Riviera. "I was horribly shy (*terrible-
ment intimidée*) the first time I met him. After dinner, he
sent for me to the smoking-room to smoke a cigarette.
I refused to smoke, but was obliged to go there. I took
Miss Stonor with me. He asked for my photograph,
which I shall delay sending him as long as possible."
She was cautious, among all those gay, dashing, smart
people. *"Cependant toutes ces femmes* 'fast' *me respectent
car je ne vais jamais nulle part sans Papa."* She was
evidently still very innocent and deliciously naïve. The
highly sophisticated Prince and his friends delighted in
her naïveté. "I did not understand what he meant by
his jokes, but they must have been funny, because everybody laughed." Then he told her that she brought him
luck at baccarat: "He made me sit at his right hand,
and indeed he won. He gave me a big gold piece of
100 francs as a mascot with his name and the date
engraved on it. . . . Then we went on to the Club, where
the Prince danced the Quadrille d'honneur with me.
He had been looking for me all over the place, while I
was sitting quietly talking with someone else. He put
me at his right hand at supper; he is amiability itself

towards me." In the Casino at Monte Carlo she was much struck by the number of *cocottes*, and especially by the lack of animation on their faces. She met one lady, who would have been so nice if only she had chosen a white wig instead of a blonde one. She was shown a clockwork ostrich,—"*une autruche à mécanique, dont j'étais complètement émerveillée*",—and met a man with neither legs nor arms, "*et il s'est marié tout de même!*" All this was very novel and amusing, but she hints that her own popularity brought certain disadvantages. It was annoying to be told by Count Sala at a luncheon party that he would give any man a week to fall in love with her: "*C'est bien peu, et je n'ai pas une si bonne opinion de moi*". It was "such a bore, everybody here thinks that one is flirting when *un homme est aimable pour vous*". She thought she would have to give up wearing her pink tulle frock trimmed with silver leaves at cotillons, as it seemed to be too much appreciated whenever she appeared in it. It was embarrassing when Mrs Bloomfield Moore, who had already given her the string of pearls at Washington, offered her a present of £10,000. "Of course, I cannot deny that the money would be very useful to me, but I cannot accept it." This thought was often present in her mind, for another day she writes: "*Je fais de tristes réflexions ce soir sur la vanité de l'argent, mais pourtant j'aimerais bien avoir un petit million à moi*". Above all, she was terribly worried by a young French marquis who was especially determined to marry her. So ardent was he, that she invented an extensive curtain as a piece of needlework which she hastily produced whenever his visit was announced, so that entrenched behind her curtain and many needles and skeins of wool she felt herself comparatively safe. "*Je les agace tous avec mon ouvrage que je traîne partout avec moi.*" Nevertheless, she was more than half inclined to accept him. The Prince of Wales eulogised him to her, saying that he was such a good fellow. Everybody brought pressure to bear on her. And she herself was not indifferent. She liked him. When he failed to return from Paris owing to some mishap, she records frankly that she was disappointed. "*Désappointée*", she writes in her sloping foreign hand in her diary; just the one word, no more; but it evidently meant a lot. Yet she was not in love,—not in love according to her full capacity. She liked him, she toyed with the idea of marrying him. "*C'est un bon garçon, très sérieux.*" That was much, but it was not enough. It was not enough to carry her off her feet. She still sat with the curtain draped across her knees, and thought the situation over. The difference in their religion was the great difficulty, for, although a Frenchman, he happened to be a Protestant. She could scarcely foresee that within the year she would be defying Cardinal Manning over precisely the same difficulty,—but not in connexion with the same man.

IX

A very different story takes us briefly back to Spain. While all these events were filling the lives of Lionel Sackville-West and his daughter, the rackety existence of Juan Antonio Oliva was drawing towards its miserable end. That gay, sleek, whiskered dancer who had courted Pepita in his youth was now approaching his sixtieth year, and although afflicted with the terrible disease of cancer in the tongue, had continued to earn his living as he had always done, by accepting any engagement he could get, whether it kept him in Spain or took him to the little republics of Central America. When his friends questioned him about his trouble he answered them lightly. He said, "Oh, I am all right; I smoke and I drink and it doesn't trouble me". For, in fact, he could not afford to give in. He had not only himself but his woman Mercedes Gomez to support, and the pair of them struggled in the deepest poverty. After his return from Guatemala his condition became so serious that he had to be taken to the public hospital of San Carlos in Madrid: he could then speak but very little, and the doctors refused to operate again. His sister and one of his brothers visited him on Sundays and other days when they could get leave from their work. Nor did his old friend Pedrosa desert him at the last, although he found the visits extremely distressing, as Oliva's speech had become almost inarticulate owing to his disease. Mercedes Gomez was constantly with him too, and it was in her arms that on a hot July day he died. They took off the ring that he was wearing and gave it to his brother Agustin; Mercedes took his watch and chain, but afterwards said that she would like Agustin to have them as a memento. They buried him in the cemetery of Nuestra Señora de Almodena.

Mercedes Gomez was left not only heart-broken but almost destitute. Oliva's family took her to live with them, in return for a small contribution towards the household expenses. She brought all her effects with her, but they consisted only of a bedstead and a trunk. She managed to earn a little money by accepting engagements in Oporto and elsewhere, but before very long she fell ill with a chest complaint,—chronic catarrh they called it,—and it became obvious that she would never dance again. "With the sale of her stage dresses, the little money she had contrived to save, and occasional help from outside, she managed to live. On three occasions when she became very bad she was taken to the hospital, and when she got better she returned to our house. Whenever she was in the hospital her trunk remained in our house." After her death, they turned out the contents of the trunk. It contained a few clothes, some old letters, and a small collection of postage stamps.

Meanwhile, in strangely striking contrast, the English family, in entire unconsciousness of what was happening to Oliva far away in Spain, was preparing to take up its residence at Knole. The treasures they were to find there differed in considerable degree and quantity from poor Oliva's ring, and Mercedes Gomez' collection of postage stamps.

CHAPTER 11

KNOLE

I

JUDGING by the entry in her diary, my mother's first visit to Knole made a most unexpected impression on her. Unlike most people, she does not appear to have been overwhelmed by its beauty or its magnificence, but by its orderliness. "*L'ordre qui règne partout dans la maison et les jardins est remarquable.*" She noticed its size and thought the house so enormous that one might easily lose oneself. She observed also that there were a great many pictures and tapestries. She also thought the housekeeper, Mrs Knox, looked very pleasant and obliging. Yet it was a summer day (July 3rd), and I should have thought the sheer loveliness of the grey Elizabethan pile rising above the brilliant turf would have struck her more forcibly than the fact that it was all so well kept or that the housekeeper was disposed to be agreeable.

After that one day spent there, she was quite content to return to London, where she was staying at Derby House. The truth is that she was enjoying herself in London as much as on the Riviera. The London season was at its height, and although she never set much store by Society, she did appreciate such fine sights as a Court ball and garden parties at Marlborough House. London was especially *en fête* that summer for the marriage of Lord Fife to Princess Louise of Wales and in celebration of the visit of the Shah of Persia. She met the Shah at Marlborough House, but did not think much of him, "*Le Shah est très laid et a l'air grognon ; il portait une énorme émeraude sur le* tummy." Her description of Queen Victoria, too, was candid rather than loyal, "The Queen looks very common and red-faced." For the Princess of Wales she had nothing but praise—so gracious, so beautiful, so wise to wear unfashionable dresses, which are so much more becoming than the outrageous modes of the moment. London held plenty of amusement for Lady Derby's attractive young ward on whom the Prince smiled with such a friendly eye, and whose romantic birth cast an extra glamour round her already romantic personality. She was a great success and was fully but quite simply aware of it. Even Aunt Bessie Bedford relented and consented to meet her. Other relations, such as Lady de la Warr and Lady Galloway, accepted her cordially as one of the family. She was taken to the Naval Review; made the acquaintance of such brilliant young men as Mr George Curzon and Lord Dufferin; of witty women like Lady Dorothy Neville; of beauties like the Duchess of Leinster and the Duchess of Rutland, whose children she thought the most exquisite she had ever seen.

All this sounds as though she were a snob, but that would not be a fair interpretation. Putting it more simply, in the 'eighties such things as Birth and Position mattered. The Proustian attitude towards the aesthetic and almost historical value of high life and elegance was the commonplace of well-bred thought; genealogies and family connexions, tables of precedence and a familiarity with country seats formed almost part of a moral code. "My child, remember who you *are*," was a phrase to be heard frequently proceeding from the lips of governess or chaperone. It is a little difficult to adjust our ideas, nowadays, to such a shape of life and not to misjudge the exaggerated importance which attached to the doings of the *beau monde*. No wonder that a young woman of twenty-seven was slightly dazzled at finding herself not only a spectator but an actual participant. And Knole in all its glory was waiting for her.

By the end of the Season their rooms there had been got ready for them. A little shy, perhaps, and a little apprehensive, she prepared to take up the reins of government. Although she had had plenty of experience in running the Legation at Washington, she now felt as though she were taking up such duties for the first time; at the Legation, she had merely arrived into an already organised and official household, but to Knole she came as a new mistress, with everything to arrange for herself. She mistrusted her own capabilities on several counts: "Laziness and indolence are my great faults. I simply can't get up early in the morning, and it costs me a great effort to look after all the details of the housekeeping as I do. But it is my duty!" The note of apprehension, however, very quickly changes to one of amusement; she evidently thought it exceedingly funny to find herself at the head of such affairs. "I keep house!" she exclaims in English in her diary; and evidently she thought both the fact and the phrase a very good joke, for she repeats it several times at intervals. No phonetics could possibly reproduce the accent in which she frequently uttered those words which seem to have become her favourite expression: "Ai kip ha-oose" perhaps approximates most nearly. She was like a child with a doll's house, and what a doll's house! The cook and the obliging Mrs Knox both came to her room for orders every morning, and in the afternoons she could rummage in the cupboards, discovering every kind of treasure, from Sèvres china to old lace. The family jewels were also brought for her inspection by the family solicitor, and she tried them all on. *"Naturellement j'ai tout essayé ce soir. Cela fait plaisir à Papa."* I think it was probably not only Papa who was pleased. She thought the diamond necklace a little skimpy (*un peu maigre*), but the tiara satisfied her, for although the stones were small the setting reminded her of a tiara worn by the Empress of Russia. No wonder, with all these toys of authority and possessions, that she should write, *"Oui, décidément j'aime Knole,"* and then a little later, *"Quel roman est ma vie!"* Yes, her life was a romance indeed. Her father let her do whatever she liked: *"Papa est si bon, il ne dit jamais rien."* Papa never did say anything; he had his own occupations, which included reading right through Gibbon every other year and whittling paper-knives from the lids of cigar-boxes. He liked the garden, where two Demoiselle cranes and a French partridge with pink legs followed him sedately about, but for the rest he was quite content to leave everything to Victoria as he had always left everything to Pepita. Victoria began to see more and more clearly that she could never leave Papa. What would he do without her? What would Knole do without her? What would she do without Knole? The chances of the young French marquis, who had pursued her to England, began to diminish daily. She was very sorry for him; very sorry indeed; she had not finally made up her mind to refuse him, but *que deviendrait mon pauvre Papa sans moi?* She made herself genuinely unhappy over the unfortunate Frenchman, for her feminine vanity was gratified and in such cases she could display a tender heart. *"Le pauvre L. C., il fait pitié à voir."* She was really in two minds about it, but she still stitched at her crewel-work curtain. It was precisely at that time of indecision that she made the acquaintance of her first cousin, Lionel Sackville-West. Pepita's story was repeating itself.

II

He was younger than she by nearly five years, being then only twenty-two, a good-looking young man, with trustful hazel eyes, and a charmingly gentle smile. A quiet and faithful person, easily hurt by an unkind word, modest and reserved, generous and idealistic; "*il est si doux, si bon*" she writes of him. He came to stay at Knole, and they played at draughts together in the library after dinner, when he watched the movement of her lovely hands over the board. She dazzled him by her gaiety, her vivacity; her foreign accent enchanted him, and her little trick of supplementing her English by French words; yet he felt her to be serious too, and honest; in fact she was an angel upon earth. Before he knew where he was, he had fallen madly, wildly in love.

For some time he tried to keep it to himself. Once she met him in a passage at Knole, and he stopped her, but she prevented him from saying what she knew he wanted to say. Then one moonlit evening they went up to the state-rooms together, and in the King's Bedroom, leaning together against the window looking out over the garden, in the shadows of that historic room with its brocades and tapestries and silver furniture, his self-control broke down.

The family, which had already suffered a slight shock over the first production of the Spanish children but which on the whole had settled down comfortably to the situation, now had to adjust itself to the disturbing idea that one of the Spanish children had captured the young heir to Knole. Not only did the close relationship dis-

tress them, but their English caution shrank from
foreign blood of so incalculable a quality. It was asking
a great deal of these conventional English ladies and
gentlemen that they should welcome such an alliance
with anything but apprehension. Who could foresee
what strange alien traits might appear in the unmen-
tionable Pepita's daughter? It was already evident that
she was a young woman of determined and forceful
character; even her charm, which they could not but
recognise, might prove to be but the mask of fascination
over hidden dangers; they *liked* her, yes, they liked her,
no one could help being charmed while in her company, but could they trust? And Lionel was so young,
so inexperienced! Victoria, on the other hand, was five
years older and had had six years of experience in
Washington. She would do exactly as she pleased with
him; he was not her match, poor boy, in any way.

Could they but have glanced into the diary the
Spanish enchantress was keeping every day, written for
no eyes but her own, their very natural anxieties might
have been considerably allayed. They would therein
have discovered a soul far less sophisticated than the
sinister background and the six years of experience in
Washington had led them to suspect. They would have
discovered, for one thing, that she frequently prayed to
God for guidance, and for another that she was deeply
distressed by the conflict which had now arisen in her
own heart over her cousin and the persistent young
French marquis, the "*pauvre L. C.*" of the diary.
They would have discovered also that she was determined to play straight by both these young men: "I
had a long talk with Lionel after dinner. I was very
frank and very loyal. *Toujours loyal!* That is one of the
family mottoes. . . . Went to the kitchen garden with
Lionel and ate green plums. . . . Went to the chapel

where Lionel so much wants our marriage to take place. He tries to be reasonable, and I try to be kind to him (*bonne pour lui*), in spite of remaining very loyal. . . . L. C. refuses to give me up. Here am I between Lionel and L. C.; each one knows about the other, for I have been very loyal towards both of them." That is not the language of a deceiver or a schemer. Lionel, for his part, was trying to behave honourably, as his letters attest. He writes that L. C. (whom they had nicknamed 'Abroad') was first in the field, so perhaps he has no right to take her away from him. All he wants is her happiness. So he writes, but he is away in Germany learning German because he is going in for a Foreign Office examination, and is quite obviously beside himself with love and anxiety. She, I think, still preferred 'Abroad', but other considerations were beginning to creep in. Lionel, after all, was the heir to Knole. ". . . I wonder whether I shall ever marry Lionel?—How much people admire Knole! I should be very lacking in ambition were I to renounce it, but one's personal happiness should come before ambition." This was all very well, but Lionel repeatedly called it Vicky's house—"It shall always be Vicky's house", and that was more than poor 'Abroad' could offer her. "I do not think I could ever accustom myself to a poor existence, now," she writes, and another day she asks herself with candid snobbishness whether she will become a French marquise or an English peeress. She was not indifferent to admiration, far from it, and records her triumphs with complacent pleasure. Thus she liked it when the servants came to see her in her finery, dressed up for a dinner-party, and when she goes to dinner with some neighbours she accepts their subservience as her due, "*Ils étaient tous* bowing and scraping *devant moi. J'étais jolie ce soir, je crois.*" The admiration of the servants and the neighbours was intoxicating her by degrees. More and more did she incline to think that her future lay at Knole as its mistress and hostess. Lionel was absolutely her slave; nothing in the world existed for him except her; his infatuation was complete. Patiently and obediently he composed his love-letters in somewhat schoolboyish French, only to have them returned to him with corrections by his lovely tyrant. Finally, one December night, after they had gone again to look at the moonlight flooding the King's Bedroom, she accepted him.

'Abroad', on receipt of this news, arrived in England, rushed down to Knole, wept, stormed, threatened suicide, and was eventually sent back to Paris in a state of collapse. She professed deep pity for him, which was genuinely felt, but which I think was not wholly un-mixed with a fresh gratification at this proof of his devotion. She also received a despairing letter from the American who, in Washington, had offered her £50,000 a year as pocket-money. But her mind was made up, and a great peace descended on her now that the un-certainty was over. She allowed herself to discover more and more qualities in her Lionel: he was so gentle, so thoughtful, so ardent; she missed him dreadfully when-ever he was obliged to go away. It was not long before she was writing that she could scarcely believe in such happiness.

There were difficulties, of course. The family as a whole had been accommodating, but the Church natur-ally proved less sympathetic. Lionel was sent to inter-view Cardinal Manning in person, who told him flatly that their idea of daughters being brought up as Catholics and sons as Protestants was "not more right than picking pockets", and that she would certainly be excommunicated and cut off from her Church for the rest of her life. It was the same difficulty as had arisen over the Frenchman, but this time her determination rendered her almost indifferent. Very well, she replied; she had done her best by offering to bring up her daughters in her own creed; but as the Church would withhold its benediction on that condition she must go forward without it, and nothing should ever persuade her that she had done wrong.

Whether the threat of excommunication was ever carried out I do not know. My mother often told me that it was; but I think that perhaps she was dramatising the situation. In any case, they were married in the chapel at Knole on June 17th, 1890, according to the rites of the English Church. The chapel was small and the accommodation limited, but the family turned up nobly to support the wedding of Pepita's daughter. Aunt Bessie Bedford absented herself indeed, but she did send a cheque as a wedding-present, and was handsomely represented by her sons Lord Tavistock and Lord Herbrand Russell. M. de Béon was also among the privileged guests. Lord and Lady Derby lent a house for the first part of the honeymoon. Triumphal arches spanned the streets of Sevenoaks; the Chinese Minister from Washington sent a cloak of Tibetan goat; a bonfire was piled round the foot of a tall fir-tree, and burnt for two hours before the tree fell. How Pepita and Catalina would have revelled in it all! How it differed from Pepita's own marriage!

Thus my mother and father set out on the first stage of their married life, and my mother's future seemed assured.

CHAPTER III

SEERY

I

It seemed not only assured, but rosy. She had youth, beauty, wealth; Knole to rule over; an unobtrusive father; an adoring husband with whom she was now passionately in love; a child whom she alternately scolded and hugged, very much as Pepita herself had done. Her sister Flora was safely married; Amalia made her home at Knole; the boys Max and Henry were, apparently, contentedly farming in South Africa on the lands which their father had given them. The sky, so far as the eye could see, was clear. There were amusing interludes: they went to Egypt once, and sailed up the Nile in a dahabiah, and on another occasion they went as members of the British Delegation to the coronation of the Czar and Czarina in Moscow, where, owing to the magnificence of her jewels, my mother, to her great enjoyment, was frequently mistaken for one of the Grand Duchesses by the crowd. Then on yet another occasion, nearer home this time, my mother, who was interested in works of art, met an exceedingly charming and exceedingly stout gentleman named Sir John Murray Scott. The significance of this meeting and of the effect it was to have upon her life was naturally hidden from her at the time. All she knew was that this Sir John Scott invited her to accompany him after luncheon to inspect the treasures at Hertford House. What she did not know until years afterwards, was that when he went home that evening he added a codicil to his will by which he left her the sum of £50,000.

The foundations of the friendship thus laid by chance were strengthened when Sir John paid a return visit to Knole. He and my mother sat out in the garden together, talking with an intimacy that surprised them both, and under the spell of her southern warmth and sympathy his admiration rapidly changed to affection and his affection to dependence and love. I do not mean that Sir John was 'in love' with my mother. I do not believe that he ever was, and during the many years when I was constantly in their company I had ample opportunity for observing them. She most certainly became, however, the centre and pivot of his life. Devoted and generous as he was to his many brothers and sisters, the sun in his heaven (and its thunderstorms also) were represented by my mother and by her alone. However often he might swear that he would have nothing more to do with her,—that he couldn't stand her temper, her fuss, and her exactions,— the simple truth remained that he couldn't live without her, and we all knew that a day or two after the angriest letter or the stormiest departure he would come abjectly back. It was impossible not to be fond of him, for of all human beings he was the most kindly, the most genial, the most lovable, and the most *grand seigneur*. His generosity and hospitality were unbounded, and proceeded from no love of ostentation,—for he was essentially simple,—but from the inherent warmth and open-handedness of his nature. A certain magnificence attended him even as he stumped down the street, blissfully unaware that everyone turned round to look at him: one might say that it was an almost Johnsonian progress, save that in contrast to the great Doctor he was always as fresh and pink as a baby, with his white mutton-chop whiskers, blue eyes, and rosy cheeks. An enormous man, six-feet-four in his stockings, he weighed over twenty-five stone, and for all my efforts as a child I never could get a five-foot measuring tape to meet round the place where his waist ought to have been. There was something monumental about him, which made everyone of normal size look mere friskers around him. Perpetually flapping a large silk handkerchief to keep away the flies, he rolled and billowed along on disproportionately tiny feet. If we ever mislaid him in an unfamiliar town, we could be pretty sure of finding him gazing wistfully at the cakes in the windows of a pastrycook, with a crowd of little boys lost in admiration of that colossal back.

He and my mother were in many ways admirably matched. Both had been brought up in France, and both spoke French and English alternately as native languages. Then, his own long association with France gave him some understanding of the tempestuous and contradictory elements in her Latin temperament; and thus when she stormed at him he did not take it nearly so much to heart as the average quiet Englishman. Symbolically, his private name for her was Josée, an abbreviation of Josefa, for, as he often said affectionately, "You're nothing but a little Spanish beggar". She half-liked, and half didn't like, that recurrent joke.

Then, again, both their early lives had been unusual. True, he had been most respectably born, the son of a Scottish doctor in Boulogne, but as a young man in the early twenties he had become involved in a series of existences quite as romantic as her own. He had, indeed, become twisted as one of the strands in one of the most curious of English family histories. Beginning with the eccentric Marquis of Hertford, immortalised as the Marquis of Steyne in *Vanity Fair*, the Hertford fortune and collections of works of art had eventually passed to one Richard Wallace. Whence Richard Wallace sprang, nobody exactly knew. Some believed him to be the illegitimate son of Lady Hertford, who had won fame of her own as the beautiful Mimi Fagnani, daughter of the Duke of Queensbury and ward of George Selwyn, the wit. Others averred that he was not Lady Hertford's son at all, but her grandson, in other words the bastard of her real son the fourth Marquis of Hertford. Whatever the truth may be, it was Wallace who, on Lord Hertford's death, benefited by a codicil to his will which enraged the whole Seymour family and has become famous in legal and social history. In the fulness of time this Richard Wallace, with his great possessions, found it necessary to employ a secretary, and it was in this capacity that the young John Murray Scott entered his household. So greatly did he endear himself to his employers, that both Sir Richard and Lady Wallace came to regard him as their adopted son rather than as their secretary. Lady Wallace, indeed, as a widow, wished to bequeath the whole of the Hertford House collection to him, but with the disinterestedness that was characteristic of him he refused this stupendous legacy, insisting that it should go to the nation instead.

His refusal was observed, but still his inheritance was princely. He had already been left £20,000 by Sir Richard Wallace; Lady Wallace left him over a million more; an estate in Ireland; another in Suffolk; house property in Paris worth about half a million, and the remainder of the lease of Hertford House.

Besides a millionaire's fortune in money, he came into possession of all the Hertford-Wallace treasures in Paris. To remember all those treasures now, as I remember them, is to look back into another age,—an age when culture and elegance seemed permanent, privileged, and secure; an age when a taste in fine books, furniture, and pictures formed part of a gentleman's equipment, as much as a taste in good food and noble wines. It scarcely seems to belong to this uneasy century at all. The connoisseurship and splendid living which descended as the mantle of Elijah on the shoulders of John Murray Scott surrounded not only him but also his friends with an atmosphere of the eighteenth rather than the twentieth century.

It was not so much in his London house as in Paris that one could savour this atmosphere to the full. In Paris he seemed to expand, as though the full flower of his jovial benevolence opened under the influence of its own congenial incarnation of benign hospitality, desirous only that everyone should be happy as his guest, dispensing, in his lavish way, all the store of courtesy, intellect, and fine fare at his disposal. For he was a great giver, and he had much to give. His vast apartment on the first floor, turning the corner of the Boulevard des Italiens and the rue Lafitte, with twenty windows opening on either street (not so very far from the hotel where my grandfather had originally made Pepita's acquaintance), was in itself a treasure-house which brought visitors from every part of Europe. I shall never forget the enchantment of that house. From the moment one had pulled the string and the big door had swung open, admitting one to the interior courtyard where grooms in wooden clogs seemed perpetually to be washing carriages, the whole house belonged to him, though he reserved only the first floor for himself and a number of odd and secret little apartments tucked away on various floors and in various corners. Thus in one corner, quite separate, were the rooms for the linen, under the charge of the *lingère*, such linen as I have never seen since, stacks and stacks of it, with lavender

bags between each layer, and blue and pink ribbons
tying it up; sheets as fine as a cambric handkerchief,
towels that you could almost have threaded through a
ring. The *lingère* used to sit there all day darning and
ironing, with a canary singing in a cage at the open
window.

But these things were not known to casual visitors,
and the real glory of the house lay in the main apartment. Room after room opened one into the other, so
that, standing in the middle, one could look down a
vista of shining brown parquet floors and ivory-coloured
boisieries on either side. Here, indeed, one had the
eighteenth-century illusion at its height. The traffic
might rumble down the boulevard outside and the cries
of Paris echo muffled beyond the slatted shutters, but
inside the rooms there was no hint, even in the smallest
detail, of the modern world. No telephone, no electric
light; nothing but wax candles in the heavy ormolu
candelabra on the tables and in the sconces on the walls;
no bells, save those that one could jangle by pulling a
thick silken rope ending in an immense tassel. Even
on the writing-tables the little sifters were always kept
full of sand, and the pens were long quills, with a knife
laid ready to sharpen them. All around, silent and
sumptuous, stood the priceless furniture of the Wallace
Collection. Chairs and sofas of brocade and *petit point*;
tables and consoles with the voluptuous curves of Louis
Quinze or the straight lines of Louis Seize; the bronze
sphinxes of the early Regency; the tortoiseshell and
buhl of Louis Quatorze; the marqueterie of rose-wood
and lemon-wood; the ormolu mouldings of Caffieri,
sporting into shells and cupids, into the horned heads of
rams and cloven hoofs of satyrs; endless clocks, all tick-
ing, and all exactly right, chiming the quarters together;
the library full of rich bindings, all stamped with the

Hertford crest; the faded gilt of the panellings; the tapestries where hirsute gods and rosy goddesses reclined on clouds; the heavy curtains,—all was untouched perfection of its kind, even to the exquisitely chased fastenings to the windows and differently modelled keys to every door.

The servants of this enchanted refuge were all of a piece with their surroundings. Save for the cook, they were all men and they were all old. To my eyes they seemed so old that had I been told that they had assisted at the taking of the Bastille I should not have been in the least surprised. I forget how many there were, five or six, I think, and in the mornings before anyone else was up I used to watch them going about in green baize aprons and waistcoats striped black and yellow like a wasp, long feather dusters in their hands and clouts tied round their shoes to polish the shining floors. When they talked they growled like old bears, especially Jacques, who was like a very hairy old monkey and whose favourite expression was, "*J'ai mes cent sous par iour et je me fiche du Pape*".

It was from them that we derived the nickname by which Sir John was always known to us: Seery. The French servants called him Seer John, or, more simply, Seer, and the anglicised diminutive arose naturally. Everybody adopted it, my mother included; we never thought of him by any other name.

The head of all the servants, M. Bénard, was far too grand to take any part in the housework and cleaning. He did not even supervise, but reserved himself for the dining-room, which was his particular province. There, with his superb white head and streaming white whiskers, directing his group of ancient acolytes by an imperious glance or a jerk of the head, he officiated as some high-priest conducting a holy rite. To see him set down some huge silver dish before Sir John, and remove the cover, and stand waiting for his master's gesture of approval before bearing it away to carve, was to learn once and for ever how such things ought to be done. To watch him bring in some bottle of precious wine, carrying it with all its cobwebs in his white-gloved hands as though some fragile and irreplaceable relic, followed by Jacques or Baptiste with the cork on a salver, to hear him murmur "Château neuf des Papes, dix-huit cent soixante-dix-huit, Château Lafitte, soixante-quatre", or whatever it might be; to watch him pour, just so much and no more, was to realise that such wine was a gift to be received with respect and, if possible, in silence.

The dining-room was large and quiet; the thick carpet muffled all footsteps; on the walls hung four large battle-pieces by Horace Vernet, representing the victories of Napoleon. Under these ferocious pictures full of struggling horses, dying men, and smoke spurting from a range of innumerable cannon, the big white circle of the dining-room tablecloth spread in luxury and peacefulness. It was a place where people might linger, delighting in the pleasures of the mind, the palate, and the eye. In the centre of that table, until my mother suppressed it as an unnecessary extravagance, an enormous silver bowl the size of a foot-bath was daily refilled with out-of-season flowers; it looked like a flower-painting, a wild improbable jumble by Fantin-Latour, lilac, tulips, carnations, roses, irises, lilies, all absurdly mixed together in profusion. Seery tried to protest against its suppression: it had always been like that, he said, and he saw no reason why it should be altered. They compromised finally on the understanding that the florist should come only three times a week instead of every day.

My mother never cared for flowers; she liked them made of paper, or silk, or feathers, or sea-shells, or beads, or painted tin, but the real flower never appealed to her in the least. This may perhaps have been why she resented the extravagance at the rue Lafitte, for she had a certain Latin shrewdness about money running through her whole composition, and did not like to see it wasted on things in which she took no pleasure. On the other hand, she never tried to suppress the dishes of little cakes, chocolates, brandy cherries, *dragées*, and *marrons glacés* which also loaded the table daily, from the most expensive of all Parisian confectioners. I was glad of this, for I liked them too.

Then apart from the rue Lafitte, Seery had inherited Bagatelle in the Bois de Boulogne. This most delicate little pavilion, standing in a garden of sixty acres, had been built for Marie Antoinette by the Comte d'Artois in a space of three months only, in obedience to her wish that she might have some resting-place between Paris and Versailles. "It shall be done", he had said, and it was. And, when she thanked him, he replied in the grand eighteenth-century manner, "*Madame, ce n'est qu'une bagatelle*".

Bagatelle is now the property of the city of Paris, but when I first knew it in the hot summer of 1900, when the great Exhibition was being held and Paris was almost unbearable by reason of the heat and of the crowds, we had the run of it entirely to ourselves. Almost every afternoon we used to drive out there, in one of Seery's big landaus, the fat horses clumping sedately up the Champs Elysées. He kept no servants there, except coachmen and gardeners, so that the expedition was always a picnic. In the shady garden I could wear an overall only and could run barefoot over the cool grasses. It was a garden which seemed

inexhaustible in its surprises. However well I thought I
had explored it, I always discovered something new.
There were grottos with statues of nymphs round
whose necks one could hang garlands of flowers; there
were little lakes with boats and bridges and islands.
There were caves which were always cool, and which
dripped water from the roof, making mud of the sandy
path beneath. There was a mound which one ascended
by a long and winding path, and from the top of which
one could overlook Paris. There were the deserted
underground quarters of Marie Antoinette's servants,
down two long passages with eighteen rooms opening
on either side. There were the stables and coach-
houses, which Seery quite unnecessarily kept full of
horses and carriages. There were gardeners' sheds and
bothies. And finally there was the pavilion itself,
empty now, but still eloquent with the monogram
M.A. under the crown, even on the *espagnolettes* of the
windows. They certainly understood the art of charming finish and detail, at the time Bagatelle was built.
Even then, when the spiders spun their webs across the
corners, and the sunlight lay in slats across the dusty
floor, you could see that it had been a present fit for a
prince to offer to a queen.

II

This friendship with Seery formed an integral part of
our lives. He was constantly at Knole; every spring we
went for about two months to stay with him in Paris;
every year from August to October my parents shared
a shooting-lodge with him in Scotland. Whenever he
and my mother were apart they wrote to one another
every day, for they were conversant with every detail of
one another's existence. He got on admirably with my

queer old grandfather, who became more and more silent as the years went on, until finally he was seldom heard to speak at all. Seery would refer to him as "the old man" behind his back, and my grandfather would sometimes say, "Good fellow, Johnnie", though to the end they never addressed each other as anything but Sir John and Lord Sackville, an old-fashioned formality which always amused us. What made it funnier to us, was that my grandfather should thus privately allude to him as Johnnie, a name we never used.

Seery, despite his enormous size and weight, was an ardent and determined sportsman, and, since it was his policy always to ignore the burden of flesh he was compelled to bear about with him, even to the extent of pretending that he was not really at all fat, nothing would deter him from taking his part in the active life led by younger men such as my father and his friends. This determination gave us many uneasy hours, for dear old Seery with his top-heavy clumsiness was frequently a source of danger both to himself and to others. How often I have seen him clambering over a loose stone wall, gun in hand, his weight bringing the whole thing down with him in a thunder of stone, and the gun going off as he rolled to the ground! How often have I seen him overbalance as he fished, and topple into the river! It took two ghillies to turn him the right way up again, while the water ran out of his waders.

Yet he was never discouraged, never in anything but a beaming good-humour. He would only be at great pains to explain why none of these mishaps had been due to his own fault,—either the wall had been badly built, or else the river-bank had been slippery. He never got rattled except when my mother came and fussed him as he sat at his writing-table, for she was always wanting something and he was always unable to find it. "Go away, go away!" he would shout, flapping at her with the handkerchief that was used to chase away the flies, and then he would start fumbling again with the huge bunch of keys which were supposed to, but never did, unlock his drawers.

"If only you would leave the stamps out", my mother would say.

"Yes, and if I did"—winking at me—"you'd take them all in one morning."

Or else she would want a shilling to give to the telegraph boy, interrupting Seery in the middle of a letter.

"*Ah, ce que tu m'embêtes,*—why have you never got any change of your own?" But he looked up at her with his kind loving eyes which showed so plainly that he was not really cross. Then he would start burrowing into his trouser-pocket for his purse. As his trousers were always much too tight, his hand much too fat, and his purse much too bulky, it always took a long time and much heaving and grunting to get it out, especially as he usually searched in the wrong pocket first. When produced, the purse matched the scale of its owner. Made of stout black leather, secured by a black elastic band an inch wide, it invariably contained forty or fifty pounds, many of them in golden sovereigns. Sometimes he spilt it,—for owing to their extreme podginess his fingers were muddling and clumsy, except when they most surprisingly roamed the piano with a delicate and sensitive touch,—and then I would go down on hands and knees to retrieve the sovereigns rolling into every corner of the room. My mother welcomed this golden shower, for she always got what she called "pickings".

"Seery, give me a pound."

"Go away, you little Spanish beggar!"

III

My mother was adorable at that time of her life. She was tiresome, of course, and wayward, and capricious, and thoroughly spoilt; but her charm and real inward gaiety enabled her to carry it all off. One forgave her everything when one heard her laugh and saw how frankly she was enjoying herself. As a child can be maddening at one moment and irresistible the next, so could my mother be maddening and irresistible by turns. For, like a child, she neither analysed nor controlled her moods: they simply blew across her, and she was first one thing, then the other, without exactly realising which side was uppermost. She never thought much; she merely lived. Whatever she was, she was with all her heart; there were no half-measures. Energy such as hers needed something to occupy it all the time, and it followed naturally that she conceived one disastrous idea after the other. Living with her was rather like living above a harbour where incoming ships would anchor for a time, stay just long enough to become familiar; then vanish, never to be seen again. There was craft of all kinds. Sometimes they were sailing-ships, light vessels, transitory visitors; sometimes great liners that made a big wash, swamped our lives, and occupied a whole quay for weeks. The difficulty was that we never knew whether the vessel meant to stay or swiftly disappear; whether it flew a respectable or a pirate flag; yet we had to adapt ourselves accordingly. Any amount of tact and adjustment was constantly needed.

One of her most inconvenient ideas arose out of a charity which originally she had called the Knole Guild. Quickly perceiving that she could persuade her friends, in the interests of charity, to buy lampshades, waste-paper baskets, and little boxes at double their value, she leapt to the idea of establishing a shop in London. It was quite a good idea, and in someone else's hands might have proved not only charitable but profitable. Unfortunately my mother was temperamentally incapable of distinguishing between charity and personal profit; friendship and business. With her, everything always conveniently merged, and she never could understand why other people failed to see things in the same way. Thus she was genuinely hurt when my father pointed out that she couldn't continue to call it the Knole Guild once she had removed it to London and was running it for the benefit of her own private pocket. The arguments they each advanced were typical: *his* point of view was that you couldn't use the name of Knole, let alone the implications of a Knole Guild, when you were setting up a shop in South Audley Street where frivolous fashionable women might buy their Christmas presents or the cushions for their drawing-rooms; *her* point of view was, why shouldn't she use the name of Knole, when it would provide an attraction to the shop and thereby increase the turn-over? The difference between them was that my father had a sense of the true dignity of Knole, and my mother had none; that my father had a sense, the Englishman's sense, of fair and decent dealing, and my mother had quite a different standard,—inherited, perhaps, from Catalina and Pepita. She simply couldn't see why she shouldn't set the words THE KNOLE GUILD over her shop in South Audley Street, although it no longer had anything to do with either Knole or a guild. It was not often that my father put his foot down, and I think it must have been torture to his gentle nature, but on this occasion he was firm, and my mother, genuinely puzzled and considerably aggrieved, had to give way. She was soon comforted by her own ingenuity in inventing the name *Spealls*, an anagram composed from the name of her first, but not last, manageress. Frankly, the Spealls period was one of the most trying we ever had to live through. For one thing, it was fertile in rows,—rows with her managers and assistants, all of whom in turn she accused of dishonesty and incompetence; rows with her friends, who either did not pay their bills promptly enough or were 'tiresome' enough to treat Spealls as an ordinary shop, where one could make complaints, ask for things on approval, or exchange unwanted goods; rows with ourselves, whenever she scented an atmosphere of disapproval or accused us of being 'disobliging'. The truth was that if one once started being 'obliging' about Spealls, there was no time left for anything else in one's life. My mother with her limitless enthusiasm for her own schemes could be an exceedingly encroaching person, and Spealls provided a glorious opportunity for her particular kind of fuss. Thus no one could leave Knole without being loaded with notes and parcels for distribution in London, 'to save postage'; every piece of brown paper and string which came into the house had to be saved; and anyone who was suspected of any hidden talent was pressed into service. I thought myself safe enough over this, for I knew I had no such useful talents at all and the clumsiest set of fingers, but nevertheless I found myself set down with a pair of scissors, a pot of paste, and a pile of horrible little note-books which I was expected to cover in silk or chintz. When this proved a failure, and everything came unstuck, I was told I wasn't trying to help; I was selfish, ungrateful, disobliging, hopeless, no use at all. My mother then unfortunately remembered that I had once written a verse on the death of a canary, so, as that seemed the only way in which I could make myself useful, I was set to compose mottoes suitable to decorate ash-trays and blotting-books. My mother was very fond of mottoes and epigrams; "Never complain, never explain", was a favourite, and so was "A camel can go for nine days without water, but who wants to be a camel?" "Do right, and fear no man; don't write, and fear no woman", was another which particularly pleased her. If I could write verses on the death of a canary, I could surely turn out such gems of neatness and wit by the dozen?

"*Mais voyons, tu passes tout ton temps à gribouiller, tu pourrais bien venir en aide à ta pauvre maman?*"

I tried, I really did. I spent anguished hours, trying. How I envied the artist who composed the mottoes for Tom Brown's Christmas crackers! How I regretted that my own literary inclinations refused to bend themselves in that direction!

The annual three months in Scotland, however, were marred by nothing except the necessity of preparing for Spealls' pre-Christmas season. Apart from Spealls, those months were perfect. My mother was very happy; the pure Highland air suited her, and whenever she liked she could go into Banchory or even to Aberdeen and buy anything she wanted, putting it down on Seery's account. As she adored shops, and really did not mind much whether she bought sixpenny-worth of picture postcards or twenty pounds-worth of Harris tweed, this occupation satisfied her endlessly. Over money as over everything else she had no sense of proportion whatsoever. I know that many people thought her grasping, and said, what could you expect with an heredity such as hers? But it would be much truer to say she was merely acquisitive. Value meant nothing to her; the fun of shopping meant everything, and of course she loved getting something for nothing.

She would quite shamelessly purloin the stationery from an hotel if she stopped there for luncheon, and came away convinced that she had effected a real economy if she could stuff half a dozen envelopes into her bag without anybody noticing, though at the same time she would readily give the waiter a five-pound note as a tip if she discovered that he had a sick wife or an ailing baby at home. On the same principle, it made very little difference to her if the five-pound note came out of Seery's pocket or her own. Money was meant to be spent; it was gratifying to save a penny stamp if by chance a letter arrived with the postmark omitted; at one time she even took to cutting up used stamps and fitting the pieces neatly together so that no smudge of postmark appeared; it was satisfactory to sneak a pinch of bath-salts if one had been staying in a country house; it was infinitely preferable to use a piece of string off a parcel than to cut a length off a bought ball, even a ball presented in desperation as a birthday gift by one's harassed daughter. "*Je n'aime pas les dépenses inutiles; ma pauvre enfant, je vois que tu n'es pas du tout* thrifty." This reproach of not being at all thrifty puzzled me, for, being young and ill-informed, I was incapable of reconciling my mother's extraordinary extravagances with her equally extraordinary economies. I couldn't see why a person ready to spend hundreds of pounds should be equally ready to stinge over a stamp or a ball of string. I had not yet reached the age when one is able to accept all idiosyncrasies, however queer, as part of a person's make-up.

It was perhaps over anything connected with stationery that she displayed her most characteristic inconsistencies. Thus although she would cheerfully buy writing-paper at £1 a quire, patronising Macmichael, who in those Edwardian days was the fashionable stationer of Mayfair, and would get the most elaborate dies cut to go with it, she would seldom write her letters on anything but the backs of catalogues or the half-sheets torn off letters she had received. One was lucky, indeed, if one got the half-sheet, for sometimes it was a puzzle to make out what she had written, all mixed up with the printing on an advertisement. I think she touched the peak when she wrote to me on the toilet-paper she had found in the Ladies Cloak-room at Harrods. She was immensely pleased by this discovery. "*Regarde*," she wrote triumphantly, "*comme ce papier prend beaucoup mieux l'encre que le Bromo.*" A stranger recommendation for a toilet-roll was surely never devised.

How my mother puzzled me, and how I loved her! She wounded and dazzled and fascinated and charmed me by turns. Sometimes she was downright unjust, and accused me of things I had never done, lies I had never told (not that I was by any means an exemplary child, only she always seemed to get my offences wrong, blaming me for those I hadn't committed, and ignoring those I had), but how she could always win me round, however unjust she had been, just by looking at me and saying: "Perhaps we have had a little misunderstanding". I remember her saying that to me once; she had been really unjust to me, accusing me of telling a lie which I happened not to have told; children are sensitive about such things, and at the bottom of their hearts they know the difference between truth and untruth; on this occasion I knew I had told the truth, but my mother made me kneel at her feet, which humiliated me and hurt my pride, and said I must ask God to forgive me, and then as I hesitated she suddenly put her fingers under my chin and turned my face upwards towards her own lovely face and said, "Never mind,

darling, perhaps we have had a little misunderstanding".
I never forgot that; she had let me off my supreme
humiliation; I felt that she had conferred an inestimable
grace upon me. Never had forgiveness for an uncom-
mitted crime been so graciously granted. I loved her the
more for it; my love for her mounted even higher and
higher, as one mounts the rungs upon an endless ladder.

Really, nobody could have failed to love her as she
was then, in her middle youth, so gay, so vital, so
amused, so absolutely herself with all her faults, all her
tiresomenesses and all her charm. At twelve o'clock in
the morning I would be saying to myself that I couldn't
bear this life any longer, that I couldn't hear the word
Spealls once again without screaming, stopping my
ears, and running away; then an hour later, having
escaped, from the top of a hill would see my mother
pounding up and down the lane, back and forth to an
old derelict farmhouse called Manallan, singing at the
top of her pure clear voice, draped in an old tweed cape
with a scarf over her head,—which she wore always in a
manner curiously reminiscent of the Spanish mantilla,
—singing the most incongruous songs of the most
sentimental description, "*Ange pur, ange radieux,*"
from Gounod's *Faust*, "*Porte mon âme, Au sein des
cieux*" or else "*Si mes vers avaient des ailes*", or else
"*Le jour où Sylvain m'a parlé. . . .*" She loved these
French songs, and they rang out over the Scotch hills
as she tramped up and down, always over the same road,
setting a pebble each time she reached her bourn. One
pebble marked one stretch; ten pebbles meant a mile.
When ten pebbles had accumulated, they were replaced by a larger stone; a proud moment. From the
distant hills would come the rattle of stone walls col-
lapsing under Seery's weight, and the subsequent ex-
plosion of his gun.

On the way up to Manallan, my mother would pass
the farmer's cottage. The farmer's wife worshipped her,
with an adoration approaching idolatry. It is no ex-
aggeration to say that that starved and suffering woman
lived for the annual three months my mother spent on
that Highland hill-top. She was the first and only
person to introduce romance into that harsh and difficult existence. I don't know how she did it; I suppose
it must have been by her sheer loveliness, under the
old tweed cape and the scarf over her head, and by the
sympathetic smile in her eyes, and the tones of her
foreign voice. She would pause outside the little granite
cottage every day on her way up to Manallan. "Meeses
Meelné?" she would call outside the window, in a voice
as soft as a cooing dove, and Mrs Milne would appear,
beaming, her Hinde's curlers stiff and rigid under her
cloth cap. Every day, regularly, Mrs Milne would ask
her to come in, and every day, regularly, my mother
would say, "No thank you, it smells much too bad inside
your cottage". An insulting remark, one would think;
but somehow my mother managed to say it in such a
way that Mrs Milne took it as a joke and almost as a
compliment. My mother, of course, was quite right: the
Milnes' cottage did smell atrociously of cooking cab-
bage and unchanged air. Living as they did in the purest
air that anyone could wish to breathe, their one idea was
to keep their windows as closely sealed as possible. My
mother tried to defeat this scheme by opening their
windows from the outside whenever Mrs Milne wasn't
looking; Mrs Milne attributed all her neuralgia to this,
but, having shut the window again, continued to worship my mother none the less. I think she would have
died for her, and she would certainly have laid out anyone that said a word against her. Mrs Milne was very
fond of me too; she accepted me as one of "the bairns",

meaning her own children, with whom I was allowed to run wild; but often she would shake her head and say I would never be a patch on my mother. It never occurred to me to take this as anything but a tribute to my mother, not as a reproach to myself.

One of the things which shocked me most, was when my mother quarrelled with Mrs Milne. She accused Mrs Milne's son of stealing a mackintosh, and when Mrs Milne very rightly resented this imputation and defended her son, she incurred my mother's wrath. It was the first time I ever realised consciously that my mother would not tolerate being contradicted or criticised in any way, and that she could be ruthlessly cruel to the person who had thus crossed her. It seemed to me horrible that she could cast a poor all-lacking woman out into the uttermost darkness for no fault at all; it seemed like kicking a dog who has become accustomed to scraps of kindness at one's hands. It was incomprehensible to me, because I had not yet estimated how much my mother liked power.

She left Mrs Milne in misery for a year, and then, after repeated pleading letters, forgave her. How she could enrich! And how she could take away!

But, after all, it was all quite consistent. There was very little difference between my mother saying that Mrs Milne's son had stolen a mackintosh, and Catalina saying that Felix Gomez Carrera had stolen a peacock. I had been accustomed since my earliest days to such sudden accusations, which no amount of contrary evidence could affect. At the age of four or five I had seen my own loved Nannie torn from me because three dozen quails having failed to arrive in time for a dinner-party my mother insisted that Nannie had eaten them. After that I took such things more or less for granted.

CHAPTER IV

TROUBLE

I

LIFE must have been extremely pleasant in the first decade of the twentieth century for those who were blessed with money and possessions, and whose ears were not tuned to catch any sound of ominous cracking going on around them. One spent the winter months in London (Mayfair, of course), then a few weeks in Paris with the chestnut trees coming out and the spring sunshine sparkling on the river, then the deep summer beauty of Knole, with week-end parties and the adulation of stray ingratiating people who wanted to 'see the house', then the freedom of Scotland and plenty of time to read,—a nice book of memoirs, or the latest novel by Mr E. F. Benson, who was so amusing, or Mr Robert Hichens, who understood so well the workings of a woman's heart,—not that horrid H. G. Wells, who was a Socialist and wrote about things which were much better left unsaid. It was all extremely agreeable. One had an enormous motor, one of the very first, reinforced at the back by three iron bands to support Seery's weight; plenty of servants, a lady's-maid and a valet who always went ahead by train and had everything laid ready for one's arrival; one had a chef, and as much *pâté de foie gras* and plovers' eggs as one wanted. My mother was not a person who cared to look beneath the surface. So long as she had her luxuries, more than enough money,—though always convinced that she was

to be pitied for being so hard-up,—Seery to bully, and
Spealls to think about, she was quite content to sing her
little songs and to persuade herself that life would
always continue exactly as it was.

Yet there were clouds massing low down on the
horizon, if ever she allowed herself to examine them.
Not the clouds of social or political unrest, for those
held no interest for her, but the clouds of more personal
troubles threatening her life. Seery was ageing, and
really by now his bulk had become alarming; though
he retained his almost babyish freshness of complexion,
he had already had one or two little attacks which
nobody liked to call strokes. They were referred to as
fainting-fits, but there was no denying that in spite of
his gallant efforts to keep up with the younger genera-
tion he was getting less and less able to do so. He would
droop off to sleep after meals without warning; the big
head would sink gradually, the big chins would pile
themselves over the collar, the ash on the cigar would
lengthen, the fat hand holding the cigar would sink
lower and lower towards the table-cloth, the kind boom-
ing voice would trail away into incoherent syllables
which soon turned into an unmistakable snore. Then it
was time to interfere. "Seery! Seery, wake up. You're
burning the table-cloth." A snort; a grunt; a great
heave; the cigar hastily carried back to the mouth; the
waistcoat hastily brushed in case of crumbs. "Eh? Eh,
what was that? Asleep? no, of course I wasn't asleep, I
heard every word you were saying,"—and then two
minutes later he would be drooping off to sleep again.
"Seery! Seery, wake up."

My grandfather was ageing too. Unlike Seery, he
was a slender old man, rather frail on the whole; and
then he was really old, approaching eighty. It was
obvious that the term of human life could not be

extended very much longer. And when the term of that frail life ran out, the most distressing troubles would inevitably ensue. In other words, it had been known now for many years that Pepita's son Henry, tired of farming in South Africa, was determined to establish his legitimacy and lay claim both to the peerage and to Knole on his father's death. Far away in Spain an unfortunate gentleman named Mr Brain was trying to disentangle the strands of truth from the appalling muddle of lies and contradictions, and to send home some clarifying reports to the family solicitor. Mr Brain was working in circumstances of extreme difficulty and discomfort and was manifestly not enjoying his job in the least; he knew scarcely any Spanish and yet spent most of his time consulting Spanish lawyers with the help of an interpreter; their highly technical language and the unfamiliar complications of Spanish legal procedure worried Mr Brain, who was conscientiously anxious not to mislead his employers at home. "I am in the position of a Spanish *procurador*", he writes piteously, "who has arrived in London to investigate a crime which has baffled the Public Prosecutor and Scotland Yard for more than a year". He found that he was expected to do work "quite outside the work of any sort of lawyer"; to go, for instance, to a certain modest tavern where a certain person might be heard of, and dine there in order to make friends with the tavern keeper. He could not even procure the ordinary materials for his correspondence in Madrid, and terminates a letter which had begun by stating: "I am writing this in bed; I can't get up to write because there is no one to light the fire", with a plaintive appeal for more foolscap envelopes, some paper-fasteners, and some Relief nibs.

Poor Mr Brain. The whole story which he had been

sent out to investigate was a very odd one. It concerned nothing less than the deliberate falsification of the register recording the marriage of Pepita Duran to Juan Antonio Oliva. Nobody disputed this falsification; the only question was, by whom it had been perpetrated, in whose interest, by whom instigated, and with what purpose in view? There it stood plainly in the register of the church of San Millan at Madrid for anyone to see; it needed no handwriting expert, though several were called. It was most curious, inexplicable, and apparently pointless. The names of the contracting parties had first been scratched out, so roughly and incompletely as to leave them still legible under a magnifying-glass, and then written in again in the same space, but in a handwriting different from the rest of the register.

Now what could have induced anyone to take the extremely difficult and dangerous step of getting the church register into his possession for the sole purpose of erasing two names which he then re-wrote? Mr Brain, in spite of his name, could not imagine. He did, however, pursue the obvious course of asking himself what person or persons could have any possible motive in tampering with the register, or in employing another person or persons thus to tamper. The finger of probability pointed, in Mr Brain's opinion, straight at Henry Sackville-West.

It was greatly to Henry Sackville-West's interest to discredit his mother's alleged marriage to Oliva. If Pepita, in short, had never really been married to Oliva, or to anyone else, there was no reason why she should not have married Lionel Sackville-West, with whom she had lived for so many years and by whom she had had so many children, in which case the children would have been legitimate and he, Henry, as the eldest son would succeed his father as Lord Sack-ville and owner of Knole.[1] It was a stake worth playing for. Unfortunately there were a number of documents in existence, all referring to this inconvenient marriage to Oliva. There was the application for the licence to marry, in the book of *entradas* kept at the Vicaria in Madrid; the application for the dispensation of banns, in the same book; a licence issued by the Vicaria author-ising the parish priest of San Millan to perform the ceremony; the actual entry in the church register, re-cording the celebration of the marriage; and finally a similar entry in the Civil Register of Marriages kept by the civil authorities in Madrid. No plotter, however un-scrupulous and daring, could hope to obtain possession of all these five pieces of evidence, two of them con-clusive, for the purpose of falsifying or destroying them.

To this day no one knows who the plotter was, nor how he went about his work. Only the most obscure hints indicate the conspiracy that was going on. Thus Manuel Guerrero, Pepita's old friend the ballet-master, was got hold of and was offered sums of money and a share in the spoil if only he would contradict the evi-dence he had already given. A "*soldado de licencia* fre-quently invited him to refreshments and once took him to the bull-fight at Aranjuez, speaking Spanish like a native but with an Andalusian accent". Guerrero, though not averse to profiting by the refreshments and the free seat at a bull-fight, remained suspicious and

---

[1] It may be objected here by a puzzled reader with a retentive memory that Maximilian was the eldest son, not Henry. This is perfectly true, but as Maximilian had been officially registered as the son of Oliva and Pepita, he was out of the running. All the other children, on the other hand, with the exception of my mother (*fille de père inconnu*), had been registered as the legitimate offspring of Lionel Sackville-West and Pepita. My grandfather declared that he had con-sented to this deception merely in order to please Pepita.

advised his acquaintance to go and consult a lawyer, but, perhaps maliciously, mentioned the name of a lawyer whom he knew to be already involved in the business on behalf of Lionel Sackville-West's family. The suggestion met with no welcome from the *soldado de licencia*. "Ah no, not I!" he replied; "better to let a sleeping dog sleep."

Three men were eventually accused, and stood their trial in Madrid, being finally acquitted because the jury could not reach an agreement. It is not for me to offer any opinion, and I prefer to state the case in the words of the Spanish Crown Prosecutor:

"The Crown Prosecutor inclines to the belief that the marriage was valid, and that the entry was tampered with in order to create a doubt as to its validity.

"After enquiry, it results that the accused, Enrique Rophon,[1] was in communication with a person living in Paris, named Henry Sackville-West, with the object of annulling the marriage celebrated in the church of San Millan on Jan. 10th, 1851, between Juan Antonio Gabriel de la Oliva and Josefa Duran. As the accused and Sackville-West were convinced that such annulment was impossible, the marriage having been celebrated with all legal formalities, they concerted a plan for the disappearance from the register of the church of the page referring to this marriage, or to forge it. Forgery was decided upon, and Rophon, accompanied by the accused, Manuel Anton, to whom he had offered a large sum of money, went to the church of San Millan, after having given notice of their intentions to the other accused, Jose Sanchez. Sanchez was the attendant of the church, who took the register of marriages from which Rophon erased the names of the parties mentioned above. Rophon then induced Anton

---

[1] This Enrique Rophon was a cousin of Pepita.

to re-write what he (Rophon) had scratched out. Anton did so, without varying anything in its sense, but making certain additions, and in such a way that the actual fact was made to appear false."

It was ingenious, this sort of double-crossing. A leading and most respectable London paper suggested that it looked like "a diabolical plot", and gave a simple illustration:

"Suppose one has a genuine cheque and erases the amount mentioned, then writes in the same amount. The cheque becomes suspicious, and nobody will cash it, except after inquiry and examination; but all the same the cheque is good because the signature, guarantee, and everything else, except the erasure, are valid. The difficulties which arise are caused without forgery in the proper sense of the term, and yet litigious matter is made out of a genuine cheque."

This is all more or less cautious, legal, and official, but a hand comes to draw aside the curtain for a moment, and to reveal the darkened stage on which these mysterious movements were taking place. Again I make no comment, and offer no opinion; I merely quote the evidence of Don Ricardo Dorremocea, a clerk in the office of the church of San Millan. He can be allowed to express, much better than I can, the sort of thing which was going on for years in the background of my mother's life, a direct though belated repercussion from the gay indiscretions of Pepita; curious chapters of cause and effect, running darkly parallel to the brilliantly illuminated existence my mother was outwardly leading.

The functions of Don Ricardo Dorremocea seem to have been somewhat varied, for apart from his employment at the church of San Millan he also attended a theatre in some ill-defined capacity.

"I was engaged", he says, "in assisting at the performances of the Guignol Theatre which was then in the Prado. One evening about dusk at the end of August or the beginning of September, a performance having just closed, I was on the stage. Someone came and told me that a person outside wished to see me. I asked who it was and he said that he did not know, but that he asked for the man who belonged to San Millan Church.

"I went out to the street door of the theatre and saw two men. They wore automobile caps, but were otherwise dressed as *chulos*.

"The *chulo* dress is a well-known distinctive dress which was, I believe, originally the costume of Andalusia. In Madrid the dress is worn by certain men of the lower classes who think well to adopt it. Some of them are of the inferior class of bull-fighters, and some others, although not bull-fighters, take great delight in running after bull-fights. The *chulo* is a sort of swaggerer or gentleman-rough. Any man is at liberty to adopt the *chulo* dress, but no one would be likely to do so without having some natural fitness for the part.

"One of the *chulos* advanced to me and said, 'You are the one who is employed in the Parish Church of San Millan?' I replied, '*Si, señor*'. He then said, 'I am come to treat of a matrimonial question'. I said, 'As the time is so short between the acts I can't attend to you now. Tell me where I can see you.' The *chulo* then gave me an appointment at a tavern in Calle San Miguel at the corner of Hortaleza at night when I left the theatre. The hour was not fixed. After the theatre was over (from 12 to 12.30) I went to the tavern. The *chulo* who had made the appointment was seated at a table on the right. Two or three other men appeared to be sitting there in company with him. I don't know whether they were *chulos* or not. I did not go to the table.

"The *chulo* rose and advanced towards me and told the tavern keeper to give me a glass of wine. We had no conversation in the tavern. After I had drunk the wine, the *chulo* took me into the street.

"He then said that what he wanted was for me to tear out the leaf from the register of the marriage of Juan Antonio de la Oliva with Josefa Duran and that we would take this leaf to a gentleman who would read it and then burn it, so that I should not be compromised, and that he would give me fifty dollars. I told him I would not do that, and he then said, 'You need not be at all afraid, for in the Vicaria it has been arranged' (or 'it is being arranged', I am not sure which) 'to make to disappear the marriage *expediente* and the names from the Index'.

"He said that he had been in the office of San Millan Church talking with Sanchez to get him to tear out the leaf and also to make to disappear the *despacho* and that he had offered him 1000 pesetas. He said that Sanchez had replied, 'No, but for 1000 dollars if you like'.

"He said that Sanchez had shown him the *despacho* and also the marriage entry. The *chulo* then added that if he had only gone there provided as he then was (taking out something which appeared to be a revolver) it would have been another thing.

"I then hurriedly said good-bye to the *chulo*, who said, 'Well, we will wait till Monday then'. I only repeated 'good-bye' and left him, and have seen nothing of him since.

"I am not positive that the two *chulos* were in company with one another, but they appeared to be so. They were both standing there—one advanced to speak to me and the other remained where he was. The one who spoke to me had what they call *coderas* on the elbows—a light jacket with patches of black cloth on the elbows.

"As to the age of the *chulo*, I am rather short-sighted, but he seemed to me something like 38 or perhaps 40 years old. He had a darkish moustache and was two or three inches taller than myself. He spoke Castilian very well, no provincial accent. I can't form any idea as to whether he was disguised or whether he was a real *chulo*.

"The automobile cap was a cap of dark cloth with a peak. In general form it resembled an automobile cap, but I think it was flatter in the head than an automobile cap. *Chulos* generally wear a broad-brimmed hat. Rather recently the other sort of cap has come into fashion. Even organ-grinders wear them, so that there is nothing strange in a *chulo* wearing one.

"Before the meeting with the *chulo* I had not heard attention called to the marriage entry. I had never heard that any proceedings were going on about that marriage. I had no idea who Antonio Oliva was.

"The *chulo* said nothing about who Oliva and Duran were. I think he mentioned that the marriage was in the year 1855, but directly I heard what he wanted done I paid no more attention to him. He said nothing as to whether he had got a certificate of the marriage. He did nothing but make me the proposition straight out, and as soon as I heard what it was I paid no more attention to him. He said nothing as to what was the object of destroying the entry. I was not with him in the street any longer than was necessary to say what I have mentioned.

"He gave me no idea where he lived, whether in Madrid or not. He said that he would be at the tavern again on the following Monday to see whether I brought him the leaf. He did not name any hour. I was only too anxious to get away from a man who had made such a proposal and did not notice what he said.

"I do not remember mentioning the *chulo* incident to anyone until after the proceedings appeared in the newspapers. I was very much occupied in various ways and did not read the newspapers. My attention was first called to the matter by two of my friends who are clerks in the Municipal Court of the Inclusa. One is named Ceferino. I do not remember his surname. The other, I cannot recollect his name at the moment. I knew them by their coming to San Millan Church respecting certificates and acts of matrimony. They told me of what had appeared in the newspapers about the Register at San Millan Church, and on their mentioning the name of Oliva it recalled to my mind the incident with the *chulo*, and I narrated it to them as I have now done in this statement.

"Being in the vicinity of Calle San Miguel, we said, 'Let us pass by the place and have a glass.' So we went to the tavern and had a glass. Until that occasion I had not been there since the interview with the *chulo*."

II

The storm had been growling ever since 1896, when the intentions of Henry Sackville-West first became apparent and steps had been taken to prepare some defence against them (in other words, the evidence had been secured, which forms the material for the first part of this book) but it was known that nothing could materialise publicly in England until the death of my grandfather should precipitate the necessary decision in the courts. Quite apart from his estates, an English peerage could not be allowed to remain in dispute; but, equally, the question of succession to an English peerage could not arise until the death of the peer.

My grandfather had always seemed to me immensely old,—he had, after all, been born in the reign of George IV, which came quite a long way back in the history books,—and although I was fond of him in the unexamining way that a child is fond of anyone to whom it has always been accustomed, it probably seemed to me more remarkable that he should be still alive than that the hour of his death should be in any way imminent. I know I was only vaguely surprised when my mother told me we should not all be going to Scotland as usual one year, but that Seery was going to a different place in Scotland with his sisters, and that I should be sent alone to stay with them. I knew, of course, that Grandpapa had recently had an operation whose nature had never been made clear to me; I knew also that he had, even more recently, fallen downstairs, which was a very serious thing for an old man to do; but I don't think it ever dawned on me that I was being sent to stay with Seery and his sisters in Scotland in order to get me out of the way. I do remember being sent in to my grandfather's little sitting-room to say good-bye and being there quite alone with him, and his looking at me in a rather strange and particular way. He, at any rate, knew that he would never see me again; for my own part, I wondered only why he left his hand lying so long, so heavily, and so affectionately on my shoulder.

The next incident embarrasses me to relate, but it sticks up in my mind so vividly that I cannot suppress it. I was in Scotland, in my bedroom in the gaunt, unfriendly house in Banffshire which Seery had taken. It was before breakfast; I was half-dressed; a servant came to the door bringing me a letter. One does not receive many letters at the age of sixteen, so any letter was an excitement, especially a letter in an unfamiliar writing. I stared at it; I stared particularly at the inaccurate superscription: "The Hon. Vita Sackville-West". Never in my life had I received a letter addressed like that.

It was in a slightly foreign-looking hand. I tore it open. I hope the distinguished author by whose name it was signed will forgive me for thus dragging her into my family history, and for recording here that she had most kindly and graciously replied to a letter from one of her many young fans. Yes, I had written to Baroness Orczy; carried away by my admiration for the Scarlet Pimpernel, I had written a fan-mail letter to his creator. And she had answered. There was the signature: Emmuska Orczy. But she oughtn't to have addressed me as the Hon. I wasn't. I was overcome with shame; I felt that somehow or other I had misled her; perhaps I shouldn't have written on Knole paper. . . .

There came a second knock at my door. Not another letter, surely? No, it was one of Seery's sisters, in a pink flannel dressing-gown, her hair not yet done,—a guise in which I had never yet been privileged to see her, and which startled me as much as the superscription on Baroness Orczy's envelope. She was exceedingly kind. She put her arms round me and very gently broke to me that a telegram had just arrived saying that my grandfather was dead. My mind absolutely refused to register this fact, and I could feel only that her sympathy was meaningless and misplaced. Yet I knew she was being very kind, and somewhere in the background of my mind I reproached myself for being ungrateful. Then she said I had better go down and see Seery, who was very much upset.

Still moving in this world of unreality, I made my way down to Seery's room. I found him sitting in front of his dressing-table, clad only in a suit of Jaeger combinations. He was sobbing uncontrolledly, and his sobs shook his loose enormous frame like a jelly. He was quite oblivious of his appearance. He was just overcome by the fact that 'the old man' was no more. I stood looking at that huge, Jaeger, sob-shaken bulk, and envied him his power of feeling things so immediately and acutely. For myself, I couldn't feel anything at all; I was just worried because I had no mourning to put on, because I felt dimly that I ought to telegraph to my mother and didn't know what one said on such occasions, and because I had already begun to wonder whether it would be disrespectful to go fishing that day, or whether I ought to stay at home and perhaps play croquet by myself?

It was only when I went upstairs again to my own room and found Baroness Orczy's envelope lying on the dressing-table that I realised she had been right in her superscription after all; right, though a little previous. My father was now Lord Sackville,—or wasn't he?

III

That was the question. The papers were soon so full of it, that it became impossible to keep the facts from my knowledge. Besides, Knole was shut up, and all its revenues put into the hands of the trustees, until this question of the succession could be settled. They could not have pretended to me that all was well. It was as though a new character had joined our family life; a new character called "The Case".

I don't think my parents ever had any real doubts as to what the outcome of "the case" would be or any real anxiety so far as that went, but they did dread the exposure of all that ancient scandal, they did mind all the

tiresome inconvenience entailed, and they did mind the
enormous and unnecessary expense. Large sums of
money had already been spent since 1896, in lawyers'
fees and in the examination of the Spanish witnesses, an
expenditure which had been going on steadily for twelve
years up to the date of my grandfather's death. Of course
the fact that many of the negotiations had to be carried
on in Spain considerably increased the cost: it meant
journeys, special envoys, the services of interpreters,
the fees of Spanish consultant lawyers; altogether I
believe that my parents' share in the total cost of the
case amounted to something like £40,000. In addition
to this they saw themselves faced with the necessity of
raising a similar sum to pay the death duties—always
supposing, of course, that they were not dispossessed
from Knole. Few estates could stand such a strain, and
Knole, although provided with an income adequate in
those days of low taxation, was by no means so rich as
people perhaps imagined.

My mother made herself genuinely unhappy over The
Case. It was seldom that she touched reality, but I think
she touched it here. Usually, she lived in an unreal
world, a world of her own creation, but here she was
brought up against facts which struck at very deep, real
feelings in her early self. For one thing, she cherished
a deep devotion to her mother's memory, and could not
bear the details of her mother's most private, intimate
life being dragged out into publicity. For another, she
had an almost morbid shrinking from the fact of her
own illegitimacy, and now here she was placed in the
position of hearing her illegitimacy and that of her
brothers and sisters insisted upon by the very men who
were working to gain a superb inheritance for her
husband. She could not look on the matter in an impersonal way; to her, it was all personal and vibrating;

it was not merely "In the High Court of Justice (Probate, Divorce, and Admiralty Division), before the Rt. Hon. Sir John Bigham, West or Sackville-West (Ernest Henri Jean Baptiste), *v.* the Attorney-General (Lord Sackville and others cited)". That sort of phraseology meant nothing to her at all. What it meant to her, was that her brother Henry was bringing a dreadful and indefensible case; and that, little as he might intend to do so, he must ultimately bring shame upon Mamma and Papa. She was torn between the most intimate ties that can humanly exist: her mother, her father, her brother, her husband, her home. For, of course, Knole was her home, the only real home she had ever known, and, to all of us, Knole meant as much as any human being.

It was different from one's love for any human being. It transcended it. I don't think my mother ever felt like that about Knole; not quite; not as my father did. She never got its values right; one could not have expected that of her. She was too Latin, somehow; too unreal; too fantastic altogether; too un-English. She exploited it for the wrong reasons; invented stories which were really not necessary to enhance the authentic legend. But still, it was her home, and in her own way she added her own legend to its grey historic walls. I often think, looking back on my mother, as one does when people have passed away and one begins to get them into perspective, all the silly little irritations fading and the real quality emerging, that although she went wrong and got every possible value wrong and made my father and me clench our fists in silence whenever she talked about Knole, still, now I see that she contributed beauty to it in her own way, and influenced people, and showed them beauty in a way which mightn't be truthful, and mightn't be ours, but which was certainly her own, and was not the less gracious for that.

And it was her home. As such, she was prepared to fight for it. It was exceedingly painful for her to hear this unpalatable squabble going on in the law-courts, and to see her own brother sitting there on the front bench as the Petitioner, but still she had given her evidence and would abide by it. Fortunately she was never called upon to go into the witness-box. I pass quickly over the six days' hearing which decided the the Romance of the Sackville Peerage (as the papers called it); it is not a subject upon which one would wish to dwell. It is enough to say that the petitioner's case collapsed half-way through and my father's case had won.

My father had vetoed my going into the court, but my mother, always a rebel, smuggled me in for ten minutes. She showed me some of the witnesses sitting there, waiting to be called. "Look", she said rather bitterly, "at your relations." I looked. They seemed to me very drab and black-suited and bowler-hatted,—not romantic at all. My Spanish relations! They looked like plumbers in their Sunday-best. Where, oh where, was Pepita, the source and origin of all this wild and inordinately expensive romance? There was nothing left of Pepita but a falsified marriage register and this gloomy troop of Spaniards perching on the uncomfortable benches of the High Court of Justice. And a lot of posters on the railings, and headlines in all the papers. It was all very strange and confusing, and I was too young to understand it rightly.

IV

Two days later my parents made their official return to Knole. They took me with them. From the moment we reached Sevenoaks, it became a triumphal progress.

We had motored from London as far as Sevenoaks,
knowing that at the foot of Tub's Hill we should be
expected to abandon the motor (with all its reinforce-
ments on the back to support the weight of Seery whenever he happened to be a traveller in it), and to transfer
ourselves into the victoria, that chic little victoria which
my father had once given to my mother as a Christmas
present, with its smart little pair of cobs, driven by our
incomparable coachman Bond, who wore his top-hat at an
angle a Regency dandy might envy and who had a figure
that any Savile Row tailor might have been proud to
dress. Where were the *chulos* of Madrid in their automobile caps, trying to bribe Don Ricardo Dorremocea in
the taverns; trying to get him to tear leaves out of
marriage-registers? The automobile cap of the *chulos* was
very far removed from the shiny top-hat of Bond as he
met us at the foot of Tub's Hill on February 16th, 1910.
Yet all that Spanish background did not seem very re-
mote to me as I sat opposite to my mother and father
on the *strapontin* of the victoria that day, driving up
Tub's Hill at Sevenoaks. It seemed to me as though
things were linking up with other things; as though
'the case' were finding its natural sequence here. . . . I
wished only that my Spanish relations hadn't looked so
like plumbers; I wished Pepita could have been in the
victoria with us to share in the fun. She was very vivid
to me just then, for her photographs had been in all the
papers. She would, I felt, have enjoyed it.

I enjoyed it myself. Never, before or since, have I
felt so much like royalty,—only without the disadvan-
tage of royalty, whose functions go on day after day,
year after year. For once in one's iife it is quite an
amusing and indeed instructive experience to arrive at
the foot of a hill in a motor-car (especially in the days
when motor-cars were still such rare objects as to cause

people to come out from their houses to stare), and then at the foot of the hill to transfer oneself into a victoria, and then on arriving at the top of the hill to have the horses taken out of the traces, and to be pulled by the local fire-brigade through the main street of Sevenoaks and then right through the park up to Knole, with cheering crowds all the way and carefully coached children presenting bouquets at intervals. And then, finally, being pulled right through the first courtyard at Knole, when normally one had always drawn up outside. It seemed odd, and somehow wrong, to sit in the victoria, still drawn on ropes by the fire-brigade, passing between lines of boy-scouts, on rubber tyres, up the smooth-paved path of the Green Court. It wasn't the natural way to arrive at home. And Bond, the elegant Bond, looked so silly, sitting up there on his box with no horses to drive. He retained all his elegance and the smart tilt of his hat, but without any horses at the end of his reins he seemed temporarily to have lost all his justification in life. He seemed to be conscious of this himself, for every now and then during the fire-brigade progression he took the whip with a nervous and accustomed gesture out of its socket; but then, suddenly realising that he had no use for it, put it back and tried to resume his air of complete detachment.

Then there were more speeches, with everyone in the most amiable humour, and as the doors shut behind us and we laid down our heavy bouquets in the familiar library we felt with relief that we had really come home. Now we could go and have dinner quietly and comfortably in the dining-room, with the oil-lamp in the middle of the table as it had always been. It must have been a very old-fashioned oil-lamp, because I remember it had a boot-button hanging from a string from its key, and whenever one of us saw the button creeping upwards towards the key we would hurriedly reach forward to wind the key, and the button on its string would descend again. If we didn't do this, it spluttered, stank, and went out. It was a very ugly lamp, with a pink china shade, more suited to a boarding-house than to the splendour of Knole. We loved it, though, as a symbol, because it appeared only when there was no party; its appearance on the table meant that no strangers were present, no intruders, no one to whom one had to be falsely polite. The hideous pink china shade meant that one could be completely at one's ease.

CHAPTER V

MORE TROUBLE

I

My impressions of my mother naturally became more vivid as I grew older. It never occurred to me to analyse her character as a whole,—my home was a completely unintellectual one, where analysis wasn't the fashion,—but as I gradually acquired a certain skill in avoiding rows we got on very happily together. She taught me the most deplorable principles,—"One must always tell the truth, darling, if one can, but not *all* the truth; *toute vérité n'est pas bonne à dire*"; "Never refuse a good offer, my child; I have refused many good offers in my life, and always regretted it",—but although I was sometimes faintly puzzled I never took very much notice, and anyhow my father in his quiet way used to put me right with little axioms of his own. I fancy that my father, discreet and loyal as he was, watched with a far shrewder eye than I ever gave him credit for.

I am sure that it was not my mother's intention to instil cynical principles in me. I see now that owing to the difficult beginnings of her life, and to the stigma which had lain over her birth, making everything delicate and doubtful, she had unconsciously absorbed the idea that the world was a hard place where one must fight one's own battle for one's own best advantage. It is not an uncommon idea, and it may with justice be observed that many people have considerably more reason for holding it than my mother, who, from the age of nineteen onwards had had everything very much her own way. But if there is any truth in the contention that the foundations of character are laid in childhood, the faint and disturbing mystery must also be remembered,— why didn't Mamma receive visitors like other ladies? Why was one forbidden to play with other children at Arcachon and in Paris? Why wouldn't Papa let Mamma accompany him to parties when she so badly wanted to go? Why did the servants look at one pityingly and sometimes say "*Pauvre petite!*"? Why couldn't Mamma, who was so good and charitable and beloved, go to church? Then came the harshness of the convent, and why didn't one go home for the holidays like the other girls? Why did M. de Béon warn one solemnly that one must never go out alone into the street because there was a man who wanted to kidnap one? Why was one always sent out of the room at Mme. de Béon's whenever visitors were announced? So far, all had been obscure, but then came the shock of Mrs Mulhall's revelation on the cross-Channel boat: "She told me our father and mother had never been married". How lucky that she had her teaching certificate in her bag! She could be independent; she could earn her living as a governess. Meanwhile, there was the renewed habit of leaving Aunt Mary Derby's drawing-room, as at Mme. de Béon's, when callers came. . . .

Then everything had been startlingly reversed. Instead of anxiety, there was security; instead of being the unwanted little foreigner, hustled away at a stranger's approach, she had become the spoilt young hostess at Washington, the autocratic young mistress of Knole. My father, with his boyish worship, had come into her life; then Seery, who gave her his entire devotion and could refuse her nothing,—at least, not for long. Yet none of this, I think, ever succeeded in obliterating those early impressions: life had treated her harshly once, and might at any moment do so again; therefore one must make the most of the opportunity when it offered, and one must, in fairness, teach one's child the same lesson as a possible safeguard when needed.

Heredity entered into it too. Although on one side of her lineage she had the opulent Sackvilles aligned behind her, on the other she had all that rapscallion Spanish background, that chaos of the underworld, tohu-bohu, struggling and scheming and bargaining and even thieving for a living. It was the descendant of all those people,—the old-clothes pedlars, the smugglers, the fruit-sellers, the gypsies, the rascals,— that her critics expected to behave as an ordinary English lady.

Whatever the ethical outlook she endeavoured to present to me, she was a very gay companion and great fun to do things with. When she was in a good temper, we did enjoy ourselves together. Of course she always put me to acute embarrassment by the unconventionality of her behaviour wherever she was; thus she always remained convinced that no one understood French except herself and me, and would make personal remarks at the top of her voice in that language. "*Mais regarde donc cette vieille horreur, ma chérie: qu'est ce qu'elle a l'air, avec cette perruque-là? Peut-on s'affubler ainsi!*" It was quite in vain that I tried to stem the flow of such comments whenever we went to a shop or to a matinée together (she rather liked going to matinées and would weep generously whenever the situation became in the least emotional). Oh yes, she was fun, she was enchanting, she was embarrassing, she made me feel hot with shame,—and then, seeing her visibly charm the tired shop-assistant behind the counter, or watching her lovely profile beside me in the darkened theatre as she fanned herself with that unmistakably Spanish gesture, wafting her very personal scent of white heliotrope towards me, I would have died for her, I would have murdered anyone that breathed a word against her, I would have suffered any injustice at her hands. But at the same time I did wish that she wouldn't make such audible and personal remarks in French.

It was odd, her mixture of unconventionality and conventionality. In some ways she took the absolutely conventional point of view about what was correct or not correct; she was the complete Edwardian lady at times, bringing me up with truly Edwardian social principles about what was "done" or "not done"; she sent me to Ascot very much against my will; she had a sort of aristocratic arrogance about her, which in her later years crystallised itself into the phrase "I am very 1792", and carried such expressions with it as *très grand seigneur* or *très talon rouge* (she liked the neat ready-made phrase, just because she was so unable to synthesise anything for herself); yet although she esteemed these qualities theoretically, she was, thank goodness, temperamentally quite incapable of living up to them. Here, again, her dual nature, the Spanish and the English, was at war. The gypsy and the Sackville came into conflict. No wonder I loved, and wondered. No wonder my father loved, and got hurt.

Then, as though it were not enough to have the disreputable Spanish and the (more or less) respectable English strains mixed in her, she must needs go and add idiosyncrasies all her own. I daresay I might trace some of them to her grandmother Catalina, if only I knew more details about Catalina. As it is, I suspect that my mother's tastes and Catalina's might have met at many points, allowing for the difference in their circumstances, fortunes, and period. Catalina would, of course, have been the ideal supporter of Spealls: she would have approved of its money-making possibilities, of its taste, and moreover would have eagerly adopted all the fuss which it entailed, the parcels, the notes, the endless daily occupation, the rows, the quarrels, the grievances,—if only Catalina had been alive at that time, what a lot of unwelcome bother could have been pushed into her ready hands! I am sure, again, that Catalina would have appreciated the collection of china birds assembled on an imitation tree of mahogany in one corner of my mother's London drawing-room. Catalina would have loved the bedroom at Knole entirely papered with postage-stamps. She would have loved the idea of a different book-plate drawn for every 'well-bound' book. (There was a book-plate with a sundial for the book on sundials, a book-plate with a view of Chenonceaux for the book about the chateaux of the Loire, and so on; so, a hundred times on.) She would have loved the books with pictures you could discern only when you slid the gilt-edged pages sideways,— hidden pictures, secret concealed pictures, which didn't show at all when the book was closed. She would have adored the collection of little tables with human legs,— buckled shoes, or naked feet with the toes showing. She would have exclaimed in delight over the tiny Fabergé plants made of jade and precious stones. She would have liked the washing-stand-set specially made from silhouettes cut by a stall-holder at Earl's Court (my mother got these cut for a shilling each to go with the really exquisite silhouettes in her collection at Knole). Above all, she would have liked the Persian Room.

The Persian Room was not really Persian at all: it was Turkish. It originated, quite unmistakably, from Damascus. My mother did not like one to say this; she had bought the room for a large sum and had decided

that it was Persian; therefore Persian it must be. After
that, no one took the risk of contradicting her. In any
case it was a singularly beautiful room, very romantic,
like something out of the Arabian Nights, with painted
panelling and views of improbably spiky cities and vases
of improbably luscious flowers; there were some latticed
windows too, and a pair of wide sliding-doors, painted
green and orange, which suggested admission to some
concealed harem.

My mother put this up in the back drawing-room of
her London house. Anything less suited to the back
drawing-room of a London house can scarcely be
imagined: it demanded the hot and shuttered sunlight
of the east. It needed a dusty street outside, with the
slippered feet of Syrians shuffling past, not the fogs and
hooting taxis of Hill Street, Berkeley Square. But my
mother was delighted with it; she possessed, more than
anybody I have ever known, the faculty of delusion.
When once she went into her Persian Room she ceased
to see the fog or to hear the taxis. She entered the only
world she knew, the world of unreality which she made
real to herself, and into which she persuaded other
people by the sheer strength of her own personality and
conviction to enter. It was only when they got out into
the street again that their critical faculty returned.

Lady Sackville. . . . Had they been mesmerised? Was
it something like the Indian rope-trick, which everybody had heard of and nobody had ever seen? They
rubbed their eyes, trying to get back to normality. Lady
Sackville was said to have taste and knowledge. Yet in
that Persian Room of hers,—which wasn't Persian,
only one couldn't say so,—she had made the most
incredible muddle. She had got hold of a truly lovely
thing in that room, with its strange painted views of
cities and its stylised lilies and tulips in vases and its

sliding-doors and suggestive lattices; and yet although she seemed to understand it in a way, she had muddled it all up by hanging cheap reproductions of Persian houris by Edmond Dulac against the panelling, and by strewing well-bound editions of FitzGerald's translation of Omar Khayyám on little *moucharabiyeh* tables. Where was the connexion, in her mind? Did she really believe that obviously Turkish room to be Persian? Did she really think that Dulac's pretty drawings bore any relation to the real Persia? or the Christmas-present editions of FitzGerald's Omar either? Yet, so long as one had stayed in there with her, one had almost been tempted to believe in all the fables she told one. The world into which she led one was matched in fantasy and in contradictions only by her Persian Room itself.

She herself was quite unaware of contradiction or incongruities. She just went gaily on her way, taking everything as it came, suffering when circumstances forced her to suffer, enjoying herself when she could, which was often. I never knew anybody who got more desperately or unnecessarily into despair or, next moment, enjoyed herself more heartily than she. It was rather confusing to anyone who took moods too seriously: one moment she would be in tears saying that my father wanted to kill her with worry because the electric lighting at Knole had broken down, and next moment she would be mopping her eyes with laughter because a gardener had stumbled over a flower-pot.

II

Seery fitted into all this crowded and agitated style of living far better than my father, who was a sober man, at heart requiring nothing of life but that it should be peaceful at home and that he should have leisure to occupy himself with his public services, his yeomanry, and the management of his estate. Passionately in love as he and my mother had been, and convinced though I am that my father was the only man my mother ever really cared for, it is idle to deny that they were ludicrously ill-matched. My father was the best type of the English country gentleman; just, courteous, and conscientious, he was truly loved and respected by all. Five days a week he devoted to the service of his county; Saturday he would give to his duties as owner of Knole and as a landlord,—not a tile came off a cottage without his knowing all about it;—Sunday he would play a round of golf or some strenuous racquets or tennis, for he believed in physical fitness, and then unobtrusively would disappear to deal with accumulations of business, for his responsibilities were many, he never employed a secretary, and wrote all his letters with his own hand. There was never any fuss or fluster; he always seemed to have plenty of time for everything and everybody, and I have often wondered since how he managed it. I was indeed astonished when I had to go through his papers after his death to find how accurately everything was filed and docketed; copies kept of all important letters, —no typed carbons, but all in the same neat handwriting; records of infinite trouble taken over any appeal that might come to him; yet nothing superfluous retained; all was methodical, intelligent, competent. The Education Committee; the Roads and Bridges Committee; the grammar-school; the hospital; the West Kent Yeomanry, which he commanded; receipted bills; letters of enquiry,—he must have been able to lay his hand on anything he wanted at any moment. Such a man, of course, ought to have had a smoothly running home; lots of children; sons whom he could teach to shoot and fish and ride and accept responsibility against

the day when it should be theirs: a woman to understand his sensitive and simple nature. My mother's
eccentricities must at moments have driven him mad,
though never by word or gesture did he allow it to
appear. Her consistent unpunctuality, the extraordinary
disorder of her bedroom, the endless fuss over insignificant matters, the vindictive grievances, the storms,—
all this was far better suited to Albolote than to Knole.
On the whole a conventional man, though far too
intelligent to be narrow-minded, he was irritated by her
inability to do the simplest thing like other people.
There was, for instance, the question of fresh air. My
father was by nature an outdoor man, and any odd half-
hour which he could spare was spent in the open; my
mother had never thought about it one way or the other,
until suddenly one of those great liners of a new idea
came to anchor in the harbour of her mind, this time,
unfortunately, to remain. Having once adopted the
theory that you ought to get as much fresh air as you
can, she pursued it with a vengeance. Door-stoppers
miraculously appeared for every door in Knole,—and,
being my mother's, they were not ordinary door-
stoppers, but were created out of every imaginable
object which had never been intended for that purpose,
statues of Nelson or the Duke of Wellington, Cupid or
Hercules, sham-books artificially weighted, regimental
drums filled with sand, all the ingenuity which delighted
her and which ran riot at Spealls. I myself was given a
door-stopper for my sitting-room: it was a wooden
figure representing Shakespeare. "You like poetry,
darling, so you will like to have Shakespeare holding
the door for you. *N'est-ce-pas que c'est bien trouvé?*"

My father, who liked real fresh air but hated
draughts, did not appreciate this new idea in the very
least. He could be seen surreptitiously shutting the

doors whenever he thought it safe. (My mother, when she discovered this, took up the line that it "was a pity dear Lionel was so frowsty".) But he endured it, as he endured many other things. My mother, however, who was not a static person, and whose ideas were apt to grow as fast as Jack's beanstalk unless, indeed, they were most mercifully dropped and forgotten altogether, improved rapidly upon her original inventiveness. Regular meals in the dining-room had always bored her, and she now hit on the double solution of having her own meals brought to her out-of-doors on a tray. My father could just understand people liking to have luncheon out-of-doors in very warm weather, but the spectacle of somebody cheerfully eating her dinner by artificial light while large snowflakes drifted on to her plate moved him to nothing but repressed exasperation. He was not even amused. I could manage to be amused so long as I was not asked to share the experience, but I must admit that the memory of such evenings as I was compelled to spend in the wintry garden is one of acute misery. The arrangement entailed heavy fur-coats which prevented any free movement of the arms; hot water-bottles piled on one's knees; a horrible fur rug terminating in a foot-muff which gave me claustrophobia; and a variety of tickly woollen things, like mufflers and mittens, which my mother knitted herself (out of odd scraps of wool) and insisted on my wearing in spite of my protests. "Now aren't you deliciously warm?" she would say, when she had turned me into something resembling a reluctant Arctic explorer. I was not deliciously warm at all; I merely felt weighted down, with my fingers like ten icicles and my nose like an eleventh one; but such was her delight that I never had the heart to say so. However uncomfortable, however cold, I never lost the sense that no ordinary mother

could introduce such fairy-tales into life. And indeed
the scene before me was one of an unusual and un-
intentional loveliness: the brightly lit table, my mother
opposite me with her dark glowing beauty, the surrounding pallor of the snowy lawns under the starlight,
fading away into the darkness of the encircling trees
beyond.

III

Seery, as I have said, accepted my mother's peculi-
arities far more philosophically than my father, who
most righteously and mistakenly (though silently) continued to apply his own standards to each new development of her behaviour. Seery just took everything for
granted as it came; he either enjoyed, or endured, or
tolerated, or disputed, but in the end always accepted
and was then lovingly amused. Seery was perhaps more
accommodating than my father, a softer, more elastic
man altogether, and therefore suited my mother better
than a man with his own austere standards always stable
at the back of his mind. In spite of all their rows and
quarrels, she could always rely on Seery to give his
kindly laugh in the end, and this, I think, gave her
the sense of support and approval which she missed
in her own home. She exacted approval, and resented
disapproval, even when negatively expressed. Rows she
could understand, and indeed provoke, and indeed enjoy; what she couldn't understand was the silent continuous unexpressed commentary of someone whose
standards she dimly felt to be completely opposed to her
own. Seery, in spite of their frequent rows, was on the
whole easier to manage than my father; Seery had time
to deal with rows; he had time to write long letters in
answer to hers; he never seemed to be too busy with

other things; he didn't go off to Maidstone on county business; he didn't say, as my father frequently and patiently said, "Well, dear, I am afraid I must be going now". My mother could not understand that attitude at all. She took it as a slight when my father bounded upstairs from his breakfast to say good-bye to her in the morning. She would have liked to detain him with endless personal chatter, and took it amiss when he was finally obliged to say that he really couldn't keep his committee waiting. She never could visualise a committee waiting, twenty miles away. He, of course, could. And so they both hurt one another, who had started by loving each other so much.

Seery had no complications in his life such as a regiment or a County Council. He had certain responsibilities,—for instance, he was a trustee of the National Gallery and, I believe, of the British Museum also,—but on the whole he was very free to be at my mother's beck and call. His days, in fact, would have been very empty without her. She amused and occupied and annoyed him, all in turn. My father was not nearly so accessible or amenable, so she fell back on Seery: Seery was always ready to come clumping along in the old one-horse brougham he maintained in London, to fetch her at any hour and at any place.

She was waiting for him at Spealls one day to fetch her before luncheon. He had been instructed to bring a bottle of port-wine with him, to give to one of her workers who was ill. It was very unlike him to be late, but she knew he had an appointment with the Keeper of the Wallace Collection that morning, so did not think much about it, when she got a telephone message to say he had collapsed and died in a chair at Hertford House.

IV

There was a peculiar rightness in the place of his death, among the treasures which his self-denial had secured for the nation, and by the manner of his death also he had been spared a painful old age, enfeebled by the strokes which would have been bound to recur. He himself had written in his diary years before that he hoped "to pass away without pain and suffering, even as my darling mother did". His wish was mercifully granted. But my mother missed him dreadfully; he had been by far her most intimate friend, and their companionship had been unbroken for over thirteen years. A tribute on the grand scale was paid to that friendship in his will: he bequeathed to her the sum of £150,000 and the contents of his house in Paris.

I cannot pass in complete silence over the storm which arose as a consequence of that legacy, for the "Million-pound lawsuit", as the newspapers liked to call it, is still fresh in many people's memory. (Actually, the newspapers were under-stating the fortune involved, for Seery died worth £1,180,000, but I suppose they preferred the round figure for their headlines.) Apart from the bequest to my mother, the bulk of this enormous fortune was to be divided amongst his brothers and sisters, with some minor legacies to other relations and personal friends.

It is not for me to judge whether his relations were justified or not in their resentment of this legacy, or in trying to upset it on a charge of undue influence; not for me to judge whether my mother was right or wrong in allowing the case to come into the courts at all, instead of offering a private compromise. Compromise was not in her nature; as the judge himself with rueful admiration observed in his summing-up,

"Lady Sackville is a lady of high mettle,—very high mettle indeed".

So the case was allowed to come on, and was decided in a blare of publicity before Sir Samuel Evans and a special jury, after a battle extending over a fortnight. Great counsel were involved: F. E. Smith on the one side, Sir Edward Carson on the other. My mother spent two half-days and one whole day in the witness-box, and F. E. Smith freely admitted afterwards that he had never had to cross-examine a witness who gave him more trouble. Her methods as a witness, I need hardly say, were completely irregular. The ingenuity she displayed in evading any question she didn't want to answer was a triumph of femineity at its best and worst. She was disconcerting, maddening, witty. At moments she had the whole court in roars of laughter, when even the judge permitted himself a smile. For one thing, she insisted on treating the opposing counsel as a person she knew socially, as indeed she did: "You would have said just the same thing yourself, Mr Smith. We meet at dinners, so I know you would."—"We will not argue that, Lady Sackville."

Then he was unwise enough to tackle her on the subject of having arranged Seery's dinner-parties. The accusation was that she had usurped the function of hostess in his house, to the exclusion of his sisters. "The order of entrance was not always determined by ceremonial precedence? Peers, Knights, Privy Councillors, and large numbers of other people, but apart from those?"—"King's Counsel too, Mr Smith!"

At other times she seemed to be taking him into her confidence. He was trying to get her to admit that she had been disappointed when Sir John threatened, as he frequently did, to cut her out of his will:

"You say you did not mind?"

"No, I did not. It is funny, but I did not. I got so sick of it. You know, Mr Smith, you do get sick when you are told five or six times a day that you are going to be cut out of a will."

When in real difficulties,—as any witness under fire from a brilliant cross-examiner must sometimes be,—she appealed direct to the Judge and the jury:

"My lord, may I ask you something? . . . My lord, you may remember, and the gentlemen of the jury. . . ."

Mr F. E. Smith (*wearily*): "I will sit down."

At times he remonstrated:

The Judge: "You are fencing with each other prettily, but these are all speeches to the jury."

Mr F. E. Smith: "My lord, the lady puts it on me."

The Judge: "Your experience ought to enable you to cast it off."

Mr F. E. Smith: "If I do, my lord, I shall get no answer, because the lady answers another question every time, which I have not asked."

At other times, her evasiveness setting their nerves on edge, the opposing counsel got cross with one another, when the Judge made peace between them:

Sir Edward Carson: "You really misinterpret every answer she gives."

Mr F. E. Smith: "That is a statement without warrant of any kind. If you think so, you can object before my lord."

Sir Edward Carson: "My lord, I do object. Over and over again my friend when she says one thing pretends to think she said another."

Mr F. E. Smith: "That is a grossly improper statement without warrant."

SIR EDWARD CARSON: "I will not take any notice of ill-
        temper. I have been too long at the Bar to do so.
        What I object to is this——"

THE JUDGE: "What is the next question?"

MR F. E. SMITH: "My friend ought not to have said
        what he said."

THE JUDGE: "It is much more agreeable to go on to the
        question."

SIR EDWARD CARSON: "I am not in the least inclined to
        be bullied."

THE JUDGE: "Now the next question?"

There were moments, however, when even the conciliatory judge grew impatient:

SIR EDWARD CARSON: "I think everybody will agree."

MR F. E. SMITH: "I would rather you spoke for your-
        self."

THE JUDGE: "I wish you would neither speak for your-
        selves nor to one another, but would ask a question
        of the witness."

v

If I have taken the more humorous incidents in the
case,—and there were many which consideration for
others prevents me from recording here,—it is only
because I have no wish to dwell on an episode which
was naturally deplorable, sordid, and painful to all concerned. The spectacle of a group of people squabbling
over money is not edifying, and the less said about it
the better. All that need be said is that the case was
decided in my mother's favour.

She was now a very rich woman, and she lost no
time in letting her extravagant tastes run riot. How
she flung money about, that year! (We are now in
1913.) It was almost terrifying to go out shopping with

her, for one never knew what would take her fancy next. I was walking down Bond Street with her one day, when she saw a chain of emeralds and diamonds in a jeweller's window. In she went.

"How much are you asking for that chain?"

"Two thousand pounds, my lady; the drop at the end is an especially fine carved emerald, as your lady-ship will see. . . ."

"I will have it.—There," she said, handing these dripping gems over to me, "that's for you."

A Socialist might not have approved, but there is no denying that my mother did things in style.

Perhaps fortunately, the terms of her marriage settle-ment did not allow her to spend the £150,000 capital, of which she could enjoy the income only, but no re-strictions were placed on the money she could obtain by the sale of the works of art in Paris. I seem always to be alluding to fabulous sums in connexion with my mother, but I cannot help it. The way in which she attracted money was equalled only by her capacity for getting rid of it. On this occasion she sold the collection *en bloc* to a Paris dealer for the sum of £270,000, which was entirely her own to do as she liked with. By any standards, it was a considerable amount, and the rate at which she contrived to spend it was correspondingly startling. For instance she met a Canadian gentleman in the train, who in the course of a forty-minutes journey managed to interest her in his gold mine to the extent of investing £60,000 in it. (I think she recovered a few hundred pounds from it, many years later. In the mean-time, she grew very much annoyed with anyone who suggested that the speculation might possibly prove injudicious.)

But an event was at hand, of such magnitude as to disconcert her completely; something of which she had no experience at all, something which she could neither control nor override nor even ignore, something against which neither charm nor beauty nor wealth nor personality could prevail, something which upset her world and disposed matters without consulting her convenience. There had been threats and rumours of course for the past month, growing in volume as the summer days went by, but up to the last moment she never believed,—she could not believe,—that they would ever materialise. And then one August evening at Knole my father was called to the telephone. He came back looking unusually stern and serious. "Mobilisation", he said briefly, in answer to our unspoken enquiry. He left us, to reappear twenty minutes later in khaki,—that uniform which we had always been accustomed to associate with his happy three weeks of annual training. I wondered even then whether he intended any irony as he came up to my mother and spoke those familiar words which had so often irritated her in the past, "Well, dear, I am afraid I must be going now". I do not think so; he was not a man ever to carry any irony in his soul.

A quick kiss; and the headlights of his motor rushed him away into the darkness across the park.

VI

The war outraged and infuriated my mother. She did not know how to cope with it in the least, so took refuge in regarding it as a personal insult. One by one, she had to watch the men at Knole being called up: the carpenters, the painters, the blacksmiths, the footmen. Even an appeal which she addressed to Lord Kitchener —for she still believed in personal appeals, and Lord Kitchener was a friend of hers, such a charming man

when you went over to Broome to have luncheon with
him,—produced no helpful result. It was terrible, she
wrote; couldn't he, who was all-powerful, give Lionel
a safe staff job, instead of sending him off to that awful
France or that awful Gallipoli? Supposing Lionel got
killed, that would mean renewed death-duties for
Knole, and he, Lord Kitchener, who had such an
appreciation of beautiful things, would realise what it
would mean to the nation if more pictures, more tapestries, had to be sold to America? But Lord Kitchener,
despite his artistic tastes, seemed to think that even
more urgent catastrophes threatened the nation. He
returned a very polite reply, dictated, typewritten on
War Office paper, to the effect that much as he would
deplore any accident to Lord Sackville, he much regretted that he was unable to interfere in the movements
of any individual officer.[1]

She wrote again. Her letter was couched in the most
conciliatory terms. She quite understood, she wrote,
that he couldn't do anything about an individual officer,
but what about Knole? Knole was suffering from this
horrible war. "I think perhaps you do not realise, my
dear Lord K., that we employ five carpenters and four
painters and two blacksmiths and two footmen, and
you are taking them all from us! I do not complain
about the footmen, although I must say that I had
never thought I would see parlourmaids at Knole! I am
putting up with them, because I know I must, but it
really does offend me to see these women hovering
round me in their starched aprons, which are not at all
what Knole is used to, instead of liveries and even

[1] The reason I am able to reproduce the text of her own letters, is
that she was in the habit of getting her maid to copy them whenever
they were specially "important", and then of inserting them between
the pages of her diary.

powdered hair! Dear Lord K., I am sure you will sympathise with me when I say that parlourmaids are so middle-class, not at all what you and me are used to. But as I said, that is not what I complain about. What I do mind, is your taking all our carpenters from us. I quite see that you must send my dear Lionel to Gallipoli; and he would be very cross with me if he knew I had written to you. Of course all the gentlemen must go. There is *noblesse oblige*, isn't there? and you and I know that—we must give an example. You are at the War Office and have got to neglect your dear Broome, which you love so much. I think you love it as much as I love Knole? and of course you must love it even more because the world says you have never loved any woman —is that true? I shall ask you next time I come to luncheon with you. But talking about luncheon reminds me of parlourmaids, and I said I would not complain about them (because I am patriotic after all), but I do complain about the way you take our workmen from us. Do you not realise, my dear Lord K., that you are ruining houses like ours? After all, there is Hatfield where Queen Elizabeth spent her time as a young princess, and that is historic too, just like Knole, and I am sure Lord Salisbury would tell you he was having frightful difficulties in keeping Hatfield going, just as we are having in keeping Knole. What can you do about it? It seems to me a national duty, just as important for us as keeping up the army and our splendid troops. I do admire them so much. Do help me all you can."

To this letter Lord Kitchener returned an equally polite and evasive reply.

Then the income-tax went up, and, undeterred by Lord Kitchener's lack of response, she wrote to the Chancellor of the Exchequer: ". . . I do wish you could see the unfairness there is in this heavy taxation on historical places. There are so very few in England that it would apply to as it would to Knole, that it would not affect the revenue at all seriously. This tax is simply ruinous on the place, and if my husband who is fighting in Palestine is killed the Death-duties paid 3 times in 30 years will be the death-blow. Can you help me to save it? I should love to show it to you any time you could come down and see for yourself how fair and patriotic my intense request is. I live here alone and in the strictest economy."

Like Lord Kitchener, the Chancellor of the Exchequer returned a polite reply:

DEAR LADY SACKVILLE,

I have received your letter and appreciate your difficulties. But I am sure you will realise that it is impossible to modify the Income Tax system at the present time.

Yours sincerely,

A. BONAR LAW

She could write to these gentlemen, and receive answers from them, however unsatisfactory, but not even she could hope to receive any redress or reply from the chief offender of all. "*Ce sale Kaiser!*" she would exclaim whenever she could momentarily not think of anybody else to abuse. The evening paper announced a rise in milk prices, and she flung the paper in a rage to the ground. "*Ce sale Kaiser,—voilà qu'il a* upset *le* milk." We all laughed so much at this disproportionate grievance, as well as at the mixture of French and English in which it was expressed, that she looked quite puzzled.

Having once realised that a European war was in progress and that she could do nothing to oppose it, she decided that she had better help. To this end she announced that she would turn the Great Hall at Knole

into a hospital ward, and would be prepared to receive
either English wounded or Belgian refugees. Arranging
the hospital ward was almost as exciting as arranging
for the Christmas sale at the now mercifully defunct
Spealls, and she entered into the new adventure in very
much the same spirit. So long as she had something
to occupy her, it did not very much matter what it was.
Her ideas as to the wants of injured soldiers or destitute
Belgians were, however, dictated by her own experience
rather than by any knowledge of suffering such as these
men might have undergone: she thought they would
each like a prettily decorated locker in which to keep
their possessions, and a new tooth-brush each. These she
provided, with a reading-lamp over each bed, and sat
back to await the first arrivals.

These happened to be five harmless and harassed
though unprepossessing Belgians. My mother was
pleased at first, because she could talk French to them
and could tell us all how abominable their accents were,
compared with her own. Which indeed was true. But
then she proceeded to become really friendly with her
refugees, and to show them all over the house, telling
them where King James I had slept, and Queen Victoria, and similar things, until in their jocose innocence
they started asking her which bedroom she would
have given to the Kaiser had he chanced to visit Knole.
She was already getting a little bored with them by that
time, and conveniently decided that they must be spies.
They were asking questions about Knole in order to
send information to the Germans. . . . They were in
German pay. . . . Knole would be bombed by the next
Zeppelin, all because *ces sales Boches* thought the Kaiser
had stayed there. . . .

Everything went very rapidly, as it always did once
my mother had got an idea into her head one way or

the other. With the same energy as she had displayed in providing the decorated lockers and new tooth-brushes for the victims of the war, she now set herself to get rid of her first contingent. They were spies; they had asked questions about the bedrooms. Worse than that, they had never used the tooth-brushes. They had been at Knole for four days, and the tooth-brushes were still as virgin as when they came out of the chemist's shop. That was quite conclusive proof for my mother, who instantly got into touch with the local police, and commanded them to remove these dangerous spies without delay.

That, so far as I know, was the beginning and end of her war service.

CHAPTER VI

THE LAST YEARS

I

When the war did eventually come to an end, my mother emerged from it with far less loss than many other people. She had no son or sons to be killed; she was not ruined; and my father, the only man for whom she truly cared, survived his various campaigns at the cost only of one serious illness. The four years of the war, it might in one sense be said, to her meant only an interlude during which life became inconvenient, controlled, and restricted. There had been the time when she couldn't get a license to buy petrol, and had fitted a gas-balloon to the roof of her Rolls-Royce sooner than give up using the car altogether. There had been the time when she couldn't order what she wanted for lunch, and had to listen to talk about food-coupons. There had been days when expected guests had failed her, either because they were suddenly ordered off somewhere else or because they were detained at their work in London. There had been the unpleasant surprise of seeing the workmen taken away, one by one, from Knole. There had been frights, and scares, and a general sense of something going madly wrong, rather like what the French aristocracy must have experienced during the Revolution. But, on the whole, she might congratulate herself on having come through the world-ordeal comparatively unhurt.

Yet the war had an effect on her life, more profound

than she at the time supposed. At the time, she was thinking only of the worry entailed, and the diminution of income, and the general incomprehensible upset of the order she was accustomed to, things which bulked very large in her mind, insignificant as they really were. What she did not see, was the psychological development which during those four years had been taking place both in herself and my father. Such developments can have effects quite as far-reaching as those which come about more dramatically and sensationally, through the accidents of life and death.

I have done my work ill, if I have not shown my mother as an entirely dominating, triumphing, warm-hearted, frequently mistaken, generous, regardless character; and my father as a quiet, sensitive, retiring, light-hid-under-a-bushel one. I hope I have shown no prejudice on either side, for the truth is that I loved them both equally, though in different ways, my mother as the more brightly coloured figure, my father as the dear steady, yet wistfully poetic one.—It is odd: I wrote that word 'poetic' almost by mistake, as one does write things down when one is thinking very intensely and not worrying about the exact word to employ, but I will let it stand, because it really does express a certain quality in my father which might easily have been missed by those who saw him only superficially.—I have done my work ill, I say, if I have not made it clear that sooner or later these two natures were bound to come to an open breach. They had once been wildly in love, and then, after the first rapture had passed, that love had modified itself for many years into a tolerable marriage; but it now seems quite obvious, as the years went on, bringing the hardening of personality with them, that the accordance of that marriage could not last. The breach had begun even before the war, but the war was really responsible for the final disruption. Until then, they had divided their mandates at Knole fairly amicably, my mother ordering the indoor matters and my father the outdoor, but with my father away for four years of the war the entire direction of affairs devolved upon her. Autocratic as she was by nature, she now had no check upon her at all; no one to object, no one to disapprove. My father for his part had found a new authority: he had been called upon to take command of men in circumstances of danger, difficulty, and discomfort; his standards had of course altered; his habit of command had grown. For the first time in his life he had really found himself as a man among men, away from the sapping feminine influence. He had seen Gallipoli, Egypt, Palestine, France; he had suffered,—I saw him through nights of agony when he steadily refused to accept morphia until he had almost lost consciousness through pain,—and naturally all these experiences developed him. He came back from the war an increased and more authoritative man, and my mother, who had also grown more autocratic during her four years of grass-widowhood, couldn't understand the change in him.

The change, had she but realised it, was very slight and very right. It meant only that as he had commanded in the field he intended now to resume command over such part of his own possessions as he had hitherto controlled. I remember very distinctly the occasion which decided the final separation of my parents. My father was home again at last. We were all three alone in the library at Knole, after dinner, talking as people do talk after months and months of separation, about the things which have happened in the interval,—not world-things, not important things, but just the things which have happened in their own home. It all seemed very friendly, in that familiar room with its comfortable sofa and armchairs and blazing fire. I looked at each of my parents in turn, thinking with some relief how well they seemed to be getting on together, when the final storm burst.

It burst very quietly, with a sort of muffled detonation which gave no hint of the effects to follow.

My father just said, "Oh, look here, dear, would you mind telling Saer (the bailiff) when you want any work done in the house? Because, if you don't give warning, it upsets all the men's work-sheets for the week on the estate, and then Saer doesn't know how he stands. He is short-handed enough already, and he doesn't know what men he can have, if you suddenly take them off on to another job."

That seemed, to me, reasonable enough, and I was all on my father's side; but then my mother suddenly lost her temper and said he had insulted her, and burst into tears and left the room, never to return.

II

I spent a miserable week-end, going up and down stairs, carrying messages between my parents. I could not really believe that my mother meant finally to leave Knole which she had so loved in her own odd way, and my father whom she had loved also; but so it turned out. I had evidently underrated my mother's power of decision. She was, I think, almost heartbroken, but having taken her decision was resolved to stick to it, whatever it might cost her. She spent the whole of that week-end shut away into her own rooms, doing her packing, and occasionally sending me downstairs with those practical, heart-breaking messages to my father, to which he returned coldly courteous replies to the effect that if she wanted to change her mind at any time the door would never be shut against her. This coldness and correctness of attitude was the last thing she could be expected to understand. Had he rushed upstairs, battered at her door, and flung himself at her feet imploring her not to desert him, she would have understood that, and, I think, stayed. But those were methods suited to Albolote and Buena Vista and the Villa Pepa, not to Knole.

Fortunately for herself, she already had her own refuge ready and waiting for her. For some years past, it had become abundantly clear that Catalina and Pepita's taste for acquiring properties and for "improvements and renovations" had been lavishly transmitted. But Albolote and Buena Vista and the German houses and the Italian villas and Villa Pepa itself were innocent and economical amusements compared with the follies on which my mother gaily embarked. It makes my head reel to try and remember the various schemes she at one time or another had on hand, some of which materialised and some of which luckily did not. Among those which materialised was a large meadow overlooking Rome, for which she paid (I think) £10,000, and on which she proposed to build herself a house; a flat in a Roman palace which she refused at the last moment to occupy,—and when I say "at the last moment", I mean that her Rolls-Royce was actually on its way to Dover when she suddenly decided that she wouldn't go to Rome at all; several houses in London, on which she spent fantastic sums enlarging basements, putting in passenger-lifts, building out dining-rooms, and so on. Then there were also the schemes which for one reason or another never came to fruition. There were the houses she meant to build at Hampstead or in Brook Street, and for which she caused endless plans to be drawn, discussed, altered, and finally scrapped. . . . At last an ill-chance led her to Brighton, where she espied a "To Be Sold" board displayed on a large and unattractive house in an unattractive square. For my mother, "to be sold" was synonymous with "I can buy it". She bought it. In order to justify the purchase to herself and to everybody else she evolved the formula that she had finally settled on Brighton "because it is so nice for my little grandsons to go to the seaside". It was quite in vain that I suggested that her little grandsons could go into lodgings if necessary, and that in any case Brighton with its shingle beach and crowds was the very last place to amuse two little boys who wanted to paddle and build sand-castles; no, she had seen a house for sale and had set her heart on it. It was a huge house, a great echoing mausoleum of a house, with vast naked staircases and still vaster drawing-rooms, large enough to accommodate four generations of descendants. I could not help reflecting that she had the whole country in which to make her choice; she could have bought some exquisite old house, with lovely matured gardens, a river, a lake, the Downs, the sea,—anything she wanted; she could have built herself a new house on some ideal site; a dream house, there was nothing to prevent her; but instead of that she must determine to acquire this impossible barrack at the corner of a Brighton square. I was dismayed, but she was enchanted. So enchanted was she, indeed, that before very long she had also purchased the two flanking houses, equally large, equally resounding, equally intractable. . . .

Since there were never any half-measures for my mother, the modest *pied-à-terre* she had taken at the seaside for her little grandsons was rapidly transformed into "my palace at Brighton". To hear her talk about it, you would really have thought she had acquired the Pavilion. She was always like that. Never did anybody's geese develop into such sumptuous, snowy swans. She almost convinced one, because she was so completely convinced herself. Thus she was persuaded that you could see the sea from her house, and indeed it was true that if you went to the top floor you could just catch a glimpse of it round the corner of another building, but the only view which the windows really commanded was a magnificent one over Brighton's gasometers.

She now flung all her energy into transforming her three houses into one habitable dwelling, a miracle no one could possibly hope to accomplish. By her own admission she spent over £50,000 in the attempt, and one thought sadly of the gems of architecture she could have acquired for that expenditure. Amongst other things she constructed a sort of underground vault, saying that it would be nice for the little grandsons to play in on a wet day; it was a windowless cavern, and so far as I know nobody was ever known to go into it. Then she put in a passenger-lift, and a central-heating system which could never be used as its furnace was found to consume a ton of coal a day. By demolishing walls she created a dining-room in which you could comfortably have seated a hundred guests, but as she never had more than one or possibly two people at a time to stay with her, and had all meals out in the loggia anyhow, this was not of much practical use either.

In all these activities she had the co-operation of an architect who seemed to have been specially created to suit her. She and Sir Edwin Lutyens together were the richest comedy. That most delightful, good-natured, irresponsible, imaginative jester of genius could keep her amused by the hour, as, with his pencil flickering over the paper and the jokes pouring endlessly from his lips, he flung domes and towers into the air, decorated them with her monogram, raised fountains and pavilions, paved garden walks with quartz and marble, and exercised all the ingenuity which she so well understood. Of course they squabbled. There were times when he tried loyally to restrain her extravagant schemes. There were times when she worried him nearly into his grave. There were times when he irritated her, for underneath all his flippancy he held certain standards from which, as an artist, he would never depart.

"You understand nothing of the *grammar* of building," he would say in despair; "now look, I'll show you . . ." but she would never look and would never even attempt to understand.

III

Thanks to gold-mines and extravagances of every kind, she occasionally found herself short of money, and the means to which she resorted in order to raise cash were various and successful. There was, of course, the obvious method of selling jewels or works of art, and I know that during one year alone she obtained £20,000 in this way, and during another year a further £25,000, all of which disappeared, I don't know how, where, or to whom. These sales were sometimes attended by incidents which somehow I do not feel would have befallen anybody else. There was, for instance, the occasion when she left £1000 in Bank of England notes in a taxi, never to be recovered. There was the other occasion when she wished to sell a diamond necklace which had once been the property of Queen Katherine Parr and sent it to a London jeweller for this purpose. In broad daylight, and in a shop full of people, it was stolen out of the window from the inside and has never been since seen; she did, however, profit by the insurance money. It fortunately never occurred to her to organise a flag-day for her own benefit, but she did conceive and put into execution the idea of raising funds among her friends for any scheme she particularly wanted to carry out. Thus in order to help towards the cost of doing up one of her many houses, she invented the fund for the Roof of Friendship and wrote to everybody she knew asking them to give her enough to buy one tile, or more than one tile if they were feeling generous. She was furious with the painter William Nicholson, when he sent her a real tile done up in a brown paper parcel.

I remember one day I was staying with her at Brighton, and a telegram was brought for her while she was in her bath. I was directed to read it to her through the door. "Handed in at Bangkok", I read. "I am commanded by His Majesty to inform you that the elephant was despatched yesterday to your address." Peals of laughter came through the door at my astonishment. "I quite forgot to tell you, darling, I have had such a good idea: a white elephant stall. You know people have them at bazaars? but I shall have this one for myself. And then I thought as elephants came from Siam I would write to the King and ask him for a white one."

It duly arrived about a month later, a chubby little elephant of solid silver, which I have no doubt she sold for a most repaying sum.

It was at about this time too that she developed a taste for gardening, but here again her methods were of the most unorthodox kind. Her knowledge of horticulture was nil, and she had no wish to increase it. All she wanted was a gay display. As I have already said, she had never cared for flowers for their own sake, though she liked the colour and sometimes the scent, but on the whole greatly preferred them made of any material other than the one which Nature had provided. Thus if she saw a gap in her border she would cheerfully stick in a group of delphiniums made of painted tin, on nice tall metal stalks, and, when I remonstrated in my dull English fashion, would quite logically point out the advantages: they flowered whenever one wanted them; they remained in flower so long as one wanted, for years if need be; they required no staking; and one didn't have to bother about "*ces détestables* slugs". There was no convincing answer to offer to these arguments.

Tin delphiniums, however, by no means exhausted her resourcefulness as a gardener. It was not long before she discovered that hawkers came round the streets with pony-carts, selling plants in pots. Plants in pots were just the thing to please her, and any flower-merchant with a barrow was sure of a lavish customer. In fact, I think the hawkers of the neighbourhood must have passed the word round to one another, for, whether in London or in Brighton, these floral barrows seemed to stroll within range of her windows with far greater frequency than anywhere else. She would tap on the window-pane, making wild signals to the flower-merchant to stop, which he was only too willing to do; and then would go down to the front door to meet him in any attire. Sometimes, if she happened to intercept him during the afternoon, she would be fully dressed; but if during the morning, she would go down in her dressing-gown and night-gown, to stand on the door-step buying the whole barrow-load off him, and finding out the whole of his family life at the same time. Then, still in the dressing-gown and night-gown, she would get him to carry his plants into her garden at the back, and would stand there talking while every plant was set in its place. I wonder whether any of these itinerant sellers ever looked at her with any sense of surprise? She surely must have seemed an odd customer? The night-gown she wore was of the very thickest and cheapest flannel, yet it was fastened at the neck by an emerald and diamond brooch of historic value; and from those gleaming gems, employed as an ordinary safety-pin, hung a police-whistle, a threepenny affair bought at Woolworth's. On the top of the flannel night-gown came a cloak of Venetian velvet,—flannel and velvet, tin-whistle and emeralds, mixed in real unself-consciousness. And over the lovely head something was always instinctively thrown,—it might be a shabby Shetland shawl, it might be a piece of black lace like a mantilla, but there was always something, as a woman of Latin race always covers her head instinctively on going into the street or into church.

In this guise she would stand, supervising her street-vendors and her own gardener, as under her instructions they planted plants as never plants were intended to grow. She outraged all their feelings; she had no regard at all for what plants were or what they wanted. Annual, biennial, perennial, meant nothing to her: it merely irritated her that plants shouldn't flower the whole time, and in exactly the right colours. Plants in pots, however, solved the difficulty. One could sink them into the ground and pretend that they had grown there.

"Look, Harold, you always told me no one could grow lilies in a town garden. Look at those!"

She and Harold then go for a stroll up and down the garden-path; and on their way back find that all the lilies have disappeared.

My mother knows quite well that the servants,

according to her instructions, have taken up the lily-pots and carried them indoors for the night, but she feels she must explain this disappearance to Harold, and anyway is never at a loss.

"If I have told them once", she says, "not to cut the lilies, I have told them twenty times."

Perhaps of all the odd corners of her garden the one she liked best was a sort of rockery entirely planted with flowers made of china.

IV

It was not so very long before she tired of her palace at Brighton, sold it for £5000 (therefore at a loss of some £45,000), and bought a smaller and more manageable house on the cliff near Roedean School. Here, at any rate, she could see the sea. Rather unexpectedly,— for she was too un-English to care much for Nature,— she really loved the sea. Incidentally, she also caught the full force of the Brighton gales, which suited her perfectly as the mania for fresh air had never deserted her and every door was still propped open and every window tied back with string. Nobody, seeing the appalling draught in which she permanently lived, could ever understand why she didn't get pneumonia over and over again. Even in the depths of winter she would never have a fire in her room.

There was a short but unfortunate period when she also owned a house at Streatham, a singularly hideous Victorian villa of yellow brick, which for some reason she said was like an Italian palazzo. Here she amused herself by making a staircase of imitation books with joke titles, also a large maze of wattle fencing. There were jokes in the maze too, such as an empty whisky-bottle suspended from a string, with the label "Departed spirits"; and she caused a most realistic half-crown to be painted on a stepping-stone. Her delight whenever anyone attempted to pick it up was great. And since a certain Sir Richard Sackville had once lived at Streatham in the reign of Mary Tudor she decided that the trees in her garden had been planted by his wife.

"Is it not curious", she would say to her guests, "that we should now be sitting under a tree planted by another Lady Sackville?"

It was very curious indeed.

I never went much to Streatham, for her time there coincided with the longest and unhappiest quarrel we ever had. It started on the day my father died, and as it seemed to be about nothing at all I can only imagine that the grief she then refused to admit drove her into this oblique method of relieving her feelings. She hurled the wildest accusations against me: I had stolen her jewels, I had refused to allow her wreath to be placed on his coffin. . . . It was useless for me to protest that I could disprove either of these things; useless to protest that a hundred witnesses could disprove them; there was nothing to do but to wait for the storm to subside. It had lasted nearly two years, when I was unaccountably taken back into favour.

Such vicissitudes fell to the lot of all those who came into any intimate contact with her, for she had the unfortunate capacity for persuading herself that she had been outrageously and ungratefully treated. I should be sorry to have to give a list of those who, after sacrificing their time, their nerves, and sometimes their health, found themselves suddenly accused of some purely imaginary offence and flung into outermost darkness. Her friends bore it with patience and pain; but other people, such as servants, secretaries, tradesmen, and professional men with their reputation to safeguard, did not at all relish the wild allegations she broadcast about them. It was seldom, in fact, that some law-suit was not pending, either for libel or slander, for wages which she had refused to pay on summary dismissal, or for bills which she had refused to settle. I think nine suits all outstanding at the same moment was the record. She herself took it lightly, and rechristened her house the Writs Hotel.

It made one a little uneasy.

It was all so very difficult to cope with; there was really nothing to be done. No amount of experience would ever teach her prudence. Nor would the logical consequences of personal inconvenience ever persuade her to curb her tongue or her pen. It was no good warning her that her entire household would walk out in a body, as actually happened several times. At the back of her mind she knew well enough that somebody would always come to the rescue, for, after all, she couldn't be left to starve, and she so managed that at least one devoted soul was always available in moments of necessity. It never surprised me in the least on arriving at the gale-swept house on the cliff, to find it completely denuded of servants, and her solicitor filling a hot-water bottle for her from a kettle.

As a matter of fact, I believe she welcomed the excitement. Anxious to protect her from herself, we always made the mistake of assuming that she would prefer to avoid these troubles, whereas I think that in reality she provoked them in the subconscious desire to give herself something to do. If one must analyse further,—and really her conduct at times was so inexplicable that one turned right and left in search of some clue,—I think that all must be ascribed to some essentially tragic failure. The bad fairy who attended the christening of Sleeping Beauty must have attended my mother's also.

Gifts had been showered on her: beauty and charm and energy, abounding vitality, courage, determination; just the little more, and she would have been truly Napoleonic. But the bad fairy ordained that she should fritter everything away. He spoke wisely, who compared her to a powerful dynamo generating nothing. There was no driving-belt attached to her whirling wheels. The force was there, but no result from the force. In politics, social work, or philanthropy, she might have been a real figure, though indeed I cannot imagine her ever working in co-operation with others: she was a dictator, not a colleague. But such things held no interest for her.

And so naturally as she came towards the end of her life there remained nothing but a sense of frustration and an immense boredom, combined with a frenzied desire to exercise authority and to fill the endless days. Because she was, as the judge had said, of high mettle, she would never accept but would always fight. She fought, lashing out even at those she loved best and striking at those who could not answer back; hurting herself, I think, as much as she hurt others, and certainly causing acute anxiety to those who felt themselves responsible for her safety and comfort. There were very black days during those years, and the cruellest blow of all came with the threat of eventual blindness.

Here, again, she was so intractable that it was impossible to help her. She would have nothing to do with doctors, oculists, or treatments. Neither would she have any companion who might read to her or help with her voluminous correspondence. For although she had estranged herself from most of her old friends,—not through any fault or wish of theirs,—her inventiveness was such that she found means to occupy herself in other ways. The memory of the Roof of Friendship fund was still with her, and of the fun she had had every morning opening her letters to see what cheque or postal-order they would contain, so she now devised a scheme which from its patriotic nature would allow her to write to complete strangers, especially to those whose birth-days she had seen announced in the daily press. This scheme had the not unambitious object of reducing the National Debt by a contribution of one million pennies. She had a number of canvassing forms lithographed, and as she used them up later on to write her private letters on the back, I am able to reproduce the text here:

DEAR ———

I am the Dowager Lady Sackville and venture to ask you if you would be kind enough (*very* kind indeed) to give me the number of pennies that correspond to the years of your life. I have noticed your age in the papers. Please be very good to my MILLION PENNY FUND by giving the TREASURY, through my collection, the small help I crave from you,—only a few pence (or shillings if you feel extra generously inclined).

I have already sent, last month, 62,000 pence representing the Brighton number of voters which gave England the largest majority.

Now I am working for England at large, through the Birth-days of her *notable* people.

Please, *please* don't refuse me. No one has done it so far and they often send their age in shillings.

May I count on your help for the TREASURY and our country, by sending me whatever you can spare, even after the awful taxes you have paid, and do give me three stamped envelopes which means one for my begging letter, one for having the pleasure of thanking you, and one for a fresh Victim.

In spite of being half blind already and practically bedridden,—though occasionally she would arise and make terrifying descents into quarters of the house where she was least expected to appear,—she brought all her old enthusiasm to the support of her fund. "It is no good doing things by halves, my child", she would say; "ask, and ye shall receive. *C'est Notre Seigneur qui l'a dit. Quoique je ne croie plus en Dieu depuis cette horrible guerre et que je n'aime pas les prêtres qui ont donné de l'argent à Henri contre nous, j'ai toujours beaucoup d'admiration pour Notre Seigneur qui avait tant de sagesse.* Knock, and they will open the door; ask, and ye shall receive. Well, I do ask and I do receive. It is really surprising how kind people are to your old Mama."

This was in a mellow mood: she must have had a good post that morning. There were stormier passages sometimes. Sometimes an innocent and ill-advised though distinguished stranger would write pointing out the proportions of the National Debt compared with even a million pennies. Then she would grow annoyed. "Does he not know, the fool," she would exclaim, "that every mickle makes a muckle?" She thought of an even better answer to such criticisms: "La Dubarry," she would say, "when she was collecting stones for her diamond necklace, always said, '*Les petits ruisseaux font les grandes rivières*'", and then, pleased with her own appositeness, would forget to be cross. There was a very awkward moment when it suddenly occurred to her that I had friends at the B.B.C. and might broadcast an appeal for her fund on the National programme. . . .

Not that she ever listened to the wireless or consented to have a set in her house. I thought, of course, that here would be the ideal solace of many hours (though at the same time I shuddered at the thought of the letters she would write to broadcasters, either of appreciation or remonstrance), but she firmly refused to have anything to do with it,—"*Cette sale boîte*", as she called it. The reason she didn't like it is obvious: she couldn't control it in any way. She couldn't control what it played or when it played it; and anything which she couldn't control was ruthlessly cut out of her life.

In the same way, she disliked Time. She had long since cut Time out of her life as far as possible, by always going everywhere in her own motor and thus rendering herself independent of trains which had a way of starting without her, by being unpunctual on principle for every possible appointment, and by detaining other people in the subconscious desire to make them unpunctual for theirs. As her eccentricities developed with age, her temperamental dislike of Time developed also, and she would sacrifice even her own pleasure and convenience in order to get the better of it. Any engagement which meant that she was pinned down to a certain hour would be cancelled, even if that involved turning away from the door someone who had been purposely summoned from London or elsewhere. Meals became more and more erratic. Supposing I went to luncheon with her, having been bidden to arrive not later than one, "because I want to give you a delicious lunch, darling",—she was always convinced that I didn't have enough to eat at home,—I would arrive at one, only to be told that her ladyship had just gone to her bath. With any luck, she might be successfully manœuvred back to her bed by three, when our luncheons would appear on two separate trays. And then she would refuse to eat hers. "These dreadful cooks! You know, my child, they do not realise that one cannot eat exactly when they want one to,—*elles sont sans pitié*,—all they think about is their evening off. Take it away, take it away", she would say, and sometimes it would be six o'clock in the evening before she felt hungry and would ask why her luncheon had not been brought. By that time, of course, it was spoiled,

and she would go back to memories of the chefs at
Knole, how reliable they had always been, how excellent, how well served she had always been in those
days. . . .

Her ideas of Time became vaguer and vaguer, or
perhaps I should say more and more antagonistic. She
thought nothing of keeping one up all night, talking:
and when I say all night, I mean till six or seven o'clock
in the morning. She would do this quite indiscrimin-
ately, to me or to a new servant to whom she happened to
take a fancy. When it was to me it didn't matter, for I
could go home and sleep it off; but to the servant who
was expected to answer the bell at eight with fresh hot-
water bottles and a cup of tea it mattered to the extent of
probably getting the sack that day or the next.

This question of her taking fancies led to endless
difficulties, because it meant that she would take anybody away from his or her own job and absorb him or
her into her personal service. Thus she would one day
send for the gardener, engage him in conversation, discover him to be an intelligent man, and henceforth use
him to write her letters for her. By some strange kink
in her mind, she preferred this system to the idea of
employing a regular secretary. The composition of her
household, whenever she had one, was the oddest ever
seen. Everybody was always doing the job meant for
somebody else. The cook was weeding the garden,
the gardener was up with her ladyship, acting as
secretary, the pantry-boy was cooking the luncheon,
—"*il fait si bien la pâtisserie, chérie, tu verras! C'est
un rêve!*"—the butler was in bed with a nervous breakdown. So far as I could make out, she never employed
a housemaid, and to this day I don't know who kept
the house clean; probably all of them, the cook, the
gardener, the pantry-boy, and the butler, all in turn.

In her restless turning about in search of an occupation which should be profitable as well as distracting, she hit upon a fresh idea, distracting in more senses than one. All her life she had been fond of maxims and neat sayings, wise or witty, and had been in the habit of writing them into albums whenever she heard them. It now occurred to her that she might make use of this collection, and the scheme of "my little books" sprang ready-armed from her brain. The "little books" were to be of two kinds: one kind was to be printed (a million copies) and sold by Woolworth's for sixpence each; the other kind was to be written by hand and sold privately to her friends and the friends of her friends. No two bindings were to be alike, and everybody she knew was requested to provide blank note-books gaily bound and decorated in coloured papers with end-papers of a different pattern. It seemed to me that the days of Spealls had returned, but I was wiser now, and instead of sitting down myself with paper, scissors, and paste, I employed professional bookbinders to exercise all the ingenuity at their command.

If I could arrive at Brighton with a parcel of bound note-books under my arm, I could always manage to divert her attention sooner or later. They were by no means certain to please her, but at any rate they would give her a few moments' entertainment, even in finding fault with them, and it was better that she should find fault with them than with her servants.

Meanwhile she was writing away with all the zest of which she was capable. Many sleepless hours of her lonely life were thus employed; if not happily, at least in forgetfulness. The unconscious pathos of that employment is a thing on which I cannot bear to dwell. She, who had been so gay, so amused, so reckless, so young, so active, so vainglorious, so feminine, so triumphant, was now old, ill, bedridden, half blind, yet still with her courage and energy unquenched, inscribing her maxims on embossed paper specially made for the blind. She could not see what she was writing, and we, alas, could not decipher what she had written. That was the most tragic part of it. She would spend half the night writing, not even troubling to turn on the light since it made but little difference to her, and in the morning she would ask one of us to read over what she had written. And we couldn't, for it was all illegible. In spite of the paper specially made for the blind, it was illegible. She would have forgotten to turn over the page, and would have written one thing over the other, so that it looked like sentences someone had wished to obliterate, like writing Egypt, Egypt, Egypt over an indiscretion. What was one to do? One couldn't say brutally, "I am afraid I can't make this out". One had to make an excuse somehow, or else to read whatever one *could* read,—but she was shrewd, and her memory was inconveniently better than one hoped. "No, no", she would say to me; "*Dieu, que tu es bête, tu lis à tort et à travers*, that isn't what I just wrote (*i.e.* wrote last night, or recently), *tu es aussi bête que tous les autres, et toi qui es supposée d'être* clever!"

But every now and then there was a phrase I *could* read, and it wrung my heart to see how often it recurred,—so often, that I realise now that it represented the sad philosophy of her later years: "What has been, has been, and I have had my hour".

v

Lest it may be thought that I exaggerate the unhappiness and discontinuity of my mother's mind, I reproduce here a typical letter from her; and it must be remembered that she wrote to me and I to her almost every day for many years. This letter, which I have selected out of many, seems to me to include the maximum number of characteristic expressions. It expresses her personal and unjustifiable grievances; her undying enterprise; her constant though erratic interest in topical events; her generosity; her oddities; her humour; her courage, take it all in all, when one realises that she was nearly blind at the time of writing; and her impatience with the unfortunate though fascinated men and women who could never satisfy her demands. Warped and wrong she may have grown; but gallant she certainly was to the end.

The text of the letter may be taken as (*sic*) throughout:

2nd July, 1934

My darling child,

This is the end of the fortnight of the worst fortnight I have known for a very long time, I have hidden from you the awful hell I have lived in, I did not want to add fuel to the purgatory I have gone through my personal attendants. It has been indescribably cruel and if it had not been for your loving letters I don't know what I have been driven to do. I prefer to live and die like a dog than to submit to doctors and nurses, and personal attendants who type, and that coarse retired soldier.[1] The Middle Ages couldn't have been more dreadful than what I have gone through.

I am thinking of going away from here, I am too utterly miserable for words, entirely brought on by those beastly heartless servants and one can get people who can read English properly much better in London. Oh! how I admire that man Hitler! If only we could take away from the World the awful wind that blows over it! I suppose one can die of boredom, from the company of ignorant people who won't exercise their brains

---

[1] I have no idea who she means by "that coarse retired soldier". Probably some gardener she sacked twenty-four hours after she engaged him.

and read a newspaper properly. I am so tired of hearing 'Her' Hitler, instead of 'Hair' Hitler.

The Brighton Murder pales before the events in Germany.

You can't imagine how my interest has revived in the Brighton murder,—a woman and a half in a trunk must be a record. The story in the *Daily Mail* and the *Evening News* is incredible. What a plot for Mrs. Belloc Lowndes! I had a horrid fright yesterday by being told that a policeman wanted to see me. I immediately imagined that it was to do with The Perfect Murder. You ought to take that for the title of your next book, darling, and imagine all sorts of atrocities.

I think the Loch Ness Monster must have swallowed the head of the murdered girl therefore he will become The Perfect Monster. You see, dearest, I must be amused. *Peu me suffit*. As far as I am concerned, *rien ne va plus*. But I won't give in, and I make poor jokes.

Please don't be disgusted.[1] If you only knew the dullness of my life you would pity me.

I can't tell you how perfectly miserable I am in this house, and how to-day almost more than ever I should like to die. Some people are too false and selfish for words, grabbing all they can get and in a very underhand way. Ah! they are not worth bothering about, and I am pretty sick with them, I can tell you, my child. I think they will end by killing me one fine morning, so be prepared for any eventuality. I am seeing my solicitor about it this afternoon and as I am very angry at the underhand way I have been treated he will be edified.

What do you do to stop a quantity of wasps that we are enjoying here? I am so afraid of being stung when I am in a coma sleep.

Oh, darling, I wish you had written your diary, life is so full of interesting incidents.

I forgot to tell you I thought of taking some house in the middle of Sussex for the winter, I have no decided plans. Do you happen to know of a little girl who would never be seen by me and do the dusting and sweeping? Do you like American peach-fed ham? Abundance helps one, especially when people come in unexpectedly. I shall send you half one, as soon as I get it from Selfridge's. I forgot to ask you how many lobsters you could

---

[1] She means "scornful". (As though I could be!) She never got her English words quite right.

manage a week. They are so fresh and cheap here; and there is a very nice horse-radish sauce that you could order at the Stores. Tell me about the peach-fed ham.

My brain-fag is so bad I can't teach anything to anybody.

Oh! that Hitler! *Il me semble que c'est un nouveau Napoléon.*

I should not at all mind buying Turner's house[1] if it is £5000. I like it for the roof-garden and the river running furiously at the foot of the garden. My life here is awful and I should prefer to begin a new life. If I got a house in London on the river there will be plenty of fresh air and you could always come and sleep at my house as I shall have a spare room. Darling, don't you think it is a good idea, to buy Turner's house? We shall talk about it on Thursday. It will give me a new thought to think about. I long for you and Thursday. I am happier now, for I am extremely patient now, I have started a new phase and it answers.

All my books have been stolen, and the cruelty to treat me like that because I am blind. The time has come when certain things must be revealed and punished.

I am very happy with little A.[2] She was not asleep at 2 o'clock, for she heard me singing as I was trying to charm away the horrid time, and she told me the tune I was singing which gave me proof of her dreadful night.

I shall advertise for a maid because W. is having a breakdown. A very curious doctor came yesterday to see him, and he and I sang beautifully some duets from Gounod. He has a magnificent voice, and he sang to me, and I suddenly began to accompany him, and he was extremely surprised at the true tone of my singing. It was Verlaine's "*La lune par-dessus les toits*"; but I can't find out who set it, it is not only Debussy and Ravel but another Writer.

Don't you think my name of Foie-gras is very good for your new Alsatian? Or you might him call Stras, short for Strasbourg, where the patés come from. I am extremely unwell this week as I have so many bothers with the two young fellows downstairs who are so stupid.

[1] Turner, the painter; his house in Cheyne Walk.
[2] "Little A." is evidently the person to whom this letter was dictated. It will be observed that she ceases to be in favour by the time the last paragraph of the letter is reached, and then becomes "my typist" and "poor girl".

I am so tired, darling, I have dictated such a long letter and my typist is so stupid I have to spell nearly every word especially if it is in French. She means well, poor girl, she can't help being stupid. Good-night, my child, I send you my butterfly kiss.

VI

The incredible disorder of her bedroom balanced the general disorder of her life. No picture of her would be complete without a picture of the untidiness and indeed squalor in which she elected to live. Suspicion, always latent in her mind, had come to stay. (I think it may not be wholly fanciful to suppose it inherited from her riff-raff Spanish ancestry?) She now suspected every-body,—she who was by nature so generous, so open-handed. This element had always been present in her character, but it now attained proportions which were really neither normal nor hygienic. It meant, in effect, that she would never have her bedroom touched or dusted; it meant that the servants had to watch their moment while she was having her daily bath to dash in and make her bed; it meant that she kept odds and ends of food standing on tables because she declared that if it were taken away it would be stolen. The most expensive bottles of pickled peaches from Fortnum and Mason stood there, half empty, for weeks. Tins of truffles from Strasbourg, jars of French mustard, pots of jam from Tiptree, samples of bath-salts, scent from Coty and Molyneux, boxes stacked with old ½d. envelopes in-tended for re-use, a stray bottle of Kümmel or cherry brandy; and then, on her bed, letters, stationery, diaries, note-books, handbags, fly-whisks, eye-shades, unopened parcels, so that the general accumulation left her only about a quarter of the bed to lie in. Yet she never seemed to notice this discomfort. She was far more concerned with the idea that the servants would read her letters and diaries, or would move her possessions out of her reach.

The clutter in the room was increased by piles of my own books, stacked on the floor, on chairs, on tables and chests-of-drawers. For one of her more persistent ambitions and enthusiasms was for my success as an author. I had the greatest difficulty in ever soothing her indignation against publishers, booksellers, reviewers, and everyone connected with the trade. No publisher ever advertised enough: why couldn't my publisher take the front page of the *Daily Mail*? It cost £500, did it? Well, she would pay for it, and gladly. No bookseller ever displayed his/my wares properly: why couldn't Messrs Bumpus, Hatchard, Lamley, and The Times Book Club each devote a window to me for a week? She had heard that that was how *If Winter Comes* had been launched on its career. And as for reviewers, it was an unlucky day for me when she discovered the existence and efficiency of Messrs Durrant's press-cutting agency. I am not aware that she ever actually wrote to a reviewer,—I tried to forestall this danger by telling her that reviewers were strange people, full of unaccountable prejudices, and that she might be doing more harm than good,—but what I could never prevent was her distribution of my books to all and sundry. Out of the real sweetness and generosity of her nature she did it, and out of the genuine desire to "help", but I must say I writhed in embarrassment when I heard of my wretched novels going to Cabinet Ministers, ambassadors, and Queen Mary. It was in vain that I begged her not to. She couldn't understand my point of view at all.

"But, darling, you want to get better and better known, don't you? You want to make money, don't you?

Sans argent on ne peut rien faire. Et Hilaire Belloc lui-même told me once *qu'un écrivain ne pouvait jamais réussir s'il ne perçait pas le* leather belt of Suburbia."

How I wished Mr Belloc had never made use of that disastrous phrase!

I said I really didn't mind about getting better known; and as for making money, it was very nice if one could, but it came second,—a long way second.

"*Je ne te comprends pas du tout, ma chérie. A un moment tu me dis que tu ne peux pas afforder d'aller* abroad, *et puis* next minute *tu me dis* that you don't care about making money. *Et puis, tu écris des livres qui ne* sell *pas.*"

I protested mildly that *The Edwardians* had sold quite well, adding that I was sorry about that, because I hated writing novels; was a bad novelist; would never be a good one; and really only cared about writing poetry and other things.

"*Oui, je sais bien: c'est très joli, la poésie, et je dois avouer que tu as écrit des choses qui me font pleurer* [as Ella Wheeler Wilcox also brought tears to her eyes I could not take this as an especial compliment], *mais enfin la poésie ça ne* sell *pas.* Now you told me you were going to write a book about Jeanne d'Arc. Has it got any love-interest?"

I said I was afraid not: St. Joan had died at the age of nineteen, and her few years of adolescence had been fully occupied by things other than love.

"*Mais enfin, ma chérie, ma niña*, you know love is the most beautiful thing on earth? *Et c'est ce qui* appeal *le plus* to most people. *Je te dis toujours que le soleil et l'amour sont les plus grands des peintres.* Now couldn't you introduce a love-story into your St. Joan? It would make it sell much better."

"But Mama, my book on St. Joan isn't a novel;

it is meant to be history. I can't introduce imaginary episodes; I simply couldn't."

She looked wistful; regretful; trying to understand. Then she brightened.

"*Tiens, j'ai une idée.* If you say Jeanne d'Arc never had a love-affair,—*ce qu'elle a manqué, la pauvre fille!* —of course I see you can't invent one. You are as tiresome as McNed [her name for Sir Edwin Lutyens] with his endless talk of grammar in architecture. 'You must have truth', he says, and it seems to me you say pretty much the same thing. *Au diable ces artistes* with their silly consciences. But now look here, my silly obstinate child,—*petite entêtée, va!*—if you can't give a love-affair to your Jeanne, couldn't you introduce one for Charles Sept with one of his ladies? He had lots, I know. I went round all his châteaux on my honeymoon, —ah, how happy your Dada and I were then, *et ce qu'il est devenu méchant pour moi depuis! enfin, n'en parlons pas,*—we were talking about Charles Sept and his ladies and a love-affair for your book. Now there was,—who was it? Diane de Poitiers? Cléo de Mérode? *j'oublie.*"

"Agnès Sorel?" I suggested.

"Of course,—Agnès Sorel. Diane de Poitiers, *c'était un autre roi,* Henri Deux I think; *mais enfin ils avaient tous des maîtresses; tu vois comme on m'enseignait bien l'histoire de France au couvent.* Cléo de Mérode, she was somebody quite different. She was what George Moore used to call *la haute cocotterie,*— oh, that old George Moore! what a bore he could be, and how amusing sometimes. Do you remember how he insisted once to come to Knole for Christmas, and how he wanted you to write a play with him, about Shakespeare I think, he shut himself into the library with you for a whole afternoon and I was quite anxious, and how he came down to dinner without his tie? And how he minded, when he found out! As though it mattered,—*et lui qui était plutôt* Bohemian. *Enfin, je disais,*—do remind me, child, it tires me so much to think of what I was going to say, and those dreadful servants they wear me out, so that I am *bonne à rien.*"

"Agnès Sorel?" I suggested again, "Cléo de Mérode?"

"Ah *oui*, Cléo de Mérode!" She forgot the dreadful servants and went off into peals of her old delicious laughter. "*Oui*, George Moore *avait raison: c'était la haute cocotterie bel et bien. C'était bien l'époque des appartements entretenus aux Champs Elysées.* And do you remember how Foch wrote to her, *quel grand homme, que ce Foch! j'aurais bien voulu le connaître,*— he just wrote, '*Quand? Où? Combien?*' and she replied, '*Ce soir. Ici. Rien.*' *C'est chic, ça, hein? Ce grand maréchal et cette grande cocotte,—ça va bien ensemble, tout de même. Ça fait chic.* I like that sort of thing. But, darling, what was I saying? You really must help me. It is such an effort for me to remember everything, and I do try to help your books in every way I can, *mais il faut aussi y mettre un peu du tien.*" [1]

VII

Reading over what I have written, I seem to have made light of it and a joke of it, but really I don't mean to convey a wrong impression of what my mother was or of what she meant to me. It was a mixture of tragedy

[1] I must disclaim all responsibility for these statements about Marshal Foch and Mme Cléo de Mérode. For all I know, they may be chronologically incompatible, and my mother may simply have been attributing a good story to two appropriate characters. All that I have done is to reproduce, almost verbatim, a conversation.—V. S.-W.

and—no, not comedy, but sheer fun. Even in the midst of her blindness and illness and general disability and hopelessness, she could still be better company than most people. Many people have told me what a clever woman my mother was, and what good taste she had; it was a sort of label tied onto her; but it was utterly wrong. She was anything but clever, and her taste was anything but good. What they never realised was that she was, above all things, herself. Wrong or right, tiresome, troublesome, turbulent, difficult, generous, mean, vindictive, revengeful, unjust, kind, lavish, enthusiastic, all in turn, she was always herself, and to be always oneself to that extent is a form of genius. "To thine own self be true",—never have I known anybody who to their own self was truer, in every detail, creditable or uncreditable.

It is not for me to write a panegyric of my mother; I hope that my love of her has been implicit in all the foregoing pages of this book; I will leave the last word to Mr Rudyard Kipling as he expressed himself in a letter to a personal friend. This letter came into my hands a short time after her death:

"*P.S.*—On mature reflection *the* most wonderful person I have ever met. And to think of that indomitable flame burning through all the dark years in those five acres of Knole buildings! And like all organisers of the highest type with no traces of pressure and apparently time in which to do personally kind things to the merest stranger. It's outside all my experiences and of a type to which I know no duplicate."